PRESS
RESET

ALSO BY JASON SCHREIER

Blood, Sweat, and Pixels:
The Triumphant, Turbulent Stories Behind How Video Games Are Made

PRESS
RESET

**Ruin and Recovery in the
Video Game Industry**

JASON SCHREIER

Copyright © 2021 by Jason Schreier

Cover design and illustration by Philip Pascuzzo
Cover copyright © 2021 by Hachette Book Group, Inc.

Grand Central Publishing
Hachette Book Group
1290 Avenue of the Americas, New York, NY 10104
grandcentralpublishing.com
twitter.com/grandcentralpub

First edition: May 2021

Grand Central Publishing is a division of Hachette Book Group, Inc. The Grand Central Publishing name and logo is a trademark of Hachette Book Group, Inc.

The publisher is not responsible for websites (or their content) that are not owned by the publisher.

The Hachette Speakers Bureau provides a wide range of authors for speaking events. To find out more, go to www.hachettespeakersbureau.com or call (866) 376-6591.

Print book interior design by Thomas Louie

Library of Congress Cataloging-in-Publication Data

Names: Schreier, Jason, author.
Title: Press reset : ruin and recovery in the video game industry / Jason Schreier.
Description: New York, NY : Grand Central Publishing, [2021]
Identifiers: LCCN 2020054028 | ISBN 9781538735497 (trade paperback) | ISBN 9781538735480 (ebook)
Subjects: LCSH: Video games industry. | Video games—Design.
Classification: LCC HD9993.E452 S37 2021 | DDC 338.4/77948—dc23
LC record available at https://lccn.loc.gov/2020054028

ISBNs: 978-1-5387-3549-7 (trade paperback); 978-1-5387-3548-0 (ebook)

Printed in the United States of America

LSC-C

Printing 1, 2021

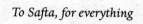

To Safta, for everything

PRESS RESET

INTRODUCTION

The success of the video game industry over the past few decades has been, by any metric, astronomical. Even calling it "success" feels understated, like saying that summers in New York City smell "bad" or that going into labor is "painful." In the 1970s, video games barely existed; in the 2020s, they make up the most lucrative and perhaps most influential industry in entertainment. By 2021, video games were generating a whopping $180 billion in global revenue per year. They had just as significant an impact on popular culture, from *Fortnite* invading schools across the world to Nintendo Direct livestreams dominating social media with big announcements and top-notch memes.

Video games are big business. And for anyone who grew up playing and loving them, it's tempting to dream about being part of that business. There's a *Far Side* comic from the 1990s in which two parents watch a young boy enraptured by *Super Mario Bros.* and imagine a set of classified ads for jobs that require elite video game skills. Back then, the idea of Nintendo proficiency translating into money made for a good punch line; today, the only piece of that comic that seems unrealistic is someone looking for jobs in a news-paper. People all across the world are now paid to go into an office and bring video games to life—sketching out characters, designing levels, and writing code to make everything function. It's an exciting prospect, and countless bright-eyed gamers want to be part of it.

I once walked into a video game studio in downtown New York City a few months before it was due to release its next game. One artist beckoned me over to his desk to "check out something really cool." Soon a crowd had gathered around the computer, craning their necks to watch a slick, realistic model of a truck roll along a drab gray surface. The artist clicked his mouse a few times and the truck exploded, tires and shards of metal flying across the screen in grisly slow motion. I couldn't muster up quite as much excitement as the designers and programmers around me, but it still made me smile to see how genuinely happy they all seemed to be. Their full-time job was to imagine things and then bring them to life on a computer screen. What could be better?

If only it were all glitz, glamour, and exploding cars. The video game industry has a darker side, one that its bosses don't like to brag about on quarterly earnings calls or at E3 press conferences. Even as game companies gobble up more and more money every year, too many of them struggle to provide stable, healthy environments for their workers. All it takes is one flop or sloppy business decision to lead that billion-dollar game publisher to enact a mass layoff or shut down a development studio, no matter how much money it made that year. Sometimes, a mistake isn't even necessary—a big company may lay people off once a project is finished (only to rehire for those same positions a few months later) or to please shareholders in time for the next fiscal quarter (fewer employees mean a cleaner balance sheet).

Volatility has become the status quo. Chat with anyone who's worked in video games for more than a few years and they'll almost certainly have a story about that time they lost their job. Maybe they worked on a game that didn't sell well enough, or they got stuck on a project mismanaged by egomaniacal directors. Maybe their publisher needed to juice the numbers on its newest quarterly earnings report. Maybe they were part of a cost-cutting measure, or a strategic resource realignment, or any of the other jargony euphemisms for "You no longer work here." Mass layoffs and studio closures have become as fundamental to the video game industry as Mario's jumps or Activision's loot boxes.

In 2017, the nonprofit International Game Developers Association asked around one thousand game workers how many employers they'd had in the previous five years. Among those who worked full-time, the average response was 2.2 employers (freelancers said 3.6), suggesting a level of instability that came as no surprise to anyone with experience in this world. The survey's authors added: "Industry churn was also reflected in the limited expectation among employees to remain with their current employers for the long term. Most respondents seemed to expect high job mobility." The following year, reporter James Batchelor at the website GamesIndustry.biz counted up all the jobs lost to game studio closures from September 2017 through September 2018 and found that the number was over one thousand—and those were just the ones that had been made public. Working in games has always meant accepting that stable employment is the exception, not the rule.

In exchange for the pleasure of creating art for a living, game developers have to accept that it might all fall apart without much notice. Sean McLaughlin, who has worked in video games since 2006, described it as a constant feeling of anxiety. "With all the layoffs I've dealt with, I get a PTSD-type thing whenever there is an email for an all-hands meeting in an office," he told me in an email. "I always think it's to announce a studio closure, even though it's just the team getting together and hearing about things going on around the studio. I'm sure it's a common thing among other developers.

"I also no longer put more things on my desk than I can carry out in one bag," McLaughlin added. "When I first got in the industry, I would have the common toys and collectibles on my desk. Now my desk is barren and only has photos and a book or two in case I get laid off again."

You might think: *Well, that sounds like any creative field.* But unlike Hollywood, in which workers shift between contracts as movies weave in and out of production, the video game industry sells the illusion of full-time employment. Job listings for massive publishers like Take-Two and EA advertise careers, not gigs. Unless a developer is on a temporary contract, there's an expectation that when they're finished with their current game, they'll move on to the next one. Keeping people around for the long haul makes sense. The tools that each studio uses to make video games are unique and complicated. Once a developer has put in the time to learn those tools, they'll be more efficient than new recruits. Plus, the chemistry developed over years of working together can be invaluable, as anyone who's worked on a collaborative creative project (or a group science experiment) can attest.

So why is it that the people making financial decisions in the video game industry don't seem to care?

I had a long chat with veteran game designer Katie Chironis about this volatility. Chironis, who has worked for the gaming giants Microsoft, Oculus, and Riot, talks often about her fears of instability. She's been through one mass layoff and watched two others happen to coworkers. In 2018, she moved from Seattle to Los Angeles, choosing her new home city in part because it was full of other big game companies—in case she's laid off again. She and her husband, also a game developer, frequently talk about their contingency plans, brainstorming lists of companies that could be attractive destinations if their current gigs go awry. "We orient our housing discussions around planning against likely layoff situations or having to move on if a project gets canceled," Chironis told me. "The common wisdom is that you want to stay in a home for at least five years. We've never worked anywhere longer than three."

Chironis says the hardest part about working in the video game industry is developing friendships that might be ripped apart with no warning. One day in 2014, Chironis arrived to work at her mobile game studio and was suddenly told to pack up her things and go home. Until then, she had thought everything was fine. "You just get pulled into an office and told to leave, and you're not even permitted to say good-bye to anybody," Chironis said. "I couldn't come back to the studio. I had friends at the studio, or people I considered friends, and I had no way to contact them."

Video games are designed to bring joy to people, yet they're created in the shadow of corporate ruthlessness. Why does such a lucrative industry treat its workers this way? Why is the video game business so successful at creating interesting art and making billions of dollars, yet such a failure at providing stable employment?

■ ■ ■

When I set out to write my first book, *Blood, Sweat, and Pixels,* I wanted to know why video games are so hard to make. I asked a whole bunch of developers and got a whole bunch of answers. The short version: games straddle the line between art and science, where technological advancements and the challenge of "finding the fun" can make it near-impossible to build accurate schedules. Whether you're developing an open-world role-playing game like *Pillars of Eternity* or a linear adventure game like *Uncharted 4*, there are so many variables that it can often feel, as the saying goes, like shooting a movie while simultaneously building the camera.

With this book, I wanted to ask a different question: Why is it so hard to maintain job security in the video game industry? I wanted to know what it's like to work in a field where you might have to suddenly pack your things and move across the country without notice. I wanted to know why layoffs and studio shutdowns keep happening, how they impact people, and how those people recover. What's it like to start a game company only to watch it fall apart? What happens to a writer, an artist, a designer, a programmer, a sound engineer, a QA tester, or a producer when their employer's studio closes? How are their lives affected? What do they do next? How do they move on? What are their stories?

This is a book about what happens when video game studios shut down. More specifically, it's about what happens to humans when video game studios shut down. Don't expect to read too much in here about financial statistics or granular business negotiations— I'm far more interested in the lives affected by all those shuffling papers. What's it like to be in the room when your boss's boss gets up in front of the whole company and says you're all getting laid off? How does it feel to look around at your coworkers, the people with whom you pulled bleary all-nighters to finish your latest game, and know that you'll never all be in the same room again? And what's it like to be in the boss's shoes—to be the person who has to inform all your staff that they'll need to find new employment?

But this book isn't just about heartbreak and tragedy—it's also about recovery. When the sun sets on a company you love, what do you do next? Do you use this as an opportunity to go off on your own and make your dream game? Do you move across the world for another studio job? Quit the video game industry for a more stable field? Some game developers used layoffs as opportunities to follow their dreams of creative independence, taking risks they never thought they'd be able to take. Others simply gave up, leaving behind an industry that didn't care to keep them.

This book examines a number of these stories. In Boston, Massachusetts, we'll look at Irrational Games, the once-mighty studio behind the seminal game *BioShock*, and meet some of the people who made it. Across the country, in the San Francisco Bay, we'll visit 2K Marin (*BioShock 2*) and Visceral (*Dead Space*), two casualties of one of the most expensive cities on the planet. We'll see how a legendary baseball player's ambitious attempt to make a *World of Warcraft* killer turned into a catastrophe not just for one but for two big companies, in Rhode Island and Maryland. Down in Virginia, we'll look at how the game studio Mythic found itself a relic of the video game industry, struggling to keep up with the hottest new trends. Then we'll talk to some people who have suffered burnout from the process of game development and also explore some solutions for all this volatility.[1]

After all, when a video game presents you with an unexpected, unfair catastrophe but you still want to play, you pretty much have two options: you can push forward, fighting through setbacks and trying to keep making progress, or you can hit the reset button and

---

1   The stories in this book are based mostly on firsthand interviews with the people involved. Unless otherwise noted, every quote was said to me directly.

try again. Maybe you'll do better this time around. Maybe you'll find a hidden path to success. Or maybe you'll find that because of circumstances you can't control, flaws built into the very code of the game, you just keep running into the same obstacles. If things don't get better, then, well, you might just decide to stop playing.

CHAPTER 1

THE JOURNEYMAN

It was late 2005, and Warren Spector thought he was going to explode. He was sitting in a conference room in Glendale, California, pitching ideas for his next video game to a handful of executives from Disney, the conglomerate behind so much entertainment that had brought him joy over the years, from Dumbo to Donald Duck. It was a thrill to be there—or at least it had been, until in the middle of his pitch Spector saw the executives looking down at their phones, texting.

Spector was already skeptical of men who wore ties and cared deeply about quarterly earnings. He'd been through this before. Nearly fifty years old, with speckled gray hair and the trademark slouch of a man who spent way too much time looking at computers, Spector was usually the oldest guy in the room during meetings. He was also usually the most famous guy in the room. Spector had made a name for himself as the director of *Deus Ex*, a game that blended the thrill of a sci-fi shooter with the deep choices and consequences of a role-playing game. Executives hadn't understood it, but he had resisted their interference, and when *Deus Ex* came out in June 2000, it was an instant success, selling more than a million copies and leading to immediate deals for sequels and even a film.[2] Spector became a celebrity in the video game industry, jaunting around the world for interviews and convention panels, and a few years later he'd started his own company, Junction Point, to make games the way he wanted to make them.

Now he was playing the role of traveling salesman. He spent his days flying from publisher to publisher, wheeling and dealing as he tried to convince various groups of men in suits that it was worth investing tens of millions of dollars into his new studio. Spector was good at pitching—he spoke with the candor of someone who believed every word he said—but he also liked to talk about risks, which could make him come off as cantankerous. "In his mind, that's what gives him comfort," said his agent, Seamus Blackley. "Here are all the problems, everything that can go wrong, how terrible it's going to be. When he has that in his mind, he feels safe, because he knows all the things he has to think about."

Blackley was the one who had suggested that they go talk to Disney. It seemed like an odd choice to Spector, who'd always loved the house of anthropomorphic cartoons but never thought their family-friendly image could jell with his M-rated games. *Deus Ex* was set in a dystopian world full of immoral hackers and violent criminals—a strange fit for the company behind Mickey Mouse. Spector balked, arguing that the trip might not even be worth the cost of the plane tickets. Yet Blackley insisted that Disney was looking to change its approach to video games, so Spector flew out to the offices in Glendale, where they were brought to a large conference table surrounded by Disney executives. Spector started

---

2   As is usually the case with video game adaptations, the film never happened.

describing the pitches he had been shopping to other game publishers. There was *Sleeping Giants*, a fantasy role-playing game set in a world in which magic had disappeared. He was working on a kung fu game called *Ninja Gold* with the film director John Woo, and he had some ideas for another sci-fi project called *Necessary Evil*—or, as Spector called it, "*Deus Ex* with the serial numbers filed off." Disney's businesspeople seemed engaged and interested—at least until they started checking their Blackberrys.

"They're looking down at their phones while I'm pitching," Spector said. "I was thinking, 'I'm going to kill Seamus when I get out of here. I'm going to kill him.'" But when Spector peeked over at Blackley, the agent was also looking at his phone.

When Spector finished pitching, the Disney executives began talking. It turned out they'd been texting each other, asking if they should talk about *the thing*. They liked Spector, and thought his ideas were okay, but they had something totally different in mind. "One of the people they were texting was me, asking if it was okay to pitch him," said Seamus Blackley. "When Warren was sitting there, they had this idea that maybe they could try *that*. Maybe they could convince him."

By Spector's recollection, the rest of the conversation unfolded like this:

"How do you feel about doing licensed games?" a Disney executive asked.

"If it's the right license," said Spector.

"Are there any Disney licenses you'd be interested in?" asked the Disney executive.

"Yeah," said Spector. "Give me the ducks. Give me Scrooge and Donald."

Truth was, Spector had always been obsessed with cartoons. He'd written his master's thesis on Warner Bros. animation, and

Disney's grouchy waterfowl were his favorite of all. He'd long fantasized about making a *DuckTales* video game, telling interactive stories about the kajillionaire Scrooge McDuck and his grandnephews, Huey, Dewey, and Louie Duck. But the people running Disney had something else in mind—something that would irrevocably change the trajectory of Warren Spector's company, his career, and his life.

"Well," the executive said, "what do you think about Mickey Mouse?"

■ ■ ■

Long before he was offered the biggest cartoon character in the world, Warren Spector was obsessing over interactive stories. Born in 1955 and raised in New York City, Spector developed an early fascination with tabletop role-playing games, in which he'd get together with a few friends and a rulebook, letting the story play out in everyone's imaginations. At twenty-two he moved to Austin, Texas, for graduate school and wound up joining a *Dungeons & Dragons* campaign that lasted for nearly ten years. He still cites this epic fantasy story as one of the biggest influences on the video games he would go on to make. "We started out as members of the Rat Gang, living in the River City of Shang, and it was great," Spector said. "Originally, we'd just do little jobs—I could talk about this forever—we'd do little jobs and steal, go into dungeons. By the end we were commanding armies, and the people who had been arresting us were our allies or bitter enemies."

At the University of Texas in Austin, Spector studied cinema and worked on his thesis, teaching classes as a graduate assistant to pay the bills, until his department chairman called with some bad news. It was someone else's turn for a teaching job, which meant Spector was out. "I hung up the phone and said, 'Oh my god, how am I going to pay my rent? I've got no income now.'" An answer arrived shortly afterward when he got another call, this time from a friend at a company called Steve Jackson Games, which developed board games and tabletop RPGs. They were looking for an assistant editor, but the job would pay only minimum wage—was he interested? *Absolutely*, Spector told them. "I was an amateur gamer," he said. "I'd been designing my own game systems and creating my own campaigns."

In 1983, Spector started at Steve Jackson Games, where he learned how to design tabletop games like Toon, in which players would battle and break the fourth wall as they role-played cartoon ducks and rabbits. Every week or so, Spector would visit Austin Books, a local comic book store and mecca for geeks in central Texas. He liked to chat up one of the clerks, Caroline, and eventually convinced her to go out with him. The two started dating and for a while worked together at Steve Jackson Games, until Spector got a call one day in late 1986 for what seemed like a dream job: TSR, the company behind *Dungeons & Dragons*, wanted him to move up to Lake Geneva, Wisconsin, and be an editor. In the world of tabletop RPGs, this was sort of like playing college basketball and then getting a surprise call from the NBA. "He looked over at me and said, 'Do you want to go to Lake Geneva with me?'" recalled Caroline. "I said, 'Not unless you marry me.' He said, 'All right.'" A few weeks later, Warren and Caroline were moving to Wisconsin. By spring, they were married, in a small ceremony at Caroline's aunt and uncle's house back in Texas, where they realized they'd rather be living.

Lake Geneva was a bad fit for both Warren and Caroline. It was frigid during the winter, and the Spectors found themselves missing their old haunts and barbecue joints. Warren Spector grew bored with the work he was doing. He yearned to be creating characters and telling stories. One day, while trying to decide what kind of dice roll to use for a game's mechanics, he had a revelation. "I had a twenty-sided die in one hand and a percentile die in the other," Spector said. "I looked at the dice in my hand and said, 'If this is the biggest decision I have to make in my professional life, I need a new way to make a living.'" Soon, he got another life-changing phone call. This time it was from a friend back in Austin, asking if he wanted to return to Texas and work for a fledgling video game company called Origin Systems.

Origin was the brainchild of a game designer named Richard Garriott. The son of astronaut Owen Garriott, Richard had grown up obsessed with computers and space travel, and in 1981 he'd released a game that combined them both: *Ultima*, a video game interpretation of tabletop RPG rules that sent the player adventuring through a fantasy world full of castles and dungeons. Playing as a human, elf, dwarf, or bobbit (a not-so-subtle attempt to dodge *Lord of the Rings* copyrights), you'd go around solving quests, fighting monsters, and eventually boarding a spaceship to battle enemies among the stars. *Ultima*, which Garriott had created with a friend over the course of a year, was successful enough to let Garriott launch Origin and turn game development into his career.

Whereas Spector was introverted and demure, Garriott was flamboyant and outspoken, with a love for hosting lavish, themed parties and exploring dangerous places.[3] Back when Spector had lived in Austin, the two men had become unlikely friends, running

---

3   In 2008, after investing millions in a private organization called Space Adventures, Garriott would become one of the first private citizens (and the first professional game designer) to travel into space, just like the *Ultima* fantasy he'd created decades earlier.

in similar circles and sharing sensibilities about game design. Now, feeling unhappy in Lake Geneva, Spector leaped at the opportunity to join his pal at Origin. "I really wanted to work with Rich," Spector said. "I think that was part of why I got the job as well. We were really simpatico in just about every way." By 1989, when Spector walked into the doors at Origin, the company was up to its sixth *Ultima* game and expanding rapidly, with offices in both Texas and New Hampshire. The video game industry was booming, particularly on personal computers, and Origin had become a burgeoning power player.

In the years that followed, Spector learned how to be a video game producer—how to lead teams, manage projects, and perform the near-impossible act of steering a bunch of stubborn people toward a single creative vision. He worked with Garriott on *Ultima VI*, helping craft an elaborate story about a horde of gargoyles who at first seemed malicious but turned out to have more complicated motivations—an innovative twist on video game storytelling for the 1980s. He helped produce *Wing Commander*, a space combat simulator in which you'd pilot a starship and gun down aliens, with the rising young star Chris Roberts, whose intractable nature taught Spector a lot about how to compromise.[4] "We'd get into ten arguments a day, and if I won three of them, that was a good day," Spector said.

It didn't take long for Spector, one of the oldest people at Origin, to move up to a senior leadership role at the company. "My business model was: I would start up four projects, two internal and two external, and I'd kill two projects every year that weren't going

---

4   Chris Roberts would go on to direct *Star Citizen*, a space opera that entered crowdfunding in 2012 and has since raised over $300 million from fans willing to spend big money on virtual starships.

well," Spector said. "I would tell people that's what I was going to do. 'Be one of the projects that's going really well.'"

One Origin partner whose projects usually went well was Looking Glass, a studio in Cambridge, Massachusetts, run by a programmer named Paul Neurath. Spector and Neurath became close creative partners, collaborating on two seminal games: *Ultima Underworld*, which came out in 1992; and *System Shock*, released in 1995. The two games had very different settings—*Ultima Underworld* took place in a fantasy dungeon, while *System Shock* unfolded on a space station—but they shared common design elements. Notably, they were both fueled by Spector's and Neurath's desires to re-create the feeling of *Dungeons & Dragons*. "We loved stories from linear fiction, film, books," said Neurath, "but games are interactive. They give you a chance to interpret that story and layer on your own sense of character."

With *Ultima Underworld* and *System Shock*, Neurath and Spector helped pioneer a genre that today we call the "immersive sim," a type of game whose influence you can see in everything from *Fallout* to *The Legend of Zelda: Breath of the Wild*. The idea was to give players the tools to overcome puzzles and obstacles in a variety of ways. Say you had to get past a door guarded by two soldiers. An action game might force you to blow the soldiers to pieces in order to proceed. In an immersive sim, though, you'd have all sorts of options. You could kill the soldiers, sure, but maybe you'd instead decide to sneak past them using a set of vents connected to a nearby alley. Or maybe you'd set off fireworks to distract the guards while you ran through the door, laughing as they missed you entirely.

In the early 1990s, this was a paradigm shift for video games. Most designers would set up a theme park ride and let the player steer the cart; immersive sims let you build the cart yourself and then pick which track to send it down. Spector, Neurath, and their cadre of talented game developers wanted to get as close as possible to re-creating the feeling of unlimited possibility that tabletop games like *Dungeons & Dragons* provided. "What we like to talk about is: two different players play a mission or adventure in a game and then they compare notes and it's like they've played a completely different game," said Neurath. "That's the litmus test."

The games were groundbreaking, but Origin was struggling, facing a cash shortage thanks to the high costs of manufacturing floppy disks.[5] In 1992, low on funds, Richard Garriott sold his company to the megapublisher Electronic Arts (EA). As is often the case with major acquisitions, the partnership started off well. "For a couple years, it was great," said Spector. "EA gave us bigger budgets and more freedom than we could even imagine." With these newfound riches, Origin expanded rapidly and started trying to produce dozens of new video games at once, some of them managed by newer, inexperienced staff. Many of these games were then canceled, and by 1995, increasingly frustrated EA executives were flying out to Austin every few weeks, asking questions about why Origin was wasting so much money. "We were not good citizens," Spector said. Origin was no longer the scrappy young publisher that had found unexpected success with the *Ultima* series; now, it was a cog in EA's massive political machine, and its developers had to deal with the executive machinations—and fiscal accountability— that came with that.

This was when Spector first began to resent some of the people who handled business development in the game industry. "One day,

---

5   In the 1980s and early 1990s, computer games shipped on thin 3.5-inch disks with limited storage capabilities. Origin's games required tons of these floppy disks—sometimes eight or even ten for a single game—which could be devastatingly pricey. It wasn't until *Myst* in 1993 that video game publishers began switching to the more versatile CD-ROM format.

a very senior EA executive who I will not name came to me and said I was not on a successful career path," said Spector. "Because even though I made money every year, I only made a little bit of money." EA was a publicly traded company, which meant that its top priority was to deliver fiduciary growth for shareholders. Simply making a profit wasn't good enough; your profits had to grow exponentially every year. Immersive sims, while beloved by those who played them, weren't reaching the types of audiences that would lead to exponential growth. Warren Spector's games were critically acclaimed but never sold as well as others in Origin's library, like Chris Roberts's *Wing Commander* series, which made Spector the odd man out. "I was the 'B-movie' guy, the guy who had the low budgets and nobody paid attention, so I got to do all these crazy projects that were cult classics," Spector said. "[The EA executive] said, 'Why would I give you a dollar knowing I'm gonna get $1.10 back when I can give Chris $10 million and either make $100 million or get a tax write-off?'"

By 1996, Warren Spector had decided to leave EA, and his old friend Paul Neurath asked if he wanted to come out to Massachusetts and work with him at Looking Glass. Spector refused to leave Texas again, so Neurath suggested he open up a new office down there. Two other Looking Glass employees already worked out of their homes in Austin, so they could join Spector's new venture. They'd call it Looking Glass Austin, and under Spector, it would get its own autonomous staff and projects.

Spector started hiring developers and planning out games, like *Junction Point*, a sci-fi multiplayer game in which you could together with groups of friends and go off on adventures—an unusual concept for 1996. "It was way ahead of its time," said Neurath. But Looking Glass ran into investment problems, and after just a few months, Neurath and Spector were facing difficult questions about how to keep the company alive. "I told Paul, 'Just shut the Austin office down,'" said Spector. "I was pretty confident I could get another deal."[6] And in 1997, Spector went through his first studio closure, asking some of his employees at Looking Glass Austin if they might stick around while he looked for a new project. (The *Junction Point* game never happened.)

They weren't unemployed for long. Shortly after the closure, Spector and his new team came close to signing a deal with a company called Westwood for a role-playing game based on the popular real-time strategy game series *Command & Conquer* (which, ironically, would later also be acquired by EA). Then Spector got a call from a brash, bombastic game designer named John Romero. Romero had also worked at Origin, although he'd left in 1988, a year before Spector started. He'd then partnered with a programmer named John Carmack to found id Software, the scrappy studio behind megahits like *Doom*, *Quake*, and *Wolfenstein 3D*. Tensions between Romero and the other employees led the rockstar designer to resign, and he founded a new studio, Ion Storm, that had already built up a substantial bank account by the time Romero and Spector got on the phone.

Romero told Spector to say no to the *Command & Conquer* deal and to come work for him instead. But it was too late, Spector said— they were about to sign. So Romero drove from his office in Dallas to Spector's in Austin and slapped down the godfather offer of all godfather offers. "Unlimited budget, a bigger marketing budget than I've ever had in my life," said Spector. "Make the game of your dreams with no interference from anybody. Who says no to that?"

What emerged from this deal was a video game called *Deus Ex*. If

---

6   Looking Glass shut down in 2000 following what Paul Neurath described as a series of unfortunate events. "In brief, our investors decided they weren't interested in being in the games industry," he said.

Ultima Underworld and *System Shock* had been blueprints for what an "immersive sim" could look like, *Deus Ex* was the building. It was such a unique blend of genres, the marketing people didn't know what to call it—was this an RPG? A shooter? An action game?

The answer turned out to be "all of the above." Playing as a supersoldier named JC Denton in a near-futuristic dystopian world full of conspiracies, nanotechnology, and nasty scientists, you could overcome each of the game's obstacles in a variety of ways. Sometimes you might gun down enemies, but you could also find ways to sneak around them, or maybe hack a nearby computer terminal to disable their defenses. The goal, Spector later wrote, was to make "a game about player expression, not about how clever we were as designers, programmers, artists, or storytellers." At one point, an executive asked Spector why he was bothering to put stealth in the game when their metrics showed that only a fraction of players used it. He ignored them. "I learned early from Chris Roberts the power of the word 'no,'" Spector said. "The way to win a negotiation is to be willing to walk away from it."

When *Deus Ex* came out in June 2000, it blew players away, teaching the world that among the monotonous shooters and platformers, there were still countless untapped visions for what a video game could look like. It sold more than a million copies and was widely seen as an all-time great. Spector rode high on *Deus Ex*'s success, running Ion Storm's Austin office even once Romero left the company in the summer of 2001 and the Dallas studio shuttered.[7] He assigned *Deus Ex*'s lead designer, Harvey Smith, to direct

---

7   There were a number of factors behind the implosion of Ion Storm Dallas, but the most memorable was an advertisement, perhaps the most infamous in gaming history, for the game *Daikatana*. Black ink splashed on a bloodred screen declared: "John Romero's about to make you his bitch." Fans did not react well.

a sequel, *Deus Ex: Invisible War*, and oversaw other projects, including a new game in the *Thief* series, a set of fantasy stealth games that had been created by Spector's old buddies at Looking Glass.

Again, corporate bureaucracy began to interfere with Warren Spector's plans. The video game publisher Eidos had purchased Ion Storm during *Deus Ex*'s development, and Spector found himself dealing with the same type of risk aversion that had bugged him so much at EA. He wanted to make a game set in the Wild West but was told by Eidos marketing execs that Western games couldn't make money. "My response was, 'Western games don't sell until someone makes one that sells,'" Spector said. (That prediction would come to fruition a few years later with Rockstar's megasuccessful *Red Dead Redemption*.) Spector hit his breaking point when the marketing people started telling him to stop talking about video game storytelling so much. "This was a quote," Spector said. "'Warren, you're not allowed to say the word 'story' anymore.'"

This was becoming a pattern for Warren Spector, one that was not uncommon in his field. The video game industry, like all artistic pursuits, is built on a tension between two factions: the creative people and the money people. The conflict between game developers trying to make art and game publishers trying to make a profit is as old as video games themselves. It's the root cause of most of the game industry's problems. "I've never made a budget and a schedule in my life, not on one project I've ever worked on," said Spector. "I've always challenged people to just answer this question: Can you name one game that has shipped on time and on budget that anybody cares about?"

It infuriated executives that Spector wasn't driven to make games that would sell millions of copies—that this cranky creative didn't seem to care about how much of their money he was blowing. From their perspective, he was stubborn and fiscally irresponsible.

Spector, however, was fine with being the "B-movie guy," even if it meant butting heads with the money types. He just wanted to make the games that he wanted to make. "One of the things I love about Warren," said Art Min, a programmer who worked with him at Ion Storm, "is that he'll say, 'The number of copies I want to sell is $N+1$, where N is the number of copies I need to sell to make my next game.'"

In 2004, seven years after starting Ion Storm Austin, Spector decided he was going to quit, and Min planned to follow him, along with a small group of other employees who called themselves the Cabal. During months of spirited debates over tamales at a Mexican restaurant in the Austin suburbs, the Cabal put together plans to start a new, independent video game company. It would be a risky move, but the freedom would be unprecedented for someone like Spector, who had watched executive after executive try to kill his ideas because they wouldn't generate enough of a profit. Spector was nearly fifty, working in an industry that seemed tailored for people in their twenties. He and his wife had decided not to have kids, which made it easier for him to put in the long hours that the video game industry demanded from its creatives, but he still often thought about the number of games he had left in him. If each of these big projects took two or three years to make, and some were canceled or otherwise went awry, how many more could he realistically finish? "I was saying, 'Jump off the cliff, jump off the cliff, jump off the cliff,'" said Caroline Spector. "This is the time to go start your own company. You're never going to have a better time to start your own company. You need to jump off the cliff now."

They called the new company Junction Point, after the multiplayer game he'd wanted to develop at Looking Glass before it shut down. Immediately, Spector and Min went to look for money, eventually hiring Seamus Blackley, an old friend of Spector's, to represent them. Blackley, a physicist and polymath, had been a programmer at Looking Glass in the 1990s before going off on his own wild career journey with a notable stop at Microsoft, where he convinced founder Bill Gates to invest billions of dollars in a console that could take on the PlayStation. (Things worked out.) These days, Blackley was an agent, working with the Creative Artists Agency to help put together game financing deals for creative people. His client list was full of people who had smart ideas but always struggled to find money, like Tim Schafer (*Psychonauts, Grim Fandango*); Lorne Lanning (*Oddworld*); and now, Warren Spector.

Blackley helped Junction Point sign a deal with the publisher Majesco to make *Sleeping Giants*, a fantasy game based on a world that Warren and Caroline Spector had conceived together decades earlier, full of dragons and an elaborate physics system based on elemental spells. The two companies worked together for over a year until Majesco, facing financial struggles, decided it no longer wanted to make premium video games. "I was sitting there going, 'Uh, what do I do?'" Spector said. "There was a kill fee, and that kept us going. So we had enough money that I hoped would carry us over until I could find us another deal." Junction Point entered crisis mode. Independence had left them cash-strapped, and Art Min resigned following some heated battles with Spector over how to move forward—he thought the only path toward sustainability was to lay people off; Spector didn't.[8]

Soon, another opportunity emerged—a call from Gabe Newell, the billionaire CEO of Valve Software, asking if Spector and his team wanted to make a brand-new episode for the iconic shooter *Half-Life 2*. That lasted a few months before it, too, was canceled.

---

8   The pair stopped talking for a few years but wound up reconciling later—
     Spector even read a poem at Min's wedding.

"So that went away, and I was out a deal again," Spector said. Here was a group of experienced game developers, including an industry legend, and they just couldn't seem to find enough money to make something new. If they had gone indie just a few years later, they might have been able to explore alternate routes of funding—Kickstarter, self-publishing, small boutique publishers—but in the mid-2000s, those avenues didn't exist. Big corporations like EA and Activision were Spector's only real option, and none of them seemed to be interested in the games he was pitching.

It was hard not to wonder: Had this whole independent venture been a mistake? Did Spector really want to spend the rest of his career searching for money? The problem with jumping off the cliff is that sometimes, you just hit rocks.

■ ■ ■

When Disney executive Graham Hopper was promoted, he had one mission: produce more video games. Hopper, a South African businessman who'd started working for Team Mickey in 1991, had a mind for finance and a belief that there was real money in the video game industry. In the past, when Disney had dabbled in video games, it had mostly licensed out characters like Mickey and Goofy to other game publishers rather than developing the games itself. But in the early 2000s, as Disney watched other companies rake in big profits by making their own games, dollar signs appeared in its cartoon doe eyes. The company launched a new division, which would later be called Disney Interactive Studios, and Hopper was put in charge. By 2002, Disney had officially entered the video game business.

Now Hopper and his staff had to figure out what to do with their most valuable property, Mickey Mouse. Disney's ubiquitous mascot had starred in video games before, most notably in the 1990s with a series of *Mario*-style platformers for the Super Nintendo and Sega Genesis, but he hadn't become an icon in gaming the way he had on the television screen. In Hollywood, Mickey was top mouse; in video games, he was just another cartoon character. Part of Disney's plans for doubling down on game development involved making a Mickey game that people would cherish and remember. "Mickey's almost a mythical thing in the game space at Disney," Hopper said. "He's one of the most famous characters in the world, yet he doesn't have a video game that helps bring him in touch with new consumers, new fans."

Hopper had his hands full, though, and the Mickey project failed to gain much traction until the summer of 2004, when it wound up in the hands of a group of Disney interns who needed a new project. The interns found themselves unimpressed by some of the pitches that Disney had received from external agencies— one, in true 1990s style, put Mickey in sunglasses and gave him a hoverboard—and decided to instead come up with their own ideas. "We wanted to make Mickey Mouse meets something like *Ocarina of Time*," said Sean Vanaman, one of the interns.[9] They wound up working with a small independent studio on the project, which was code-named *Mickey Epic*, a title signaling their ambitions. It'd be an old-fashioned look for Mickey, reminiscent of black-and-white cartoons like *Steamboat Willie*, in which the iconic mouse had wide eyes and a pronounced jaw. The player, as Mickey, would go around slashing up monsters and accumulating special powers.

The game would also spotlight a pivotal part of Disney history.

---

9   Vanaman would go on to have a remarkable career in the video game industry, directing *Firewatch*, a charming, beautiful mystery set in the forests of Wyoming. He'd later sell his company to Valve and go on to work on a new *Half-Life* game, many years after Warren Spector's canceled project.

During Disney's orientation for new hires, the interns had learned about a character that most people didn't know existed: Oswald the Lucky Rabbit, an anthropomorphic bunny created by Walt Disney in 1927. With large, protruding ears and a peppy personality, Oswald became more popular than the other, flatter cartoon characters (mostly cats) who dominated the animation circuit of the 1920s. But then, as the story went, a nasty contract dispute led Walt Disney to strike off on his own. He started scribbling early sketches of a cartoon mouse to which he'd retain the rights and quit Universal, leaving Oswald in the hands of other artists. By 2004, the world had mostly forgotten about Oswald, although the Disney corporation made sure to share the story with all of its employees. "It's the first thing they tell you, day one, coffee's still warm in the cups," said Vanaman. "We were like, 'Who's the bad guy? Oh, the guy we first heard about.'"

It made for the perfect hook. Oswald, lost and abandoned, could be the game's tragic antagonist. Vanaman and the other interns envisioned an Oswald who was angry and jealous, forgotten by the world and driven to make his place in it. Envious of his more successful younger brother, Oswald would build a theme park of his own—a skewed take on Disney's Magic Kingdom, made out of cardboard and spare parts. "It was like he heard about Disneyland through the telephone and decided to make his own version," said Vanaman.

Graham Hopper and the other higher-ups in Disney's new video game division were excited about the project, but there were two lingering problems. The first was that Disney still didn't have the rights to Oswald. Since 1927, Universal had owned Mickey's older brother, and although the film titan had long ago stopped making Oswald cartoons, Universal's decision makers saw the value in keeping him around. Question was, could Disney get it back? Graham

Hopper pitched the game idea to Disney president Bob Iger, who liked it, and called Universal to ask if they could get the rights to Oswald. Universal's executives immediately said no. They figured that if Disney wanted Oswald, he must be valuable. "That was the end of that for a while," said Hopper. But Iger never forgot about it. "He kept it in his back pocket for when the time came he had something they wanted."

The Mickey video game project sat dormant, and then something unusual happened. Al Michaels, the legendary sports broadcaster best known for calling the United States hockey team's victory in the 1980 Olympics ("Do you believe in miracles?"), wanted to get out of his long-running ABC contract and join his old pal John Madden at NBC for *Sunday Night Football*. Disney, which owned ABC, quietly started negotiating with NBC, which also happened to be part of Universal. And on February 9, 2006, Disney announced that it had "traded" Al Michaels to its rival media conglomerate in exchange for a few small licensing deals as well as, inexplicably, the rights to Oswald the Lucky Rabbit. It was perhaps the only time in recorded history that a human being had been swapped for a cartoon character. ("I'm going to be a trivia answer someday," Michaels later joked.)

What nobody outside Disney's walls knew at the time—and what many people still don't realize—was that Bob Iger had asked for Oswald solely to use him for the Mickey Mouse video game. "He was very happy to call me and tell me we now had the rights back," said Hopper. "There were no other reasons. It was to make this game. It was sufficiently cool and interesting to everybody involved."

Project *Mickey Epic*, which would later be changed to *Epic Mickey*, would finally be able to get off the ground—except for the second big problem. "We didn't have a studio capable of making this game happen," said Hopper. The original prototype that the Disney interns had helped make with that outside independent studio was impressive—"I haven't played a six-month prototype that played and felt like this since," said Vanaman—but Disney didn't have faith in that company to carry it forward. It was too small, and didn't have the clout that Disney's executives wanted. "People saw it and said, 'This is cool. Let's get someone else to make it,'" said Vanaman. In the months before the Oswald deal, Hopper and his team had been hunting for a developer who might be a good fit, someone who was famous enough in the video game industry to make a big splash when Disney announced that it would be jumping into games.

Turned out there was someone available.

■ ■ ■

When he heard the whole story, it became clear to Warren Spector why Disney's executives were texting while he was trying to pitch them his game ideas. They weren't all that interested in his pitches. What they really wanted was for him to direct the Mickey Mouse video game, and they'd actually been texting one another to ask if they should pull out the proposal. Once Seamus Blackley, the agent, gave them the green light, Graham Hopper and the other Disney executives took out some of the *Epic Mickey* proposals they'd been putting together in recent months. "We'd learned from that conversation that Warren was a big fan of Disney in general," said Hopper. "Watching him present to us and engaging with him, it felt like a little bit of a long shot that he'd be interested, but it seemed worth the effort."

So, then, did Spector want to work on a Mickey game? He could barely hold in his excitement. "I just looked at them and said, 'Yeah,'" Spector said. "Mickey Mouse is the most recognizable icon on Planet Earth. Who doesn't say yes to that?" Hopper gave Spector the materials they'd already put together for *Epic Mickey*—concept art, a basic story, other assorted notes and ideas—and they agreed to the framework of a deal. Disney would pay Spector and Junction Point to spend the next few months putting together concept art and design for the Mickey project. If Disney liked it, both companies would move forward. If not, no hard feelings. "I just said, 'You've just given me an acorn, and I'm going to grow that into an oak tree,'" Spector said.

When he got back to Texas toward the end of 2005, Spector began working with two other Junction Point developers on the Mickey project, taking the Oswald premise and adding some of their own twists. They spent a great deal of time figuring out how Mickey would look, how his movements would be animated, and what he'd be able to do in the game. The game's world, the Cartoon Wasteland, would be a gathering place for unused and forgotten Disney characters. They played around with other titles like "Mouse Trapped," but *Epic Mickey* stuck. The trade for Oswald was finalized a few months later, showing Junction Point that Disney was serious about developing this game.

In April 2006, when Spector flew back to California to show Disney what they'd made, Graham Hopper and the other executives told them they were pleased with the results. There was just one catch. "That's when it got weird," said Spector. "They said, 'We love your concept. We want you to make this game. The only way you get to make this game is if we acquire you.'"

This wasn't what Warren Spector wanted to hear. He'd already been part of two different studios that were acquired by big corporations: Origin (EA) and Ion Storm (Eidos). Neither acquisition had worked out very well for him. Executives, looking for home runs rather than Spector's singles and doubles, had never given him the leeway he wanted, and Spector was not shy about letting them know how he felt. During social situations he often felt introverted, but in meetings, he wasn't afraid to let loose. Spector had started his own studio—jumped off the cliff—so that he would have the creative freedom to make the games that made him happy, without having to deal with executives demanding that he sell millions of copies.

Over sushi dinner in Glendale, one of Disney's executives made Spector an offer for Junction Point. The number was so low, Spector found himself genuinely offended. "I said no," Spector recalled. "He said, 'What do you mean, 'No'? No one says no to Disney.'" Spector thought it'd be perfectly fine to say no to Disney. He was obstinate, the company had some promising leads, and he'd learned during his days at Origin that the only way to win a negotiation was to be willing to walk away.

The tactic worked. Months later, in 2007, a Disney vice president called up Spector and asked if he would meet for dinner. Spector said sure, and the vice president was on a plane to Austin the next day. "He said they'd spent a year trying to find someone to execute on our proposal, but hadn't found anyone—would I come back and do it?" said Spector. "They still wanted me to sell Junction Point and join Disney, but this time they came back with a deal that was just good enough to convince me."

For Spector, the proposition was bittersweet. In addition to cash, Disney would allow Junction Point to scale up to the hundreds of staff they'd need in order to make *Epic Mickey*, but it wasn't the type of "eff you" money that often comes coupled with acquisitions. "I was thinking, 'I'm not ready to get acquired,'" Spector said. "But the reality of the games business is, there are four endgames: You go public, which nobody does. You survive for decades like Valve. You get acquired. Or you go out of business."

Spector didn't want to go out of business, and Junction Point's other projects hadn't gotten very far, as they still hadn't found a new publisher for *Sleeping Giants* or the John Woo game. After conferring with his wife, Spector decided he'd sell his company, and he and Seamus Blackley started what would become a very long process of piecing together a Disney acquisition contract. "It's very difficult to negotiate with them," said Blackley. "They're meticulous, have a lot of attorneys, and negotiate for every point like it's death."

That summer, at the 2007 E3 convention, Graham Hopper wanted to shock the video game world, informing them all that Disney was entering gaming in a big way. They'd hold a press conference full of announcements, unveiling the division's new name—Disney Interactive Studios—and showing off games for both kids (*High School Musical*) and adults (*Turok*). One of the marquee announcements would be that Disney had made a big investment in Warren Spector, who was recognized by most video game fans as an industry legend—the guy who had helped bring the world *Ultima Underworld*, *System Shock*, and *Deus Ex*.

Problem was, the deal still wasn't finalized. Spector was antsy about giving up his independence, and there were still a couple of items left to negotiate. "It was absolutely down to the wire," said Hopper. "Even I didn't know at that stage whether he was actually going to go through."

On the morning of July 13, 2007, Graham Hopper and Warren Spector stood together at a loading dock behind the Fairmont Hotel in Santa Monica, California. Hopper held the acquisition contract, waiting for Spector to sign it. In front of the hotel, journalists were already filing in for a Disney news briefing. "They're letting the press into the room where the announcement is going to be made, while I'm outside with Graham and a contract I had not yet signed," Spector said. "I had one phone with my lawyer on one ear, and Seamus on another phone on my other ear." Minutes before the deal was set to be announced, Spector still wasn't sure if he was ready to give up his independence. Was this really a good idea?

Blackley told Spector that there was only one real question he needed to answer: Did he like these guys? Did he want to work with them? In other words, did he trust Hopper and the rest of Disney Interactive Studios to help him try to make a great game? If the answer was yes, Blackley said, the rest would work itself out. Spector thought about it, then decided, once again, to jump off the cliff. "And so I signed the contract," said Spector, "walked into the room, and got introduced."

The journalists in attendance, who had no idea how close to the wire the deal had come, were impressed by Disney's moxie, although they thought it was a strange fit. They asked many of the same questions that Spector had asked two years earlier. Why would the director of the violent, gritty *Deus Ex* work for a company best known for cartoons and kids' games? He'd later tell the press that he'd always loved cartoons—that he'd written his master's thesis on them—and that this was a dream opportunity for him. Hopper didn't tell the world what Spector was actually working on, just that he was making a game for Disney, leaving pundits to wonder and speculate. "Then I got to go back to the office that was working on an epic fantasy role-playing game," said Spector, "and say, 'Guys, we're making a Mickey Mouse game.'"

Not everyone back in Austin was elated about the acquisition, and a few of Junction Point's original developers quit, telling Spector they didn't want to work on a cartoon game. For everyone else, however, this meant stability. They no longer had to go out and pitch new projects to publishers and investors—they could just make a video game. Warren Spector no longer had to be a salesman;

he could be a director. "We were thrilled," said Caroline Spector. "It was a very big deal. It meant Junction Point could continue. They could stop worrying about money."

As the studio expanded, from a dozen people to multiple dozens and eventually to over one hundred, the game titled *Epic Mickey* began to take shape. It would be a Wii exclusive, designed for the wand-like Wiimote and its waggling motion controls. It'd be a platforming game, like *Super Mario Bros.*, and you'd have to leap across precarious cliffs and ledges as you explored Oswald's malformed catalog of Disney history. Mickey's main tool was a magical paintbrush that could be used either to paint or to thin out large swaths of the world, giving players the choice of how to deal with obstacles and enemies—you could help bring them back to life with paint or obliterate them with your thinner. Your choices would have consequences that resonated throughout the game, influencing the story and dialogue. *Epic Mickey* wouldn't give you quite as many options as Spector's previous immersive sims had, but it was still driven by his philosophy to create games in which the player's choices actually made a difference.

For the next three years, Spector led development on *Epic Mickey*, expanding his team and battling with Disney executives over time and resources. Spector had never worked well with financial constraints—this was the man who, by his own admission, had never been on time or on budget in his life—and for a tightly wound company like Disney, that could lead to a lot of tension. "There were times when executives would call me into the office and try to say, 'This is the way you should make this game,'" said Spector, "and I would just say, 'No.'" They fought over scaling back the budget, tightening the schedule, and even over the way Mickey should look and move. After all, Mickey was the crown jewel— the most important character in Disney's vault. "I don't know why

I wasn't fired six times at Disney, but I wasn't," said Spector. "And they let me make the game I wanted to make."

Epic Mickey came out for the Wii on November 30, 2010. It had some issues—notably, the jerky camera movements, which made it tough to see what was going on—but it was a charming adventure that players seemed to enjoy.[10] The game sold well, moving 1.3 million copies in its first month, and by Graham Hopper's recollection it came very close to breaking even. This was a success for a game that launched on just one console, and with the fundamentals and technology they'd developed already, Spector's team was in a good position to make a sequel.

Yet, at the same time, there were radical shifts happening in Disney's video game division. Everyone was still feeling the fallout from the 2008 US recession, and video games were exploding on phones and Facebook, with analysts prognosticating that the traditional video game console would soon be dead. In the summer of 2010, Disney had put together a $763 million deal for Playdom, a company that made social games, and as part of a restructuring that fall, Playdom boss John Pleasants was installed above Graham Hopper in Disney's video game division. "I think there were people in the corporate group at Disney who had come to the conclusion that it was really important for Disney not to be left behind by, shall we say, the online revolution," said Hopper. "And console games were a dying industry. That's a conclusion they

---

10   Says Spector: "Everybody's got a problem with the camera. I will go to my
      grave defending my camera.... You could erase a part of a wall and walk
      through it and be on the other side of a wall. What is the camera supposed
      to do? The wall was there a minute ago, and now it's not. Or there's a little
      hole in the wall, and the character is standing a foot away from that hole—
      what is the camera supposed to do? There were dozens of problems like
      that that we created for ourselves. Could we have done better? Sure, I guess,
      with more time, but I'm still proud of the camera team."

reached by themselves, and it's not one I supported or agreed with."

By the fall of 2010, even as Junction Point's developers crunched long hours to finish *Epic Mickey*, Disney's executives were putting out signals that they no longer cared about console video games. Disney Interactive Studios had been losing a great deal of money, and the company wanted to take a different approach to game development. "After that Playdom acquisition was done, it was very clear that the interest in console games was not there anymore," said Hopper. "I even heard words said like, 'It's dead.' That was not something I could agree with and stay."

A few weeks before the release of *Epic Mickey*, Hopper—who had shepherded Disney Interactive Studios and been a champion for video games at the company—resigned. Hopper was the one who had brought Spector and Junction Point to Disney. And Hopper was the one who had pushed for Disney to make games on consoles like the Wii, games like *Epic Mickey* that would appeal to both hard-core and casual video game fans. Now he was gone.

Spector and Hopper had plenty of disagreements, but it was clear that Hopper loved and cared deeply about video games, which Spector always respected. Pleasants, on the other hand, was a business guy, with a background running numbers and branding at companies like Pepsi and Ticketmaster.[11] He looked at the spreadsheets for Disney Interactive Studios and saw a company bleeding many millions of dollars in an industry that appeared to be moving toward mobile games, social games, and live services—games that could be updated and monetized for months and months after release rather than generating revenue only when they launched.

---

11   Pleasants declined to comment for this book.

From Pleasants's perspective, making huge investments in console games didn't make much sense. Even if *Epic Mickey* was a big success, Junction Point would have to spend the next three years working on something new, burning cash until the sequel came out. Why not invest in games that could make money every year?

Pleasants was blunt when he first met Spector, telling the *Epic Mickey* director that Disney's strategy was changing. "He came right out and told me he didn't think people who were making console games were going to have jobs much longer," Spector said. "Not that he was going to fire us, but console games and PC games were not the future. He told me that the day I met him."

It raised an obvious but troubling question. If Junction Point made console games, but console games weren't the future, then what did that mean for Junction Point?

■ ■ ■

Chase Jones didn't mind living like a nomad, which made him a good fit for the video game industry. As a kid he shuffled between schools often—his parents were divorced, and his dad's job at the phone company led them to move around frequently. In 1999 he began attending DigiPen, a private college for game developers in Redmond, Washington, and when he graduated, he moved out to Los Angeles, California. There he worked as a game tester for a couple of big publishers before flying across the country for a job at an independent studio in Brooklyn, New York, called Mind Engine. It wasn't exactly glamorous. "There were days when I'd get off the subway, walk the ten blocks to work, and open up and the lights weren't on, because the electricity wasn't paid," Jones said. "So you grabbed your tower, hopped back on the subway, and just worked from home."

The founders of Mind Engine, unable to find proper funding, shut it down in 2004, and Jones went on the road once again, this time moving to Cary, North Carolina, to work at Red Storm Entertainment, a Ubisoft studio that worked mostly on military games based on the works of novelist Tom Clancy. In 2006, Chase Jones got another job offer, this time in Novato, California, at the publisher 2K's flagship studio, Visual Concepts. The offer was enticing: if Jones came and helped the team finish a movie tie-in game, *Fantastic Four: Rise of the Silver Surfer*, then he'd get to help them start a brand-new franchise once they were done. "What I didn't realize was that I was the third lead designer being brought in, with ten months to go," Jones said. "That was full-on crunch, nonstop, no holidays, no time down. Most times I'd leave the office at three in the morning to go back home, sleep, wake up, then get back at 8:00 a.m. to do it all over again."

It would have been tough enough to crunch like that for a game Jones thought could be great, but *Fantastic Four: Rise of the Silver Surfer* wasn't designed to push creative boundaries or hit new artistic heights. It was designed to sell copies to kids who watched the new *Fantastic Four* movie and wanted to play the video game. "I think we all had realistic expectations," Jones said. "It's not like we thought we were going to win Game of the Year or anything." What helped him and his teammates get through the extensive overtime was the hope of getting to do something new and exciting afterward. Visual Concepts was mainly known for making sports games like the *NBA 2K* series; with *Fantastic Four*, they were hoping to branch out into action-adventure games and maybe more.

Then came the layoffs. In June 2007, when the *Fantastic Four* video game was finished but before it had actually been released, 2K let go of nearly the entire team behind it.[12] Only two people were kept around: the game's director, Paul Weaver; and Chase Jones, who was confounded. "Me and Paul were sitting in half of an airplane hangar, looking at all of the cleared desks, just staring at each other, wondering why they even kept us," Jones said. "They'd told me they wanted to find a place for me with the sports franchises, but I wasn't into designing sports games. A couple weeks later they put me in an office by myself, and I ended up just sitting there playing games until I could find another gig, driving myself crazy."

Eventually he did find another gig—in Champaign, Illinois, where he became a designer at Volition, a studio best known for a quirky series of *Grand Theft Auto*–inspired games called *Saints Row*. Jones was there for about a year before his project was canceled by Volition's parent company, THQ, which had been hit hard by the US recession. (THQ would go bankrupt just a few years later.) Searching yet again for a new job, Jones got in touch with his old friend Paul Weaver, who had moved to Austin, Texas, to be the studio director of a company called Junction Point Studios.

Weaver said they were looking for a lead designer for their new Mickey Mouse project, and in the fall of 2008, Chase Jones found himself driving down to Austin, Texas—his sixth city (and fifth state) of residence in seven years of game development. "I'd already come to the mind-set that, whether they tell you it's full-time or not, this industry is contractual," Jones said. "You finish your title, then

---

12   Michael Stribling, the lead concept artist on *Fantastic Four*, told me in an email he was disappointed at how 2K handled the layoffs, explaining that the company escorted everyone out the door without giving them a chance to go back to their desks and grab their things. "I was just generally irritated at the whole situation," he said. "You have a whole team killing themselves to produce and release a game in a stupid amount of time with very little help from anyone, and then you let all of them go. No 'attaboy' or 'good job.' Nothing."

you worry about whether there's going to be another title or not. 401(k)s don't matter. They're all just going to be in microchunks that you then consolidate. Because that's just not the way this industry runs." Junction Point at least seemed like a place where Jones could stay for a while. It was owned by Disney, after all. Few companies were richer. Few companies were more stable.

For the next two years, Jones worked as the lead designer on *Epic Mickey*, helping Warren Spector execute his vision for the ambitious platformer. It was an intense process, exacerbated by some turnover in the design department that had happened before Jones got to Austin. "We needed to define the gameplay and pull a vertical slice together I think within a month and a half of me landing here," Jones said. A vertical slice is essentially a demo, usually a mission or a level, meant to show everyone how the game will ultimately function. To make a vertical slice, the game's developers need to figure out the fundamentals—in *Epic Mickey*'s case, how Mickey would look, how he'd move, how he'd swing his paintbrush and hop from platform to platform. What that meant for Jones and the rest of the development team was a whole lot of overtime.

Once they'd finished *Epic Mickey* in the fall of 2010, the tired staff at Junction Point split into a few teams. Some worked on secretive new projects; others started conceiving and designing a family-friendly game in which all of Disney's characters competed against one another at the Olympics. A handful of people started working on tools and other processes to make the studio run more efficiently. Chase Jones, meanwhile, was told to take charge of the sequel to *Epic Mickey*. "Paul and Warren looked at me and said: 'Go ahead and start concepting what *Mickey 2* will be like,'" Jones said. They gave him a team of a dozen people to start building a prototype—some sort of rough, playable demo for what the game could become. (Unlike a vertical slice, it's okay for a prototype to look janky and unfinished.)

The big new feature would be co-op multiplayer. In addition to playing solo as Mickey, you'd be able to bring along a buddy to play as Oswald the Lucky Rabbit, who had evolved from tragic villain to helpful ally. Where Mickey had a magical paintbrush, Oswald would get a remote control, allowing him to power up switches and electrocute enemies. Mickey and Oswald would be able to perform cooperative attacks and even revive one another during tight battles. By the time Junction Point's staff took off for Christmas break at the end of 2010, Jones and his team had designed a co-op prototype and sketched out the basics of a story for the second game. The hope was that with a standard development period of two and a half or three years, *Epic Mickey 2* could be really special.

What was most important at this point was for the team to stay small, so they could change things without having to worry about too much wasted work. Even for a sequel like *Epic Mickey 2*, which would be built on art and technology from the first game, there were still new stories to write, mechanics to design, and levels to build. They needed some time to experiment before growing their team to hundreds of people. John Pleasants and the other Disney executives wanted *Epic Mickey 2* to be on more platforms than just the Wii, which was the smart business decision but would create more technological challenges for them to solve before they went into full production.

A few days into Christmas vacation, Jones got a call from his old friend Paul Weaver, who dropped a bomb in his lap. "He said, 'Think about what would happen to your plans if, say, the second week in January you got 110 people,'" Jones recalled. As it turned out, Disney wasn't interested in moving Junction Point's other projects forward; the executives just wanted to release a sequel to *Epic Mickey* as quickly as possible. "Because we had the team, the tools, outsourcing relationships, and we could just crank out the game," said Jones. "If we push hard enough, yes, we can get something out that allows them to start making that money." Jones began frantically making decisions over the break, returning to the office with hurried assignments for the newly massive *Epic Mickey 2* team.

Meanwhile, Spector checked out. He didn't have much interest in sequels—he preferred to put his energy into brand-new things—so when he wasn't doing big-picture work to keep Junction Point operating, he was playing around with other prototypes and ideas. He was still obsessed with Disney's ducks, and he spent some time pitching an "Epic Donald" video game that would do for the cranky, pantless Donald Duck what *Epic Mickey* had accomplished for the mouse. Spector also began angling for a larger role at Disney, writing *DuckTales* comics and even trying to pitch his own ideas for cartoon series and feature films. (He refused to move to California, which hampered many of those plans.)

But it was becoming clear that with Graham Hopper gone, there were very few people on Disney's leadership team who wanted to keep making traditional video games. In November 2010, before the first *Epic Mickey* even came out, Disney chief executive Bob Iger told the press that they were investing less money in console games, preferring instead to focus on mobile and Facebook apps.[13] In January 2011, Disney shut down one of its studios, Propaganda Games, which had been making console games based on movies such as *Tron* and *Pirates of the Caribbean*. A few months later, Disney shut down Black Rock Studios, a development house in the United Kingdom that specialized in racing games including *MotoGP* and *Split/Second*. "There were people at Disney in executive positions

---

13   Said Iger: "We've seen a pretty big shift in games from console to what I'll call multiplatform, everything from mobile apps to social networking games, and by putting John Pleasants in to run games, not only will the focus be on turning those businesses into profitability, but diversifying our presence in the business."

who'd come right out and tell you, 'I don't like games,'" Spector said. "I'd be like, 'Why are you involved in running a game division then?'"

Yet, bizarrely, those same Disney executives were demanding that Junction Point go on a hiring spree. They'd done the financial mapping and determined that *Epic Mickey 2* could be profitable as long as it was finished by the fall of 2012, so they threw money at the studio in order to make that happen. Disney Interactive Studios was shrinking, but Junction Point was growing. By 2012, more than two hundred people worked at the studio, and they were also paying for hundreds of outsourcers across the world. "We spent a lot of money on that game," said Spector. "A lot of money."

Spector tried to argue to Disney that they needed more time— that it was impossible to make a high-quality *Epic Mickey 2* in less than two years, especially if they wanted it on multiple platforms. Disney gave the game an extra couple of months, but they wouldn't budge further. "What they don't understand is that no two games are alike," said Spector. "I always tell potential partners, every game I've worked on has taken about three years. If I tell you I'm going to make a game in less than that, I'm lying." As a result of the compressed schedule, the developers of *Epic Mickey 2* wound up trapped by decisions they'd made before having enough information to determine whether they were the right calls. "You always have this hope that when they finally see the scope of the game, they're going to say, 'Okay, in order to get this to quality, we're going to have a reasonable discussion about how long this takes,' which never happens," said Chase Jones. "People have a date for all of their financials to work, and most of the time you work backwards."

Junction Point was struggling. The influx of new people triggered cultural conflicts, the time constraints caused a lot of stress, and Disney's executives would frequently come in and ask the developers to experiment with whatever trends were making the most money that month. "We were exploring a free-to-play version; an always-online version," said Jones. "Whatever the whistle of the day was, we had to create another deck that showed: Should we or shouldn't we do this?" Games like *FarmVille* and *League of Legends* were making billions of dollars, and Disney wanted to emulate those successes.

Spector had started Junction Point because he wanted the freedom to make his own "B-movie" games without having to worry about what might make kajillions of dollars. Now, it was EA and Eidos all over again.

One day in early 2012, the leaders of Disney and Junction Point had a meeting to discuss the future. They sat in a conference room on the bottom floor of Junction Point's offices in Austin, Texas. It was Spector, Jones, some other Junction Point leads, and a group of Disney executives including John Pleasants. Spector said he thought his plan for *Epic Mickey 2* and other Junction Point console games could be profitable. Pleasants didn't. Pleasants wanted Junction Point to adapt to Disney's vision for the future—mobile, free-to-play, and other business models that didn't involve traditional console games.[14]

As they battled back and forth about the studio's future, Spector and Pleasants started raising their voices. Soon they were screaming. At one point, in the middle of a conversation, Pleasants's phone rang. Spector was shocked to see Pleasants pick up and answer it,

---

14 One of Disney's big bets was a game called *Disney Infinity*, a "toys-to-life" game in which you could play in big sandbox worlds based on Disney franchises like *Aladdin* and *Pirates of the Caribbean* and buy physical toys associated with each one. The first game, released in 2013, grossed $500 million, according to Disney. But the series lasted only three games, and Disney shut down the studio behind it, Avalanche Software, in 2016. (Avalanche would later be revived by Warner Bros.)

and something in his brain went off. "Next thing I know, the controller for the pointer comes whizzing across the room, flies past my head, and hits the wall and breaks open," Jones said. "And Warren storms out the door. We're sitting there, like, 'Do we continue?'"

Thanks to his screaming matches and hurling projectiles, Warren Spector's relationship with Disney fractured. "I think at some point I became persona non grata there," Spector said. "I probably doomed the studio." Later in the year, as Junction Point's staff were working long overtime hours to finish *Epic Mickey 2*, Disney gave Spector and his leadership team a new mandate: cut costs. It was time for Junction Point to lay people off. This led to weeks of negotiation between Disney and Junction Point. What would the studio look like if they reduced from hundreds of employees to just twenty-five? What if they got fifty? Seventy-five? "There was one discussion where it got down to, 'Well, what if we only got to keep ten?'" said Chase Jones. "I remember saying in that meeting, 'Then just shut the whole thing down. If we're talking about ten people then there's no point.'"

By the fall of 2012, it became clear to Spector that Disney did indeed plan to shut the whole thing down. All of his proposals for the future of Junction Point had been rejected ("Sixty-two spreadsheets, and we couldn't get anything approved," he said), and even though *Epic Mickey 2* was planned for release in November, Disney hadn't green-lit any of their other projects. One week that fall, Spector flew out to California for one last-ditch meeting with Disney executives to try to keep Junction Point alive. "I came out there with a plan that would have saved seventy-five people's jobs," he said. "And they said, 'No, we're giving you'—I don't remember the number, but way less than that." By this point, Spector had realized that what Disney was actually saying was that Junction Point was finished. Nothing he could say or do would prevent that.

Another screaming match ensued. "There was about a forty-five-minute argument that got really loud," Spector said. "I had an out-of-body experience that day. I've never had that happen before—I really saw myself on the ceiling, looking down on myself, thinking, 'This is the coolest and stupidest thing I've ever done in my life.'" As Warren Spector flew back to Texas, he left with the knowledge that the next few months would be Junction Point's last. Before they'd even gotten a chance to see if *Epic Mickey 2* was a success, the studio was doomed.

In just two years, Junction Point had gone from the vanguard of Disney's battle for console gaming to another casualty in the chase for hot new trends. And, for legal reasons involving employee severance, Spector couldn't tell anyone about it. As a producer and a leader, Spector thought of himself as "transparent to a fault"—since his days at Origin, he'd always believed in being up front about risks and problems. Now, he was sworn to secrecy. "It was a little slice of hell," he said. "One of the worst experiences of my life."

When *Epic Mickey 2* came out on November 18, 2012, it was clear that it had been the product of rushed development. Critics slammed the repetitive gameplay and Oswald's wonky artificial intelligence. ("He's able to fumble his way through the game for the most part, but leaves you wishing for a proper, communicative partner," wrote critic Lucy O'Brien in her review for the gaming website IGN.) Worst of all, the game's sales were just a fraction of *Epic Mickey*'s, which was catastrophic given that *Epic Mickey* had been on a single console, the Wii, while *Epic Mickey 2* was also on Xbox and PlayStation. If there were any lingering hopes that Junction Point might survive, they were dashed by *Epic Mickey 2*'s tepid critical and commercial response.[15]

---

15   The first *Epic Mickey* sold around 1.3 million copies in its first couple of months on the market. *Epic Mickey 2* sold 270,000 copies in a similar launch period, according to a report by the *L.A. Times*. That's what experienced video game analysts might call "not good."

Spector, who still couldn't tell Junction Point's staff about the closure, gave everyone a long break and then told them to brainstorm some ideas for mobile games. "I guess there was a part of me that hoped if we went mobile we could maybe survive," Spector said. Really, he knew that they were just killing time.

On January 29, 2013, two months after *Epic Mickey 2* came out, Spector gathered two hundred Junction Point staff in the break room—the Fantasia room—and told them the studio was closing. Just months after crunching nights and weekends to finish *Epic Mickey 2*, they were all losing their jobs. Junction Point's employees were told to meet with HR to discuss their individual severance packages. Later, there would be a job fair.

Some of the departing employees remained in Austin, working at some of the few nearby game companies or moving into other fields, while others relocated so they could remain in the video game industry. Even those who had read the tea leaves following *Epic Mickey 2*'s failure were devastated. "I said I was really proud of them," Spector said, "and really sorry it ended up that way."

Warren Spector sank into a funk. He had been through rocky endings before—at Origin, at Looking Glass, at Ion Storm—but this was the worst yet. "I was reeling," he said. "I sat on a couch for months with a remote control in my hand just clicking. I was depressed as hell. I couldn't do anything." The idea of starting a new company and making more video games was too exhausting to even imagine. "I was done emotionally," Spector said. "I describe Disney as the best experience of my professional life and the worst experience of my professional life, and nothing in the middle ever...I couldn't see myself getting lucky enough to do that again."

In many ways, Spector was fortunate. He had done well for himself financially over the years, especially at Disney, and unlike his former employees, he didn't have to worry about finding a new job or uprooting his family. But he also had to wrestle with the guilt of letting all those people down and laying them off, of having built something that ultimately collapsed. As he stewed, Spector blamed himself for what had happened. Why did he have to get in all those screaming matches? Would things have gone differently if he had taken a larger role in *Epic Mickey 2*'s development?

Spector was now fifty-seven, older than most of his peers in the video game industry. He briefly thought about retiring, until he got yet another fortuitous phone call, just like he had back in the old days. His alma mater, the University of Texas in Austin, had just received a grant for a video game development program, and they wanted Spector to help put it together. "I always assumed I would end up teaching," he said. "So I thought, 'Maybe this is the time.'"

Spector spent the next year building a program and curriculum, then two more years teaching courses on business and game design. Although he found it rewarding, it was hard to suppress the urge to go back to designing and producing his own video games. "About halfway through that, I realized I still wanted to make some stuff," Spector said. "It's great molding young minds, but there's no box at the end. There's nothing to download digitally." Plus, the program was running out of money, and despite Spector's best efforts to raise funds, he couldn't convince many people to donate. "I spent a lot of those three years trying to raise money and discovering that (a) people in the game business don't value education very much," he said, "and (b) they're really cheap sons of bitches."

When Spector turned sixty, he knew he was entering the final arc of his career. It would be a poetic one. Soon he'd find a way to rejoin the video game industry and start making things again, thanks to the return of an old friend.

■ ■ ■

Between 2004, when Spector founded Junction Point, and January 2013, when it shut down, the gaming landscape had shifted in some big ways. The rise of mobile and Facebook games had led pundits to believe that console gaming would go obsolete, but instead it had the opposite effect, bringing games to brand-new audiences just in time for the launch of a new generation of consoles, the PlayStation 4 and Xbox One, in the fall of 2013.

At the same time, the barriers for making and releasing games were collapsing thanks to widespread development tools and digital distribution. Developers no longer had to call up EA or Activision to get their games placed in Target and GameStop. By the early 2010s, anyone could develop a game and sell it to people on digital platforms like Steam and Xbox Live, whether they were a twenty-something hobbyist or a team of grizzled veterans.

Paul Neurath got to see this shift in trends firsthand. Since making games like *System Shock* with Warren Spector in the 1990s, Neurath had spent a few years at Zynga, the social gaming titan behind *FarmVille*, *CityVille*, and many other games for Facebook and phones. Zynga took off like a rocket ship and then came crashing back to earth when Facebook changed a few algorithms, and by 2013, the once-mighty company had shuttered the Boston office where Neurath worked.

At the same time, a new model emerged that seemed perfect for someone like Neurath: crowdfunding. Kickstarter, a website that allowed fans to fund creative projects directly, enabled game developers to bypass restrictive publishers—those executives who cared only about exponential growth—and go straight to the players. The most effective way to do this was to appeal to nostalgia. The creative people behind franchises like *Mega Man* and *Castlevania*, beloved but abandoned by their publishers, raised millions of dollars on Kickstarter from fans who missed those games and wanted to play new ones. Neurath thought he could find similar success by bringing back his own classics.

After long negotiations with EA, Neurath won back the rights to one of his old franchises: *Underworld*, based on the groundbreaking *Ultima Underworld*, which he'd made back in the Origin days with Warren Spector. (EA kept the *Ultima* franchise.) In 2014, Neurath started a new company, Otherside Games, and a year later he launched a Kickstarter for *Underworld Ascendant*, raising over $800,000 for a spiritual successor to the games that he used to make.[16] Following some more complicated negotiations, Otherside also obtained the rights to develop a new *System Shock* game.

Who better to lead this *System Shock 3* than Neurath's old pal, who was itching to get out of teaching and make video games again? Neurath had stayed close to Warren Spector over the years, and the two talked frequently about their old aspirations to re-create *Dungeons & Dragons* and make video games that gave players real choices. Toward the end of 2015, Neurath called up Spector and made him a proposition. "I said, 'Hey Warren, we're ready to start making a *System Shock 3*; are you interested?'" Neurath recalled. "He thought for a minute and then he said yes." A few months later, once Spector had wound down his teaching work, he started a new Otherside office—Otherside Austin—where he would build a team to make a brand-new *System Shock*. Back in 1996, Spector had started an Austin office of Paul Neurath's Looking Glass, but it had shuttered before they

---

16 Sadly, the game turned out to be a flop. Wrote reviewer Rick Lane, for *PC Gamer*: "*Underworld Ascendant* is phenomenally bad, a catastrophic mess of poor design ideas, woeful execution, and bugs the size of buildings."

could release any games. Twenty years later, they had a chance to try again.

Once again, however, Spector found himself facing money problems. In 2016, Otherside struck an agreement with a Swedish publisher named Starbreeze Studios to fund *System Shock 3*, allowing Spector to hire a dozen staff and open an office in the gorgeous Austin Arboretum, surrounded by large glass windows and fresh greenery. Things went swimmingly until the fall of 2018, when Starbreeze filed for reconstruction, the Swedish version of bankruptcy. The next few days were dramatic. Swedish authorities arrested Starbreeze's CEO on suspicions of insider trading, though he was later released and cleared of charges. In the following weeks, realizing that Starbreeze no longer had the funds to pay them, Paul Neurath and Warren Spector pulled out of the deal.

Suddenly, Spector was back on the road again, pitching *System Shock 3* to publishers as if he were back in the 1990s. But he was older now, and tired of flying around to different cities to beg for money. Publishers never said yes or no—they'd always offer non-committal responses like "We'll be in touch"—and by the end of 2019, Otherside had failed to find funding and had to lay off most of the Austin office.

Chase Jones, who had reunited with his old boss to be the design director on *System Shock 3*, was again forced to make a tough decision. After leaving Junction Point in 2012, a few months before the studio closed, Jones had moved to Redmond, Washington, for a job on Microsoft's publishing team, and then took a brief hiatus from the gaming industry to work at a software company in Australia. In 2018, he'd rejoined Spector at Otherside, where he was thrilled to work on a new *System Shock*, until the money troubles started. The company asked Jones to cut his hours in half, but there wasn't much for him to do without a full design team in place, and he couldn't afford the pay cut. He had a baby on the way. So Jones quit Otherside to join a new game studio that some of his old friends had started.

Meanwhile, Spector found a new savior. In May 2020, the Chinese conglomerate Tencent, which owned and invested in many video game companies, announced that it was taking over *System Shock 3*. Spector would again be beholden to a giant corporation. As of this writing, it remains to be seen what will happen with the game. There's reason to be optimistic; few companies are more financially stable than Tencent. Then again, the same thing was true of Disney.

■ ■ ■

There aren't a lot of people who have worked in the video game industry for more than thirty years, and Warren Spector's rocky journey may help explain why. The four game studios at which he spent most of his career—Origin, Looking Glass, Ion Storm, and Junction Point—shut down either while he was still there or a few years after he left. His immersive sim games were critically acclaimed but never achieved the sales success that many of his peers enjoyed. His journey, while extraordinary in many ways, was also emblematic of the volatility that all video game developers have to face. At least he got to stay in one city.

Spector has also had an outsize impact on the video game industry. Countless developers have been influenced by the games he's directed and produced—*Ultima Underworld*, *System Shock*, *Deus Ex*. Just down the road from his house in Texas, a studio called Arkane Austin carried on his legacy with immersive sims like *Prey* and *Dishonored*, led by one of his former disciples, Harvey Smith. Up in Montreal, Eidos developed new games in the *Deus Ex* and *Thief* series, both of which had lain dormant for years after the death of Ion Storm but were revitalized in the 2010s. Countless game developers have drawn inspiration from Spector's desire to re-create the feeling of unlimited possibility that *Dungeons & Dragons* creates.

Perhaps the most influential member of Spector's video game family tree was a sci-fi horror game that sprang directly from the loins of *System Shock*. It was a game that shook up the industry. It changed the way many people thought about video games. But it also took after Spector's trajectory in a less pleasant way. Its fame, and the pressures and responsibilities that came with that, would lead to the death of the studio that made it.

CHAPTER 2

PROJECT ICARUS

It's almost hard to imagine today, but there was once a time, in the 1990s and early 2000s, when well-respected critics questioned the narrative value of video games. Games were *fun*, went the refrain, but could they tell a story? Could they make you cry? Could they offer emotional resonance on top of the mindless satisfaction and gratuitous violence? The questions were absurd from the get-go— anyone who had seen a certain death in 1997's *Final Fantasy VII* knew that games could make you cry—but they grew quieter in 2007, when a game came out that pretty much put an end to the debate.

Set in a dystopian underwater city built by an Ayn Rand– worshipping tycoon, *BioShock* was in some ways a typical video game. You'd spend most of your time staring down the barrel of a gun, casting spells and shooting up mutants as you blasted your way from corridor to corridor. But it was also unlike anything anyone had played before. *BioShock* was a feast of sights and sounds, from the half-destroyed art deco murals spread throughout the ruined buildings of Rapture, the city that was once envisioned as a free market utopia, to the metallic clangs of a hulking Big Daddy, one of the monstrosities who now inhabited it. Whereas the stories of other video game shooters were about as philosophically ambitious as a Disney ride, *BioShock* explored Orwellian dystopia and Randian objectivism. A haunting twist toward the end of the game revealed that you weren't making quite as many decisions as you'd thought you were, raising questions about the choices we make in video games. As a Vox article declared in 2016, "*BioShock* proved that video games could be art."

Like many great works of art, *BioShock* also came from a great deal of sacrifice. The game's path began at Looking Glass, Paul Neurath's studio, where three game developers named Ken Levine, Jonathan Chey, and Robert Fermier helped make *Thief* and *System Shock*. In 1997 the three men struck out to start their own company, Irrational Games. Working out of an old loft in Boston, Massachusetts, this newly independent game studio led development on *System Shock 2*, which iterated on what had worked so well in the first game, adding more role-playing elements to the formula. *System Shock 2* was critically acclaimed but a commercial flop, and when the Irrational crew tried to convince EA to fund a *System Shock 3*, the publisher wasn't interested. The last game just hadn't sold well enough. So Irrational decided to make a *System Shock* game that wasn't actually called *System Shock*, bypassing potential rights issues by giving it a brand-new name and setting.

To finish the game that would become *BioShock*, Irrational's employees had to spend endless nights and weekends at the office (which eventually moved from Boston to Quincy, a few miles south). The game was constantly changing, as developers battled over design and art direction. One of the biggest points of tension was accessibility; Levine, worrying that the density of *System Shock 2* had turned players off, pushed his team to design *BioShock* as a shooter that anyone could play, stripping out many of the numbers and RPG mechanics they'd originally envisioned. Halfway through development, the video game publisher 2K acquired Irrational, announcing the news in January 2006. This meant financial security, but it also brought more cooks into the kitchen in the form of 2K executives, who pushed for *BioShock* to have the mass appeal of megapopular shooters like *Halo* and *Call of Duty*. By 2007, Levine had told the *BioShock* development team that seven-day workweeks were mandatory. "We basically added a lot of time to our schedule without actually having time in our schedule," said Joe Faulstick, an assistant producer on *BioShock*. "At that point it was basically, 'Yeah, come in on the weekends.'"

A week before *BioShock* launched, Irrational put out a demo to give prospective buyers a taste of the game. So many people downloaded it, the Xbox Live servers crashed—a sign that Irrational had tapped into something big. When the game finally came out on August 21, 2007, critics suggested that it was one of the greatest games of all time, up there with the likes of *Tetris* and *Super Mario Bros.* This stunned nobody more than the people who made it. "I think we spent the better part of several months kind of in shock," said Bill Gardner, a lead level designer on *BioShock*. "There's always that little bit of waiting for the other shoe to drop, where it's like, 'Okay, is this real?'"

This was Gardner's first job in game development. A few years earlier, he'd been working at a video game store in Boston when he'd overheard his boss chatting with an intense man about *System Shock 2*, a game that Gardner had enjoyed. The man spoke with a unique cadence, like a cross between a college professor and the Joker. Gardner's boss called him over and introduced him: it was Ken Levine, the lead designer of *System Shock 2*. The two men bonded over their shared love for video games, and eventually

Levine suggested that Gardner apply for a QA job at Irrational. When he got the job in 2002, Gardner was first assigned to work on a game called *The Lost*, which was completed but never actually released, an experience he calls heartbreaking, but essential. "Given the quality level and given the reputation the company had, it was a no-brainer to not release it," Gardner said. Now, in 2007, they'd gone from a video game so bad they didn't want to sell it to one of the most celebrated video games of all time.

What made *BioShock* special was the way in which its story unfolded. The city of Rapture was full of audio diaries—recordings that shed light on the world's characters and history—to which you could listen as you crept through the flooded streets, as if you were getting a guided tour of an art museum. *BioShock*, following in the footsteps of Warren Spector and Looking Glass, was all about situational decision making and environmental storytelling. Rather than just tell you exactly how Rapture had fallen apart, the game let you piece together the city's history for yourself. It wasn't exactly subtle, but it made you feel smart, largely by following the long-standing mantra of immersive sims: "Say yes to the player." By the end, Irrational had pulled off an impressive balancing act, making *BioShock* feel accessible without dumbing it down too much.

Amid *BioShock*'s accolades (2.2 million copies shipped! 96 on Metacritic![1]), representatives from 2K came to Irrational asking what their next project might look like. *BioShock*'s success led to a natural question: Did Irrational want to do a *BioShock 2*? 2K boss Christoph Hartmann viewed *BioShock* as their cash cow, and he expected them to be making new games in the series for years and

---

1   Metacritic, a website that aggregates review scores, is a flawed but frequently used metric in the video game industry as a barometer of critical success.

years to come.[2] "They asked us whether or not we wanted to do a sequel," said Gardner. "Talk about panic, performance anxiety—how do you follow this up?"

It was the fall of 2007, and Irrational's staff were burned out. Some had left the studio, sick of the crunch and of Ken Levine, who was now both head of the studio and the creative director of their games. Levine had become known for having a difficult leadership style, occasionally punctuated by screaming and cursing when he wasn't happy with how a level or scene was shaping up. Plenty of developers at Irrational tolerated or even liked this kind of atmosphere—after all, it was in the service of art, and they'd just made an all-time classic—but working in a pressure cooker could have negative effects on one's mental health.

After some debate, Levine and his team decided they didn't want to make a new *BioShock* just yet, and they eventually struck a compromise with 2K. A handful of people from Irrational would move out to 2K's offices in the San Francisco Bay Area to form a studio called 2K Marin, which would immediately start developing *BioShock 2*. This would free up Levine and his remaining staff to do something different.

A couple of years earlier, 2K parent company Take-Two had acquired the rights to an old strategy game series called *XCOM*, in which you'd play as an organization of soldiers and scientists defending the planet from an alien invasion. *XCOM* also happened to be one of Ken Levine's favorite video games, and a small team at Irrational's second office in Canberra, Australia, had been quietly working on an *XCOM* shooter since 2005. Now, the Boston

---

2   Christoph Hartmann told press that he wanted *BioShock* to get at least six sequels, following in the footsteps of another famous sci-fi series. "Look at *Star Wars*," Hartmann said. "It's a fight between good and evil, just like *BioShock*." (*BioShock* was not, in fact, a fight between good and evil.)

team would join them and develop the *XCOM* game as their next big project.

As they recovered from *BioShock*'s development, Irrational began hiring new staff to replace the people who had left. One of those newcomers was Chad LaClair, an ambitious artist and film school graduate who quickly realized that Hollywood wasn't for him. He'd gotten his video game industry break a few years earlier as a QA tester for Electronic Arts in Los Angeles, where he was first exposed to the brutal crunch that's so prevalent in video games. "I got to the point where I said, 'I'm getting burned out; this can't continue,'" LaClair said. He applied for other gigs within EA and eventually got a job as a junior level designer, where he worked for three years on games like *Medal of Honor: Airborne* before growing restless, sick of Los Angeles, and frustrated with the direction of his team's next project. "I wanted something different," LaClair said. "I was a young designer who thought, 'I'm really talented. I've gotta go out there and find artistic studios.'"

Few studios were quite as artistic as the people behind *BioShock*, which LaClair had played on release ("It just blew my mind"). So it felt serendipitous when LaClair got a message from one of Irrational's recruiters asking if he knew any artists or designers looking for work at a game studio. The recruiter saw that he had gone to college in Boston and thought he might have contacts in the area. "I said, 'Well, I don't,'" recalled LaClair, "'but I'm interested.'" He sent over his art portfolio, went through a gauntlet of interviews, and soon found himself moving back across the country for a job as a level artist at Irrational Games.

LaClair liked working at Irrational. The studio was small, maybe a couple dozen people, and there was a breezy, collaborative energy on the *XCOM* project that he really enjoyed. After the torturous production of *BioShock*, the developers remaining at Irrational were now trying to take it easy. "It was a superfun time when in the middle of the day, Ken would say, 'Hey I have this idea, I want to share it with everybody,'" said LaClair. "We'd hear his pitch, give him feedback. It was great." One day, LaClair started to notice something strange: Ken Levine and the other studio leaders kept leaving the floor, huddling in a meeting room away from the rest of the developers, sometimes for hours.

Soon, LaClair found out what was happening—Irrational was done with *XCOM*. Instead, they'd be revisiting their most successful franchise. "I remember Ken announcing to the team: 'We're going to make another *BioShock* game,'" LaClair said. "And then he came by and talked to me afterward. 'I know we hired you for this one thing. Are you okay working on a *BioShock* property?' I'm like, 'Absolutely.'"

During the summer of 2008, Ken Levine's agents had renegotiated his contract with Take-Two, according to reports from *Variety* and the *New York Post*, to secure more money and creative freedom. Although details of the contract only trickled out secondhand, word at the studio was that Levine had lost interest in the *XCOM* project and gotten the urge to make another *BioShock*. During negotiations, he'd convinced Take-Two to allow Irrational to develop its own *BioShock* sequel, one that would come out after *BioShock 2*.

There was also resentment growing among some Irrational veterans at the idea that another studio was making a new *BioShock* game and they weren't. "I was definitely a little bit pissy about the idea that people were taking our baby, something I'd spent all this time on," said Bill Gardner, the lead level designer. Sure, Irrational had turned down the chance to make *BioShock 2* in the first place, but it was like breaking up with a significant other and then watching them date someone else. Even if it had been your choice to leave, it still sucked. "The franchise is going on and living happily without us, and I think a lot of us got a little bit frustrated," said Gardner. "We worked on *XCOM* for I think the better part of a year, then we started saying, 'Fuck it, let's do a sequel of our own.'"

By 2009, there was a concrete plan in place. Irrational's Australia office would again take over the *XCOM* project. 2K Marin, the studio formed by ex-Irrational employees in the San Francisco Bay Area, would keep working on *BioShock 2*, which would come out in 2010. And the staff of Irrational would dream up ideas for what their own sequel to *BioShock* might look like.

This third *BioShock* didn't have a title yet, so, like other development projects, it got a code name, one that in retrospect might have been the perfect ironic fit for some wild initiative in Rapture—one of those ambitious Andrew Ryan projects that was destined to fail from the moment it started. They called it Project *Icarus*.

■ ■ ■

The development of a video game can be roughly divided into two phases, both borrowed from the film world: preproduction and production. Definitions vary from game studio to studio, but, loosely, preproduction is when people plan out the game, while production is when people make it. There's no clear line between the two, and each phase can be as short or as long as time and money allow. One guy making a farming game in his bedroom, for example, might just start placing tiles on the screen with no formal preproduction, even if production takes him half a decade. A team of two hundred people developing a brand-new sci-fi franchise might spend years in preproduction before they actually start building anything real.

There's a school of thought among many game developers that on a new video game, the preproduction process should take a very long time. After all, the belief goes, creativity needs to be nurtured, and great art comes from iteration. This might mean a concept artist draws beautiful, inspiring images of monsters and castles, only to discard them all because they feel like they could do even better on the next go. It could mean gameplay designers spend months on a cool new laser-shooting ability that seemed so damn fun in their heads but doesn't hold up when they prototype it on their computers (but maybe if they try replacing all the lasers with missiles...). The directors of this hypothetical project might be making new high-level decisions every day, cutting and scrapping and reworking as they try to imagine what might hold up over 10, 15, 20, or even 100 hours of gameplay.

The number of variables is enough to trigger a migraine for anyone who's worked in project management, especially the big one: fun. What is "fun," exactly? Even the biggest video game enthusiast might struggle with that question—is it fun to grind for loot in *Destiny*? To slog through the zombie-infested highways of *The Last of Us*? When you're trying to make something completely new, with no recipe to follow, that question is for the most part impossible to answer. How do you quantify fun? Jumping or dancing or swinging a sword might feel satisfying for a week or two, but will it get stale after you've played the game for a dozen hours straight? How do you know if squishing enemies will feel better or worse once you've added levels and obstacles? And what if there are no graphics or sound effects yet? Can you operate on blind faith that it'll feel better once everything's finished?

To an outside observer this all might sound like a floundering, inefficient process, one that leads to months of wasted work and a great deal of stress. Is the only way to make a game as great as *BioShock* to first spend two years figuring out what it is? Who the hell would want to pay developers for that? Then there's the cyclical aspect of it all. If you've just come off a three-year game project where your team spent the first half prototyping and experimenting, then the second half crunching and building, you're going to be drained for a while. You'll be exhausted. Even if you take a couple of weeks off work, the last thing you'll want to do when you get back is return to intense development mode. The thought of spending the next year or two messing around in a low-stress environment might sound like paradise—until you find yourself once again a year away from your deadline with nothing to show.

At the beginning of 2009, when the developers of Irrational started debating what a new *BioShock* should look like, they entered this idea mode. From the beginning they'd known they didn't want to go back to Rapture; this would be a sequel in tone and feel, not in setting. (Besides, *BioShock 2* was also set in Rapture—three games in the same city might feel stale.) One idea seemed to click with everyone: a floating city, nestled among the clouds. "All kinds of settings were thrown around," said Bill Gardner. "The idea of a city in the sky took off pretty quickly."

In the coming months, Irrational kept expanding, hiring more and more new developers to help them make the game that would soon be called *BioShock Infinite.*[3] It wasn't hard to find people who wanted to work on a new *BioShock* game. What was much harder was trying to figure out what it actually meant for something to *be* a new *BioShock* game. Did *BioShock* just mean "shooter that makes you think"? The toughest question was the same one they'd asked a couple of years earlier when 2K initially approached them about a sequel: How do you follow up a game like the first *BioShock*?

---

3   Ken Levine, who often butted heads with 2K's leadership, was said to be unhappy with the publisher's plan to get endless sequels out of *BioShock.* One common theory among Irrational employees was that the title *BioShock Infinite* was a cheeky way to stave off more sequels—after all, you can't have a *BioShock Infinite 2.*

What would this new game try to say? And just how could they surpass those drill-armed behemoths, the Big Daddies, who had become so iconic that one would even appear on an episode of *The Simpsons*?

The answers kept changing. Irrational played around with several different time periods, art styles, and settings. For a while their city in the clouds was a tableau of 1800s European art, like a cross between London and Paris, and for a while it looked a lot like Rapture in the sky. The story, which Ken Levine has said was inspired by a hodgepodge of media ranging from the interactive play *Sleep No More* to Erik Larson's *The Devil in the White City*, a book about the 1893 Chicago World's Fair, was shifting constantly. "We were just in preproduction for a while, experimenting with different ways of building the city and trying to figure out what type of architecture sets we need to make," said LaClair. "It was very early preproduction, blue sky, everything's great, going to be wonderful, everyone's happy. The fun times."

Those fun times begat not-so-fun times. Over the course of *BioShock Infinite*'s development, the game changed constantly as Levine scrapped and overhauled ideas both big and small. The city in the sky remained constant, but everything else was in flux: the story, the time period, the way in which a character's abilities would function. This could be a frustrating process for designers and artists, who'd spend weeks or months working on a chunk of the game only for it to be axed in a matter of minutes. "What we did for the better part of that year was really break down what *BioShock* was," said Bill Gardner. "A lot of people who came in as we started to ramp up, they were a little bit spooked: 'What's going on here? We're not really making forward progress.' But I think the more seasoned people knew we were used to having pretty big reboots to find the fun."

This was Ken Levine's—and, subsequently, Irrational's—approach to game development. It was how they had made their previous games, and it was how they were making this one. Levine didn't try to hide this philosophy or keep it secret, and the company expected new hires to know what they were getting into. "We basically develop our games by failing," he would tell Leigh Alexander, a journalist for the video game trade website Gamasutra, during *BioShock Infinite*'s production. "We'll just throw things away all the time. . . . We try things, and are incredibly open to failing, and learning from that and moving on." It could be an expensive process, he acknowledged, but "you can't care about sunk cost."

■ ■ ■

On August 12, 2010, at a press event in the swanky Plaza Hotel near Central Park in New York City, journalists gathered to watch the trailer for the next *BioShock* game. The video opened with a delightful fakeout, zooming in on the silhouette of a familiar-looking underwater city before pulling back to reveal that the camera was actually inside of a fish tank. Good-bye, Rapture. Hello, *BioShock Infinite*. After the trailer, Ken Levine gave the press a basic outline of the game. *BioShock Infinite* was set in Columbia, a city in the sky devoted to the celebration of American exceptionalism, during July 1912. It would star the former Pinkerton agent Booker DeWitt, sent to rescue a raven-haired girl named Elizabeth. Guarding her tower prison was a flying robotic hulk called the Songbird, who would make for a good mascot (and merchandising opportunity) in lieu of those Big Daddies.

What was nice about this announcement wasn't just that the developers could finally be open about what they were doing. It was that they now had to stick with the details they'd announced.

Columbia was Columbia. Elizabeth was Elizabeth. None of the major details could be overturned anymore.

For Forrest Dowling, the timing couldn't have been better. Dowling had just started at Irrational, signing up as a level designer a month before *BioShock Infinite*'s big reveal. As a *BioShock* fan, Dowling was stoked to see what they were doing—it had been three years of silence since the first game came out. And as a new Irrational employee, he was happy to see that they'd actually committed to the game's core ideas. "I'd joined at a time when suddenly the team was inoculated against complete swings," Dowling said. "There was no chance at that point that the entire time, setting, place, conflict would change."

Dowling was big and bearded, with a muppety voice and a pragmatic attitude. He'd grown up in western New York, knowing he wanted to be an artist but not sure where to start. After high school he went to a fine arts college—the type of place where "they're not going to even talk about the fact that maybe you want to make money and eat food some day"—and experimented with crafts like iron-casting and sculpting before growing disillusioned with the art world. By his senior year of college, Dowling had switched course, falling in love with video games like *Deus Ex* and wondering what it might look like if he made them for a living.

In the 1990s and early 2000s, one of the best ways to learn how to develop video games was to make mods—fan-made alterations that changed the way a game looked or felt to play. Some of these modders did it for fun, but others saw it as a potential career path. In 2003, a group of modders for *Battlefield*, a popular series of first-person shooter games, banded together to start their own company in New York City, Trauma Studios. The actual developers of *Battlefield*, at a company called DICE, took notice, and the following year they purchased Trauma, although they went on to shut it down less than a year later.[4] Executives at competing publisher THQ saw an opportunity, hiring members of the Trauma team to form a new game development company, which they called Kaos Studios.

Kaos seemed like a good fit for Dowling, who had been making his own mods for games like *Half-Life* while working at an Apple Store and trying to crack into the video game industry. "It was a young studio that was made up of former mod-makers who found themselves suddenly having an AAA budget to build a game," Dowling said.[5] "So they were very open to hiring an idiot like myself." Dowling couldn't afford a New York City apartment, so he spent a few months living with his in-laws in central New Jersey and making the brutal two-hour commute into Manhattan every day. First he worked on a shooter called *Frontlines: Fuel of War*, which came out in 2008, and then he went on to *Homefront*, a game set in a near-future dystopian universe in which North Korea invades the United States.

By 2010, THQ was in trouble. The US economic recession had hit the publisher hard, and it was cutting costs across all of its studios, including Kaos. When a recruiter from Irrational reached out to Dowling and asked if he might be interested in helping make a new *BioShock*, he didn't have to give it much thought. There was a phone screener, followed by a design test, then more calls and a day full of interviews at Irrational's Quincy office, where staff grilled him about his work and career. "I guess I have a stupid amount of confidence so it wasn't that intimidating for me, even though it

---

4   The CEO behind this decision was Patrick Söderlund, who would go on to join EA when it acquired DICE. There he'd become the executive overseeing studios like Visceral Games, a story that we'll look at later in the book.

5   "AAA" is a description you'll see a lot in the video game industry. It means different things to different people, but in general, game developers and executives use it to mean "expensive."

should have been," Dowling said. "I felt like I nailed the design test and felt really good about the work I did, so I felt that put me on good footing with them."

Before Dowling had even gotten in the car to drive home, Bill Gardner pulled him aside and told him he'd be getting an offer, which he accepted. Dowling felt awful about quitting Kaos during the final year of *Homefront*—"It's not cool to leave a project before it's done, particularly when people are going into crunch mode on it," he said—but he knew he had to get out of there. His gut told him something was wrong at Kaos, and that THQ wasn't going to last much longer. "*BioShock* was such a humongous game in my mind," Dowling said. "I loved it so much and I thought it was one of the smartest games of the generation.... I wasn't going to say no to that so I could stay on a project on a team where I didn't think there was a future." Dowling's instincts would turn out to be correct. THQ shut down Kaos a year later and eventually went bankrupt.[6]

When he started at Irrational, just a few weeks before the Plaza reveal event, Dowling found a team that was tired but excited to show their game to the world. The *BioShock Infinite* reveal had been months in the making, and they were all relieved that the major decisions were now locked into place. This was a game set in the floating city of Columbia. It was 1912. Booker had to rescue Elizabeth. Ken Levine couldn't change his mind about those big-picture ideas anymore, which meant they wouldn't have to keep scrapping work they'd done on the project.

Of course, plenty of other things could change. In the coming months, progress on *BioShock Infinite* moved slowly, even by

---

6   One commenter on the industry website Gamasutra wrote after the news: "If this is what happens when you give your team names like Trauma and Kaos, then I'm calling my game company Everything's Fine Studios."

Irrational's standards, due to frequent cuts, shifts, and reboots. The company was growing, but the game wasn't. Levine would tell his staff to overhaul large chunks of levels or sections of the city, seemingly at a whim, based on what he thought would be best for the game. Every cut or change Levine made had trickle-down effects for the lower-level designers, artists, and programmers. It was demoralizing to put weeks of your life into something only to watch it get flushed down the drain. "It is tough when stuff gets cut or changed dramatically that people have worked on for months," said Dowling. "That was definitely a thing that happened a lot at Irrational."

To convince 2K to expand their headcount further for *BioShock Infinite*, which was growing bigger and more expensive every day, Irrational needed to come up with ways to make the game feel more evergreen—more indefinitely replayable. Part of that plan involved two big multiplayer modes that 2K's executives hoped players would keep using even after they'd finished *BioShock Infinite*'s campaign. But these multiplayer modes weren't quite coalescing, and the single-player campaign was behind schedule, so Irrational took a drastic step, cutting the multiplayer and moving all of its staff onto the main game. "You spend a lot of time and put your heart and soul into something just to have it disappear in the span of a meeting," said Bill Gardner, who had helped lead the multiplayer team. "You never really get over that."

Public demos of *BioShock Infinite* in 2011 left fans impressed, showcasing the lively citizens of Columbia and Elizabeth's seemingly magical powers, which allowed her to rip holes in the fabric of reality to conjure objects from other dimensions. (Much of what fans saw in the demos never actually made it into the final product, which was testament to the game's turbulent development.) At the same time, the developers of *BioShock Infinite* worried that they might never be able to finish the game. Even after several delays, it was clear they needed to take more drastic measures. A number of senior staff were quitting Irrational, frustrated with the constant overhauls and Levine's directorial style. To replace them—and to try to wrangle the game into shape—Irrational kept hiring.

In March 2012, Irrational brought in Don Roy, a veteran game producer, who had some experience closing out games at big publishers like Sony and Microsoft. He was shocked to see just how bad things were. "I get there and there was essentially no game," Roy said. "A tremendous amount of work had been done. It just hadn't been stood up as a game in any particular form. To the point where the first thing I did was go, 'Can I play a build of the game?' The answer was no. They said, 'You can play these pieces of things, but there's not an actual functioning game.'"

What baffled Roy most, he said, was the disorganization. Irrational's bloat—from a few dozen people in 2008 to nearly two hundred by the end of 2012, plus support studios and outsourcing houses—had led to all sorts of deficiencies in their production pipelines. It was chaos. "We were outsourcing a lot of stuff and it was never making it in the game because the process wasn't established," Roy said. "People were asking for things, and they'd eventually get made, but then they moved on, so then the [art] came back and they said, 'No, I don't actually need that anymore.'" One of Roy's tasks was to create a workflow to prevent the company from wasting all that time and money.

In the summer of 2012, Irrational made its biggest and most publicized hire: Rod Fergusson, of Epic Games, who had cultivated a reputation within the video game industry as a "closer," someone who could come in and make the tough cuts and decisions needed to complete a game. Fergusson looked at *BioShock Infinite*, broke down the tasks they had left, and put together a schedule—

including mandatory crunch—that would result in a finished video game. "The game does not ship without Rod Fergusson," said one Irrational staffer.

What was just as important as Fergusson's scheduling, according to those who worked with him, was that Fergusson knew how to talk to Ken Levine. "Ken is a creative genius, and that comes with pros and cons," said Mike Snight, who worked on *BioShock Infinite*. "Ken is a terrible leader, he really is, and he'd be the first to admit that to you. He's a creative; he's not a leader by any means."

Levine has been the subject of much public scrutiny since the days of the first *BioShock*. Ask anyone who's worked with him what it was like and they'll probably throw out two words: "genius" and "challenging." He was the type of director whose vision could lead to masterpieces like *BioShock*, but he could also take a very long time to conceive that vision, and he often had trouble articulating ideas to his staff. "This is not meant as an insult, but I believe he's a better editor than author," said Joe Faulstick. "He's not the best off on a blank page. If he's in a situation where he doesn't know what he wants yet, he's not always the best to work with." Some ex-Irrational employees shared stories about arguments and screaming matches between Levine and other leads. Others said they watched him grow frustrated and yell when employees weren't executing on the ideas in his head. "He's brilliant," said another person who worked with him, "but he doesn't always know how to tell you what he wants."

Fergusson was able to speak with Levine, figure out what the director wanted the game to look like, and translate that message to the rest of the staff. "Rod made the right calls," said Don Roy, "and *Infinite* turned out the way it did because he was able to come in and do for production what was necessary to deliver what was in Ken's head."

In an interview with the gaming website Polygon, Ken Levine analogized his development process to carving a statue. "The way I create video games, it's more like sculpture," he said. In other words, he'd have to break off chunks of marble to carve the figure he wanted. Levine's background was in plays and screenplays, where one commonly quoted mantra is "Writing is rewriting"—the first draft is never what shows up on the stage or the screen. In games, however, where the script is written while other parts of the game are in production, constant rewriting means burning months of other people's work. "He essentially makes a tremendous amount of a game so he can evaluate it, which makes sense," said Roy. "But when you're doing it on paper, that's one thing. When you're doing it with real humans, time, money, emotions, obligations, it's a completely different thing."

Levine would make even more revealing comments a few years later, during a Eurogamer convention in London. "In almost every game I've ever worked on, you realize you're running out of time, and then you make the game," Levine said. "You sort of dick around for years"—he laughed as he said this—"and then you're like, 'Oh my god, we're almost out of time,' and it forces you to make these decisions. And that's when the magic happens, is when the gun's at your head and you've gotta make the decisions, because people, we tend to procrastinate, and we tend to put things off. I find that when it's time to [ask] what do we keep, what do we cut, what do we focus on, what do we polish, that's really when the game's made."

The people who worked for Ken Levine had mixed and sometimes conflicting feelings about this style of development. Chad LaClair said working at Irrational made him a significantly better artist and designer, yet he also called *BioShock Infinite* the toughest thing he'd ever done. "There were times when I thought, 'I don't know how we're going to be able to show this to the world,'" LaClair said. "We have so much further to go." Like the rest of Irrational's staff during those final months of development in 2012 and 2013, LaClair had to put in a great deal of overtime in order to finish the lengthy list of tasks that needed to be completed to finish the game. "I've never crunched on a game as much as I crunched on *BioShock Infinite*," said LaClair, who estimated that he was in the office twelve hours a day for most of the final year. If there was a bright side, it was that his wife had also taken a job at Irrational, so at least the two of them could have lunch and dinner together at the office.

Forrest Dowling also went into heavy crunch mode, working six days a week during the game's final months. "My house was kind of a mess at that point," he said. "I couldn't even be bothered to do dishes. I would just get laundry done and then watch a movie or something, and basically be a slug on the day off. Because when you're down to one day a week off, that's kind of your energy level." Both LaClair and Dowling had one big advantage over some of the older staff at Irrational, an advantage that made this kind of lifestyle more tolerable: neither of them had kids yet. "I still felt pretty young to the industry," said LaClair. "I think my mind-set now is much different."

Besides, LaClair figured, he was just putting in his dues. "I didn't have any idea," he said, "that the company would be going away pretty soon."

■ ■ ■

BioShock Infinite came out on March 26, 2013. Critics raved about it, and 2K shipped 3.7 million copies to retailers in the game's first year, according to a Take-Two earnings report. (The earnings report didn't say how many of those copies were actually sold, just "shipped"—a common game industry tactic to obfuscate real sales numbers.) At first it was awash with superlatives, with a *Game Informer* reviewer calling it "one of the best games I've ever played." In the weeks and months that followed other critics would slam the game's narrative foibles and hearty embrace of bothsidesism, but at launch, *BioShock Infinite* was widely beloved.[7]

Yet those veterans who remained at the studio felt like their culture had changed. Irrational's size swelling to two hundred people was a morale drain for the veterans. No longer could they all sit in a single room, swiveling their chairs when Ken Levine wanted to bat ideas around. Now, many of them didn't even know one another. "You'd walk down the hall and, not to be a jerk or exclusionary, but you'd be like, 'Who are these people?'" said Bill Gardner. "I think that was one of the problems. We lost the culture."

Some of the developers who had worked on *BioShock Infinite* left for other jobs, while others took long breaks or began working on the game's downloadable content (DLC).[8] Forrest Dowling led the first DLC, *Clash in the Clouds*, which he made with a small team on a compressed schedule after the game launched. This was a combat-only mode in which you'd rack up points by shooting your way through enemies, and although it didn't make much of an impact on fans, Dowling was proud to get it out the door. The second and final DLC, *Burial at Sea*, was released in two parts that took players back to the underwater city of Rapture, allowing you to play as Elizabeth for the first time. It was a solid expansion that tied *BioShock* and *BioShock Infinite* together in some cool ways.

---

7   Daisy Fitzroy, the black leader of a group of revolutionary populists that fights against Columbia's racism and fascism, is later presented as an antagonist just as malevolent as the oppressors she's battling against—a disappointing revelation that undercuts many of the game's more interesting themes.

8   A small team at 2K Marin, the developer of *BioShock 2*, was originally assigned to make the first *BioShock Infinite* DLC, but that version was canceled.

Throughout 2013, as Irrational's employees worked on this DLC, one question lingered: What was next? Ken Levine would grumble that the process of making *Infinite* had been miserable for him, and he talked often about how strange it was to be in a company where he didn't recognize many of his own employees. Rod Fergusson announced shortly after *BioShock Infinite*'s launch that he was leaving Irrational, which seemed like a bad sign. People began to openly wonder what their future looked like, and management didn't offer many assurances. They had to work on another game, didn't they? Were they going to make another *BioShock*? Something brand-new? This became the dominant conversation as Irrational employees ate lunch and walked through the hallways. *What was the plan?*

Soon, Don Roy learned why there were no answers. He'd been traveling with Levine to help market and promote *Infinite*, and over the course of those trips, the two men had grown close. At one point, Levine told Roy that he had been unhappy for a while and that he didn't want to make another game with a team this big. What would it look like, Levine asked, if he took a handful of Irrational employees and pivoted to something smaller? Later in 2013, while the two were chatting at Levine's house, Levine said he was going to quit and start a small studio of his own. "It was loose at first and then it became solid pretty quickly," said Roy. "Then it became, 'Okay, how would we do the thing?'"

When Levine told his publishing bosses that he planned to quit, they demurred. Losing Ken Levine could tank their stock. He was a brand, a face, a personality that gamers knew and loved. How, they asked, could they convince him to stick around? After some negotiations, the executives agreed to create a new company for Levine outside of their traditional corporate structure. Rather than reporting to 2K's executives, with whom he had argued often over the years, Levine would work directly for Take-Two, the umbrella corporation that owned them all.[9] He was happy with this arrangement, and immediately began making plans to start a new studio that would employ fewer than twenty people. Then the other shoe dropped. "Initially, I told them I was leaving the company," Levine would later tell the journalist Chris Suellentrop in a *Rolling Stone* interview. "I said I wanted to do a much smaller thing. It's very experimental. They asked me to stay. I figured they would keep Irrational for the next *BioShock*. That's not what happened."

Don Roy was floored when he heard the news: Levine wasn't just leaving Irrational. Irrational was shutting down. It wasn't clear what ultimately drove the decision—was Take-Two going to close the studio anyway, no matter what Ken Levine wanted to do?—but it was clear that the executives had no interest in Irrational continuing without its boss. Irrational was a collection of smart, talented people, sure, but it was also the Ken Levine studio. He had unparalleled authority and autonomy there. People who worked there could contribute their own ideas to projects like *BioShock Infinite*, but if Levine didn't like something, it was gone. He always got the final word. What was nice about that reality was that Levine had the sway to insulate them from a lot of 2K's executive pressure; what was less nice was that without Ken Levine, 2K didn't think Irrational could exist.

As Irrational's developers worked to finish the *Burial at Sea* DLC, Ken Levine and Don Roy started pulling people aside and asking if they wanted to join Levine's new initiative. The studio would be closing, they said, but this hand-selected group could come along to whatever was next. They just couldn't tell anyone else at Irrational, they were told, or it might risk everyone's severance pay. By the end

---

9   Take-Two had a similar arrangement with Rockstar Games, the makers of
     Grand Theft Auto, which was its own subsidiary alongside 2K.

of this process, they had a team of just over a dozen people, many of whom had been leads on *BioShock Infinite*, and all of whom now had a devastating secret to keep. "I was not ready for that," Roy said. "We had a lot of people with families."

Mike Snight, a world-builder on *BioShock Infinite*, was one of the people picked for Levine's new studio.[10] He was excited about the opportunity but dreaded having to keep it secret. "It made me feel really gross," Snight said. "All my morals were going against it. These people that are close to me—this life-altering event is going to happen to them, and I can't really tell them."

Throughout 2013 and into 2014, there were departures and lay-offs. Temporary employees, including most of the quality-assurance testers, were told their contracts would not be renewed. Some of the remaining staff just figured Irrational was downsizing to prepare for its next game. Soon, they thought, it would be time to enter preproduction again, to relax and spend the next year or two brainstorming ideas with Levine. Others could see warning signs, though, like the sudden silence surrounding an office move that the company had been planning for a while. One day, to celebrate the completion of the *Burial at Sea* DLC, the studio served a giant, three-foot cake designed to look like *BioShock Infinite*'s Songbird. To some, this was an omen. "They always say [it's a bad sign] when you see these random acts of, 'Hey, let's get the team together for no reason and just have cake,'" said Bill Gardner.

On Tuesday, February 18, 2014, Ken Levine called the whole studio into the upstairs kitchen for an all-hands meeting. Irrational had just returned from a long weekend for Presidents' Day. As soon

---

10   One of the video game industry's quirks is that every company has different nomenclature for its jobs. At Irrational, "world-builders" were responsible for laying out and lighting levels, sort of like a cross between artists and designers.

as the staff started filing in, it became clear that something was wrong. "We walked in, and it was dread," said Gardner. "You could feel something in the air."

Irrational now employed less than a hundred people, so everyone in the room could see Levine's hands shaking as he read from a piece of paper. He was closing Irrational, he said, and he'd be starting a new studio with a handful of people. Everyone else would be laid off. A blog post on the company's website echoed his remarks to staff, with Levine taking full responsibility for the decision, writing:

> Seventeen years is a long time to do any job, even the best one. And working with the incredible team at Irrational Games is indeed the best job I've ever had. While I'm deeply proud of what we've accomplished together, my passion has turned to making a different kind of game than we've done before. To meet the challenge ahead, I need to refocus my energy on a smaller team with a flatter structure and a more direct relationship with gamers. In many ways, it will be a return to how we started: a small team making games for the core gaming audience. I am winding down Irrational Games as you know it. I'll be starting a smaller, more entrepreneurial endeavor at Take-Two.

Irrational's employees were stunned. The silence about their next project had been a hint that something wasn't right, but many had assumed that Levine had been off in a room somewhere, quietly working on design documents and proposals, like he had back in the early days of *BioShock Infinite*. Most of the staff had no clue that Levine and Roy had been secretly planning to start a new studio. "It was surprising," said Dowling. "But I guess it wasn't a total sucker punch. I was close enough to know that Ken was unhappy. I didn't really know what form that would take, or how it would manifest. I wasn't expecting to get a packet that day."

Once Levine stopped talking, there were questions from furious, stupefied employees. Hadn't *BioShock Infinite* been a success? Hadn't it made money? Hadn't they proven their talent? Wasn't Irrational a prestigious enough studio to keep making games without Levine? "I think I was still recovering from crunch exhaustion at that point," said LaClair. "There was disbelief. I think I was angry.... Personal worries. What am I going to do now?"

Many of the veteran game developers at Irrational had been through layoffs and even studio closures before, but those were usually the result of financial woes. When a publisher canceled a game, developers knew to start updating their résumés. When a game failed to sell enough copies, the studio behind it could be in danger. Those events made sense. But with Irrational, as perhaps befit its name, logic had flown out the window. This was the studio behind *BioShock*, still, six years later, considered one of the greatest games ever made. Sure, the process of making *BioShock Infinite* had been painful and expensive, but the game sold millions and had earned a 94 on Metacritic. They'd given up countless hours of personal and family time to finish it. Their reward for that was to lose their jobs? It just felt so *unfair*.[11]

Once Levine had finished speaking, Irrational's human resources people came up and started walking everyone through the logistics. Everyone laid off would get severance packages based on the length of their time at Irrational. Some would get paid for at least the next three or four months. Some were able to negotiate their benefits,

---

11   2K declined to make executives available for interviews or to provide any sort of comment for this book.

too, like Chad LaClair, who had gotten sick with cancer in 2011 (and had since fully recovered). He was able to convince the company to give him an extension on his health insurance. Many former Irrational employees agreed that the shutdown was handled humanely, all things considered. Levine even spotlighted individual staff on his Twitter page, encouraging other companies to hire them.

Yet those who hadn't been invited to join the new studio felt like they'd been left out of the cool kids' table. How could they not? Levine had picked a small group of developers with whom he wanted to make games, and dozens of Irrational staff weren't included. "They took one level builder, and he had been the lead on part of the final DLC, so it made sense to me," said LaClair. "They didn't have the room for other people. But yeah, at the time, I thought, 'Aw man, I wasn't chosen; I wish that I had been.'"

Bill Gardner, who had been at Irrational for over a decade and considered Ken Levine a close personal friend, was also upset he wasn't brought along. Although he and Levine had butted heads throughout the development of *BioShock Infinite*—"We had reached a point where we weren't really seeing eye-to-eye fully on the creative vision of what Columbia was," Gardner said—it was still tough to see Levine go off without him. "I was a little bit frankly hurt about the fact that he didn't feel that he could confide in me or talk about what the next steps were," Gardner said. "But at the same time, I knew things weren't working out as a company."

In the days following Irrational's closure, dozens of big video game companies flew representatives to Boston to try to get their hands on some of the people behind *BioShock*. Irrational's leadership organized a job fair at a nearby hotel, and game studios from all across the world showed up to collect résumés. "The job fair was nuts," said Forrest Dowling. "Recruiters descended and it was like a race to get to everybody." Some uprooted their lives, moving across the country for new game development gigs. Others left the video game industry for more stable fields. And a few, like Bill Gardner, used the opportunity to go independent. In the months following Irrational's closure, Gardner began working out of his basement with his wife, Amanda, and in 2017 the two of them released a horror game called *Perception*, in which you'd play as a blind woman who used echolocation to navigate the world. The game sold decently— "several tens of thousands, which is enough for a small company to keep the lights on"—but Gardner had been hoping for more. "It's brutal out there," he said.

Meanwhile, in Irrational's now-empty offices, Levine and his remaining staff began building the studio that would eventually become known as Ghost Story Games. Their plan was to make a game based on what Levine called "narrative LEGOs"—pieces of story that could fit together in different sequences so that every player had a unique experience. It was an ambitious idea that, at least on paper, could be yet another evolution of Warren Spector's vision of a game with countless possibilities. And, as anyone who has worked with Levine might have predicted, it's taken way longer than expected.

Don Roy, who had helped launch Ghost Story, wound up quitting in the summer of 2017 after a falling-out with Levine. "I felt like I kept creating miracles for him," Roy said, "and then he wasn't doing what he said he would." Seven years after Irrational's closure, Levine's new studio has still not yet said or shown anything publicly about the game. Those who have worked there say the project has been delayed multiple times, and as of this writing, it's not clear if or when it will come out.

These days, some who worked at Irrational say they'd think twice before going to a game studio so strongly associated with a single person, unalterably linked to that person's decisions and whims.

With the first *BioShock* and a whole lot of savvy press exposure, Ken Levine cemented himself as one of the video game industry's few renowned auteurs. To fans, players, and even to executives at 2K, Levine was Irrational. Irrational was Levine. People who worked there had to accept that, and some even grew to love it, but at the end of it all, when Levine wanted to turn off the lights, they all had to go home. Working for a "AAA" game studio like Irrational meant accepting that reality. It meant getting to work on an ambitious, beautiful shooting game with hundreds of people and a budget of many millions, with good salaries and ample snacks, but it also meant being tied to the fate of one man. At another studio, the departure of a creative director might have led to an opportunity for someone else to step up. At Irrational, it meant the end.

CHAPTER 3

RAFTING UPSTREAM

Gwen Frey had been working in the video game industry for about six months when she went through her first studio shutdown.

Frey was a proficient artist, with bright blue eyes and a knack for complicated technical challenges. Growing up, making video games had never seemed like a feasible career to her, despite a compulsive *World of Warcraft* habit ("I played it way too much....It was a full-time job"). Then, while studying at the Rochester Institute of Technology, Frey discovered a club for aspiring game developers. She offered to make art for them, then had an epiphany. "It never occurred to me that I could make games until that day, and I just immediately fell in love with it," she said. "I realized, 'Oh, I'm doing this for a living.'" In March 2009, just before her graduation, Frey scrounged up some money to fly to the Game Developers Conference (GDC) in San Francisco, where developers from across the world gathered to schmooze and swap stories. She slept on a friend's couch at night and bounced from booth to booth during the day, offering her services to any game studio that was hiring.

Eventually she got a bite: Slipgate Ironworks, founded by the legendary designer John Romero a few years after his departure from Ion Storm, offered her a job as a junior artist. Soon Frey was shipping her things across the country, moving from Rochester, New York, to San Mateo, California, for her first job in the video game industry. Six months later, in October 2009, Frey was sitting at her desk, animating a character, when her boss told her to come to an all-hands meeting. "I said, 'Hold on, I need to just finish this,'" Frey recalled. "And he has this dead look in his eyes. 'No, Gwen, just go to the meeting.'" Then came the news: The studio was shutting down. They were all laid off.

Frey was terrified, suddenly out of work and thousands of miles away from her family. "I didn't have money at this point," she said. "I didn't really know anybody or have much of a plan there. It was just a daze." At least she could commiserate with her now-former colleagues. "A weird thing happens when there's a studio closure like that," Frey said. "There's a huge amount of camaraderie." That evening, many of them got together for a farewell party and played *The Beatles: Rock Band*, strumming along to classic tunes on cheap plastic instruments. "We sang 'I get by with a little help from my friends' and cried and drank," Frey said. "That night was actually one of the best nights of my life."

It didn't take long for Frey to find a new job in San Mateo. She had become friendly with some of the developers at Secret Identity, a studio in the same building that shared a parent company with Slipgate Ironworks, and they brought her on as a technical artist for a multiplayer superhero game that would later be called *Marvel Heroes*.[1] She would be a character rigger, taking the big, complicated

---

1   Gazillion, the parent company of Secret Identity, would shut down at the end of 2017 after Disney pulled out of the *Marvel Heroes* deal, putting an end to the game.

models (or "3-D meshes") that artists would make for heroes like Iron Man and Thor and giving them digital joints and bones so the animators could make them move. Rigging a character meant turning it from a static image into something like a puppet, capable of dangling its arms and legs in different directions. Then, the animators could decide how to pull the strings.

Frey liked working at Secret Identity, although over time she grew bored with the work she was doing. Most of the superheroes she was rigging were bipedal humans, which didn't make for much of a challenge; there were only so many ways you could put joints on two legs and two arms. At the same time, Frey was meeting entrepreneur after entrepreneur in San Mateo, where during the day people would work at start-ups and then at night get together to talk about leaving those start-ups to launch their own start-ups. The ambition was rubbing off.

By 2011, Frey had decided to look for new jobs, and at the E3 trade show that June, she pored over every splashy trailer and announcement, looking for games that she might want to help develop. One trailer stood out: *BioShock Infinite*, the newest game from the studio behind an all-time classic. "So many games are dark and gritty, and this was a game that's bright and colorful," said Frey. "I knew some of the people on the team, knew they were fantastic." Her roommate happened to be friends with one of the animators at Irrational, so Frey passed along her demo reel, which landed in front of *BioShock Infinite*'s art director. That led to an interview, which led to a job offer, and then Gwen Frey was moving back to the East Coast to work as a technical artist on *BioShock Infinite*.

In the fall of 2011, as Frey arrived in Quincy, Massachusetts, most of Irrational's developers were stressing about the state of *BioShock Infinite*. There wasn't much of a game at that point, and it seemed impossible to many of the artists and designers that they'd be able to finish making it in the next year. For some people the crunch had already started; for others, six- and seven-day workweeks loomed. For Frey, however, it was a dream job. She'd never worked on a game this ambitious or beautiful. "I loved it," she said. "And I know not everybody did, but I loved it." After two years of rigging the same animations over and over again, the variety of technical challenges on *BioShock Infinite* was refreshing for Frey. She wound up taking ownership over one key element: the background characters.

In a video game, every nonplayer character (NPC) has its own artificial intelligence, a set of scripted rules that tell it how to behave based on the player's actions. An enemy NPC might see you shooting at them, for example, and know to take cover behind some nearby debris. A neutral-minded character might know to be congenial if you're nice to them or to pull out a knife if you start making threats. The more important the NPC, the more complicated these rules; in *BioShock Infinite*, Elizabeth's AI was so elaborate that Irrational had an entire team of people, the Liz Squad, dedicated to making her feel like a real partner as she followed you through the streets and alleys of Columbia.

Originally, the developers of *BioShock Infinite* had wanted to fill the entire world with elaborate AI-driven characters who knew how to do all sorts of complex things, like find paths and take cover behind objects. The more complicated an AI got, however, the more processing power it would soak up. If too many NPCs were trying to run too many scripts at once, the game would slow to a crawl, like a horse trying to pull an overloaded cart down the street. To get *BioShock Infinite* to function, they needed to take weight out of the cart. Most of the game's NPCs—especially the ones you'd see only in crowds or in the background as you explored the city—had to be *dumb*.

Frey was in charge of these dumb NPCs, which she called

chumps—background characters with no AI, scripted to perform just one or two tasks. At first she started taking NPCs and giving them brief animation loops, like a kid who would just keep digging sand on the beach until the end of time, but something felt off. "If you walk up to a character and they don't look at you, it doesn't feel right," said Frey. So she started writing basic AI to make her NPCs turn to watch the player as they drew near. "Just very simple scripting." Over time she filled Columbia with all sorts of these chumps, from beggars to carnival barkers to crowds of angry citizens. Like the rest of her coworkers at Irrational, Frey put in a lot of hours, but she didn't mind. "I had such a clear ownership over what I was doing," she said. "When you have that ownership, the crunch doesn't sting as much."

On February 18, 2014, Frey was supposed to be on vacation. She had an early flight the next day that would take her from Boston to Vancouver, and then she had to drive to Whistler Mountain for a friend's wedding over the weekend, so she was preparing for a long week of traveling. Then she got a call from her boss. "He said, 'I've got some news. Irrational Games is closing down,'" Frey recalled. Then her phone started blowing up with condolences. She'd missed the meeting where Ken Levine had addressed everyone, and now the news was already out in the world: Irrational was no more.

When she was done signing paperwork, Frey walked over to Kama, a dive bar near the office where some of Irrational's former staff were drinking. "None of the people I regularly hang out with were super surprised," she said. "Nobody knew for sure that we would shut down, but nobody was shocked it happened." Later, as Frey read through the severance packet, she started calculating how much money she had left and how much longer she'd get to stay on Irrational's insurance. "You don't really have the time to feel outrage or fear or anything, because you're just busy with all of the work," Frey said. "They say a thing people experience is when they go through something really awful, in the moment, you have so much adrenaline and stuff running through you that you don't panic yet. You tend to panic later." She had originally planned to hang out in Canada for a few extra days after the wedding, but she cut her trip short so she could sort out her future.

A couple of weeks later, Frey went to the job fair that Irrational had set up at a nearby hotel. She tried to keep an open mind as she talked to other big game developers and publishers about potential jobs, but the conversations made her uneasy. She started feeling like she'd been through this before. "I was walking around, looking at these studios," Frey said. "And, okay, I'm going to put several years of my life into a game, and then maybe it'll do well and maybe it won't. Then I'm going to move, and I'm going to do it again, and maybe it'll do well and maybe it won't, but nothing will ever be mine. And this will never end. I'm on this treadmill that will never end."

As Frey handed out her résumé and talked to recruiters, that feeling kept gnawing at her. Did she really want to keep going through this? Did she really want to waste more years of her life on games that ultimately belonged to other people? She kept thinking back to her days in San Mateo, surrounded by start-ups and entrepreneurs. "I've always had that thing in me," Frey said. "I just want to make something that's mine."

■ ■ ■

On the day Irrational shut down, Forrest Dowling planned to get lunch with an old buddy. *BioShock Infinite*'s art director, Scott Sinclair, had quit a few months earlier when the studio's future seemed hazy, and he and Dowling had stayed in touch. Then the whole company was called upstairs for an all-hands meeting. "I texted him: 'Hey dude, I might be a little late. There's a company meeting. Not sure what's going on,'" Dowling said. "And then I was like, 'Ah. So. We can go long on lunch if you want.'"

Sitting at Chipotle in a mall near the office, the pair reminisced about the good and the bad times of *BioShock Infinite*'s development and lamented the studio's closure. They talked about life post-Irrational and how they'd both been playing around with ideas on the side. Dowling had been prototyping a little game about surviving in the wilderness, while Sinclair had been designing an art project involving "tiny worlds"—small, self-contained spaces with distinct aesthetic sensibilities. "We said: 'These ideas seem like they fit together pretty well,'" Dowling said. "And then we just went our separate ways."

Dowling spent the next week on his sofa, playing *Battlefield* games. "You feel deflated," Dowling said. "You don't know what's next at that point. Because essentially those words mean that there's going to be a big change in your life, and you don't know what it's going to be." He wasn't too worried, though. Between the job fair, the press, and Twitter hashtags following the closure, there were recruiters from companies big and small reaching out to just about everyone who had worked at Irrational. "I didn't have a kid in high school or something that I couldn't move," Dowling said. "I'd just shipped a Game of the Year–quality game as a lead. That meant, 'Okay, where am I gonna work?' Not, 'Am I going to work?'"

As time went on, Dowling found himself obsessing over the ideas that he and Sinclair had discussed over lunch. They exchanged energetic texts, brainstorming ways in which their respective pieces could fit together. What if they made a game in which you had to survive the wilderness, exploring a series of handcrafted "tiny worlds" as you went? What if these little spaces were connected by a river? And what if the game took place in the American South? "We started talking about how maybe we could try to do this together," Dowling said. "We always had a great working relationship. I think we really respected each other and really liked working together." Soon the "ifs" started turning into "whens," and they were making plans to fund and design their own independent game. It was the spring of 2014, and indie development seemed more like a viable career than ever before. Going indie would mean making big financial sacrifices, but Dowling could envision a path to success.

This was a huge shift from the early days of his career. In the mid-2000s, when Dowling was working on first-person shooters at Kaos in New York, the only feasible way to sell a video game had been to print it on a disc and sell it through a retail store like GameStop or Walmart. In order to package discs, you needed a publisher, which meant you needed to operate on a significant scale. If you were a two-person operation working out of your basement, you'd have a hard time even getting Sony to give you access to development kits for the PlayStation 3, let alone convincing Target that your game should be on their shelves.

As high-speed internet became more widely available and game publishers invested in their own online infrastructure, everything changed. Sony, Microsoft, and Nintendo built digital stores for their consoles. By 2010, downloadable indie games like *Braid* and *Castle Crashers* had sold millions of copies, despite the fact that they were made by tiny teams of people with little support from big publishers. Platforms like Steam and Xbox Live gave developers the freedom to sell their games digitally at whatever prices they wanted, opening the floodgates for everyone. You no longer had to make a game for tens of millions of dollars and sell it for $60 a pop, praying to the video game gods that you'd sell a million copies and avoid going bankrupt. Dowling and Sinclair could conceivably make a game on a much smaller scale than *BioShock Infinite*, sell it for a fraction of the price, and still generate enough revenue to run a small studio.

But they needed a few more people. High on their list was Chad LaClair, the designer and artist whom they had befriended on *BioShock Infinite*. Just after Irrational closed, Dowling had mentioned to LaClair that he was considering going independent, and LaClair seemed enamored of the idea. "I remember running into [Dowling] on the bridge out to the parking lot and just feeling jealous," said LaClair. Back when he was starting his career, LaClair had been inspired by the seminal book *Masters of Doom* by David Kushner, which told the iconic story of id Software. LaClair had loved reading about the two founders, John Carmack and John Romero, and how they'd cranked out legendary games like *Doom* and *Quake* with a tiny team of people, more like a rock band than the giant corporate monoliths that made up modern game development. He'd always hoped that one day he could be part of a company like that.

Money was a concern, though. LaClair and his wife had both worked at Irrational, so now they both needed new jobs. They didn't have any kids, but they planned to have one soon, and LaClair felt compelled to work for a stable company with a dependable salary and guaranteed health insurance. In the weeks following Irrational's shutdown, he flew out to big game companies for interviews. At the same time, Dowling and Sinclair asked if he wanted to join them. It was tempting, LaClair said, but he'd have to think about it. And he did. Often. "It just colored every interview I was in," LaClair said. "Do I want to go to AAA again or try to do something on our own?"

As he talked to the big companies, LaClair started noticing a strange trend: jobs in the big-budget video game industry had grown more specialized. Graphical fidelity had improved at unprecedented rates, transforming video game characters from messes of polygons into uncanny depictions of people. Back in the 1990s, *Tomb Raider* hero Lara Croft's face had looked like someone smudged some makeup on a coconut; in 2013, she almost resembled a real woman. As the graphics got better, players' standards grew higher. Even games like *BioShock Infinite*, which aimed for stylized, colorful graphics rather than ultrarealistic grit, were expected to look richer and more beautiful than any game before them.

To create those vibrant worlds, teams of twenty had grown to teams of two hundred. What had been just a task on an artist's checklist might now be one person's entire job. "I had interviewed somewhere where they knew I was a level builder, artist, and designer," LaClair said. "They said, 'We'd like you to come in and be a lighter.'" In other words, they wanted him to be solely responsible for designing and placing lighting effects throughout a game's world. "I said, 'That'd be really fun, but I don't know if I'd be bored doing just that. I want to do other things.' They said, 'No, we really need a lighter.'"

Not unlike his former boss Ken Levine, LaClair had grown weary of big teams and bloated budgets. He wanted to be on a small team of rockstar developers, like Carmack and Romero. "Even being in a thirty-person room at Irrational in the very beginning was such a different vibe than when we got to our one hundredth or two hundredth employee," LaClair said. Back in 2011, when LaClair had gotten sick with cancer, he spent a lot of his days getting treatment after work, so it had taken him a while to notice how unfamiliar the office had become. "It was: focus, focus, focus, then go to the hospital," LaClair said. "Suddenly I look up and there are fifty-plus people that I didn't even know anymore." After some pondering, LaClair told Dowling and Sinclair he was in. "I wanted to work somewhere where I could be part of a small team and we could be in control of our destiny," LaClair said.

Gwen Frey was an easier sell. She'd grown exhausted at the thought of getting back on the AAA treadmill. At going-away parties for the former staff of Irrational, Frey would tell her colleagues that she had grand plans to go solo.[2] "I'm saying, 'I'm going to go indie. It's time,'" Frey recalled. Then she ran into Dowling, who said he was also going indie, but he was going to bring along Scott Sinclair, and hey, it turned out they needed an animator. "I said, 'Oh, never mind. I'm going to be your animator,'" said Frey.

By the summer of 2014, they were a team of six: Forrest Dowling, Scott Sinclair, Chad LaClair, Gwen Frey, and two other friends they'd recruited—Bryn Bennett, a programmer and guitarist who'd worked at Harmonix, the studio behind *Rock Band*, alongside Sinclair; and Damian Isla, an AI specialist who had contracted on *BioShock Infinite*. All six of them would share equity in this new independent company, and they'd all take paychecks based on their individual needs. "We did not pay ourselves anywhere near what any of us made when we worked for a big AAA studio," said Dowling. "We just put our cards on the table, and said, 'All right, here's literally what I need to live. I'm not going to contribute to a 401(k); I'm going to forgo any luxuries. This is the baseline of what I need.'" The hope was that whatever they sacrificed now they'd get back in the future, once their game had launched and the company was generating revenue.

On June 5, 2014, just under four months after Irrational shut down, Dowling registered a trademark for their new company, The

---

2   Many of the post-Irrational parties took place at a charming Cambridge bar called Meadhall, which former employees now associate with sadness and despair. "I feel like I just can't go to Meadhall anymore," said Frey. "It's where people say good-bye to leave the state."

Molasses Flood, named after a 1919 molasses tank explosion that had become part of Boston folklore.[3] It was a day to celebrate. They had officially gone indie.

■ ■ ■

The dream goes something like this. You, a talented and creative person with the next Big Idea for the Great American Video Game, quit your job to live off savings for a couple of years while you lock yourself in a room and work. You make absolutely no artistic compromises. Your vision is pure. Some time later you emerge, unwashed and covered in sandwich crumbs, with the video game that will make you billions of dollars. The people will see and play your work, and then you will have made the next *Minecraft*, *Undertale*, or *Stardew Valley*, selling millions of copies and setting yourself up for life. Best of all, you won't have to share a cent, because you'll be free from the yoke of big corporations taking your profits and telling you what to do.

Dowling and crew took a more pragmatic approach. They wanted to make a game they thought was great, yes, but they also wanted to make a game with a reasonable scope and marketing appeal. "We thought up the company with the understanding that we are not going to be making artsy bullshit," said Frey. "We believed we would make a game that is good and profitable. We wanted to do both." Their first game, *The Flame in the Flood*, would

---

3   Why name their new studio after a tragedy that killed twenty-one people? "The pithy answer is because it was available," said Dowling. "Nobody names their company after industrial accidents. The real answer is that I think it fits a lot of things that are important to us. It's a story that, when people first hear about it, it's funny and light. It feels like a joke. But when you actually learn about it, it becomes really interesting and complicated."

be about surviving and exploring the wilderness, like Dowling and Sinclair had initially imagined. You'd play as a wanderer named Scout, rafting down a river that would look different every new game. You'd have to scavenge for supplies, stave off dangerous wild animals, and search for survivors in run-down gas stations and abandoned hardware stores across the game's postapocalyptic, flooded version of America. It was a cartoony, lo-fi game with isometric graphics—a far cry from the massive airships of Columbia, but lovely nonetheless.

On October 7, 2014, once they'd mapped out their plans for the game, Dowling and crew launched a Kickstarter for *The Flame in the Flood*, asking for $150,000 and immediately driving buzz from video game news outlets. *Laid-off Irrational developers strike it out on their own!* By the end of their Kickstarter campaign, they had reached almost twice their goal, bringing in over a quarter of a million dollars from more than seven thousand empathetic and curious backers. It was a success by any measure, but they all knew the money wouldn't go very far. Divided by six, their earnings of $251,647 came out to just around $42,000 per person—less than half what each of them might make at an AAA studio—and that was before Kickstarter fees, backer rewards, and other expenses.[4] The Molasses Flood struck a deal with Microsoft for additional funding in exchange for temporary console exclusivity on the Xbox, but money was still a big stress point, which meant that they didn't have much time. In that sense, being independent was a lot like entering production at Irrational. "It's less different than people might think," said Dowling. "You always have a fixed amount of money that you

---

4   Kickstarter took a 5 percent fee and added a 3 to 5 percent cash-processing fee on top of that. Backer rewards—which for *The Flame in the Flood* consisted of posters, art books, and T-shirts—drained even more money from the tank.

can work with, you always have a clock that's ticking, and time is always running out. The numbers are just much smaller."

For the next year they plugged away at *The Flame in the Flood*, working out of a small office they'd rented just outside Boston. The hours were long and the pay was low. To save money and keep their team as small as possible, everyone at The Molasses Flood handled multiple jobs. Dowling was both a designer and the president of the company, and he also did their PR and marketing. Frey animated the game's characters and somehow also found the time to crunch the numbers and pay everyone's taxes.

Buoyed by the support of a small but hard-core community and the buzz they'd gotten around the launch of the Kickstarter, the team put *The Flame in the Flood* into Steam Early Access in late 2015, allowing players to buy and play before it officially launched. The developers continued to fix bugs and update the game, heading into 2016 with high hopes. The official release would be February. "We had this just never-ending confidence that this was going to be just fine," said Gwen Frey. "We never thought we'd be Notch"— the billionaire creator of *Minecraft*—"but we did think we'd break even."

On February 24, 2016, *The Flame in the Flood* came out on PC and Xbox. It did not break even. "It didn't hit those numbers," Frey said. "Not even a little."

For a team of people who had just spent years in the world of big-budget game development, it was shocking to have a launch this underwhelming. Back at Irrational, they'd commanded attention. When *BioShock Infinite* came out, the world looked up. There were television commercials, *New York Times* features, and big, splashy advertisements everywhere. During the game's release in March 2013, many of Irrational's staff had been at GDC in downtown San Francisco, where they'd gone to a GameStop and signed artwork for an eager crowd who had lined up at midnight just to get their hands on the game. In contrast, *The Flame in the Flood* was just a bullet point on the list of dozens of games that hit Steam every week. "Launching an indie game is like—I just picture a lonely dude in a party hat and a folding chair," said Dowling. "A single confetti falls from the ceiling."

Maybe it was the lack of marketing buzz, the mouthful of a name, or the glut of other indie games in 2016. Maybe not enough people liked the game. (Reviews were solid, but didn't stand out.) Whatever the reasons, *The Flame in the Flood* wasn't the sales success that the developers at The Molasses Flood had hoped it would be. They weren't going to be able to take back pay and make up for the salaries they'd sacrificed over the past two years. Over the next few days, the six of them gloomily started to realize that they might not even have enough money to keep functioning as a game development studio. One day, Frey sat down with Chad LaClair, whose wife had just given birth to their first child, to tell him the company wouldn't be able to pay back any of the salary he'd sacrificed. "I had to look him in the eye and say, 'I can't even you out yet,'" Frey said. "That was extremely painful. That failure was so much worse than ever being laid off, or anything else. Because you're responsible."

Soon they were talking about contingency plans, and what it might look like if The Molasses Flood had to shut down. Bryn Bennett left for another company, in part because of the instability and in part because he wasn't enjoying his role there.[5] The five other founders started to wonder if they should look for other jobs too.

---

5   "My background is mostly graphics," Bennett said. "I was finding a difficult spot in that company to really use what interests me....Most of what I think was needed from me was a ton of gameplay programming. That's fine, but it's just generally not what I'm interested in. My skill set wasn't exactly a great fit."

In May 2016, three months after the launch of *The Flame in the Flood*, Dowling noticed a handful of job listings at Double Fine, an independent studio in San Francisco. In a fortuitous twist, Double Fine was looking for five developers whose descriptions exactly matched theirs. Dowling sent them an email offering to make their lives easier: What if, instead of interviewing and hiring dozens of candidates for each role, they filled all five positions in one shot? *Sure*, the Double Fine people wrote back, and suddenly The Molasses Flood had a financial lifeboat. For the next few months, Dowling and crew worked on *Psychonauts 2*, the long-awaited sequel to Double Fine's cult-classic platformer. "It gave us the money we needed to at least breathe a little bit," Dowling said.

At the end of the summer, when the *Psychonauts 2* contract ended, Damian Isla also quit. "At that point we thought, 'Okay, we have no engineers in our video game company. This is not good,'" said Dowling. Recognizing how dire their financial situation was, the remaining cofounders mulled over closing the studio, but they couldn't bring themselves to give up just yet. Instead, they decided to take a six-week hiatus to reflect and recharge. Dowling went to Spain—the first proper vacation he'd taken in years. "You hear a lot about burnout as a result of crunch, but I also think that burnout can be the result of creative exhaustion," Dowling said. "We needed a little time away from just making a game to think about what individually each of us wanted at that point."

When they got back from their break, in the fall of 2016, the founders of The Molasses Flood decided they wanted to keep fighting to survive. They still only had the funds to pay everyone a fraction of what they'd made in AAA development, but something funny was happening. *The Flame in the Flood* was still selling. The team had expected that, just like *BioShock Infinite* and the other big-budget games they'd developed in the past, *The Flame in the*

Flood would make most of its money in the first few weeks after launch. After all, that was when $60 retail games did most of their business—when GameStop put up big posters and Best Buy stuck copies in prime positions at the front of their stores. After that, there would always be a big drop in sales, which was what Dowling and Frey had expected from *The Flame in the Flood*. Yet their little indie was still selling. The revenue wasn't enough to make them financially comfortable, but the game's sales were hitting a steady cadence, like Scout rafting down the river, trying not to crash.

They signed a deal with a small publisher to put *The Flame in the Flood* on the other major consoles, and in January 2017 the game hit PlayStation 4, which helped boost sales a bit more. "Our knowledge about how a game performs when it comes into the market was based entirely on the way that AAA worked, which is that you launch a game and get the lion's share of sales on month one, and then diminishing numbers in a linear fashion into nothing," said Dowling. "Which is not how it works when you don't have a $40 million marketing budget. Because you launch and it turns out that when you've spent $20,000 on marketing, nobody's heard of you. So it takes time for people to hear of you."

With some newfound leeway to keep the company operating, The Molasses Flood now had to decide what to make next. After their hiatus, they had started prototyping a multiplayer action game about high school kids battling one another using the items you'd see on the backs of comic books in the 1980s, like x-ray specs and hoverboards. In the fiction of this game, these items wouldn't be the disappointing cheap knockoffs of their real-life childhoods—they'd actually work. "It was a fun idea, but I think I was the only one that really loved it on the team," Dowling said. "There just wasn't a lot of passion for it." In the spring of 2017, they scrapped the comic book game and decided to instead start developing a sequel to *The*

Flame in the Flood. Scott Sinclair quit shortly afterward, leaving The Molasses Flood as a team of four: Dowling, Frey, LaClair, and a new engineer they'd hired, Alan Villani.[6]

The Flame in the Flood 2 didn't last very long either. Soon the game had transformed from a sequel into something else entirely. "I think a strength and a weakness that we have as a group is challenging assumptions," said Dowling. What started off as "Let's just do a sequel and fix the things we didn't like about it" turned into a complete overhaul of everything they'd done in *The Flame in the Flood*. "We started saying, 'Well, does there really need to be a river?'" Eventually, the project turned into what would be called *Drake Hollow*, a multiplayer game in which you'd team up with friends to build settlements and defend little anthropomorphic vegetables from menacing monsters.

That summer at Gamescom, the massive annual gaming convention in Germany, The Molasses Flood's founders started pitching *Drake Hollow* to publishers—a long, drawn-out process involving endless meetings, flashy PowerPoint presentations, and executives who were allergic to straight answers. "It was stressful," said Gwen Frey. "You get all these promises, and everybody's like, 'Yeah, yeah, we're interested; not right now, though. Maybe in six months.' We kept hearing that. Sometimes they won't ever say no, they'll just say, 'Maybe come back later.'" In the coming months Frey and the team kept building and pitching, hoping to convince some video game publisher to take a bet on their new game, but it was starting to feel hopeless. Low on funds and burned out, they decided to take The Molasses Flood part-time, giving each employee a couple of days every week to take freelance contracts or work on their own

---

6   Sinclair took a job in a 2K hangar in Novato, California, where—in a move that took him full circle—he began working on the next *BioShock*.

personal projects. Dowling did some level design work for their old boss, Ken Levine, at Ghost Story Games, the studio that had emerged from Irrational's ashes. Frey started dreaming up her own small game.

By the fall of 2017, after months of pitching, those remaining at The Molasses Flood were starting to wonder if they'd ever find money for *Drake Hollow*. The endless pitching was like paddling against a current, and few things were quite as demoralizing as hearing the words "maybe later." Would they ever get funded? Soon they were setting deadlines for themselves. If they couldn't sign a deal by December, they all agreed that they'd close the company. Just three years earlier, they had been the victims of a studio shutdown. Now they were days away from having to shut down their own studio.

Then came an unlikely savior.

A year earlier, when Dowling and team had signed the deal to bring *The Flame in the Flood* to consoles, they didn't think too much about the planned Nintendo Switch version. Nintendo's previous console, the Wii U, was a big flop, and there were few indications that the Switch would turn out any differently. Yet, when it launched in March 2017, the Nintendo Switch became a runaway success. Thanks to its sleek portability and lineup of fantastic games like *Zelda: Breath of the Wild*, the Switch immediately sold millions, beating the Wii U's entire lifetime of sales in just one year. Switch owners grew hungry for new games to play, and when a port of *The Flame in the Flood* launched on October 12, 2017, it arrived at the perfect time. Once an afterthought, the Switch version of *The Flame in the Flood* was now the defibrillator jolt that kept them alive. "It helped our pitching," said Dowling. "I could update how many units *The Flame in the Flood* had sold, and I could add a couple hundred thousand, which was nice."

When that December deadline came around, Dowling and crew

still hadn't found a financier for *Drake Hollow*, but their success on Switch bought them more time. They pushed back their self-imposed final day a few months, giving themselves until March 2018 to find a deal. If they couldn't get traction at the Game Developers Conference, they said, they would call it quits. They also decided to go back to working at The Molasses Flood full-time. It had become difficult to make serious progress on *Drake Hollow* when they were all there just a few days a week, and the company now had enough money to pay everyone properly. "If we were going to go full-time, then we needed to be able to continue living our lives, so we brought ourselves all up to reasonable salaries," said Dowling. "'Maybe this'll be for nothing,' [we thought], 'but we'd might as well pay ourselves what we deserve for people of our experience level. Go out in a blaze of glory of getting paid a little bit.'"

San Francisco was buzzing as game developers descended on the Moscone Center for GDC in March 2018. Nintendo's Switch was the hottest console in town, while Microsoft and Sony were briefing a handful of developers about their plans for the new Xbox and PlayStation, both slated for 2020. And another megacorporation was quietly meeting with companies to pitch them on a new gaming platform that they hoped would change the industry: Google.

The tech giant had been secretly hiring game developers and executives to launch a new streaming platform, which it would later call Stadia. Unlike previous gaming platforms, Stadia wouldn't be a console or computer in your home—instead, Stadia games would run on clusters of computers located in Google nodes across the world, and you'd play them by streaming the data to the device of your choice. It was an ambitious service, one that Google hoped would bring video games to hundreds of millions of people who wouldn't otherwise be able to play them. Google was on the hunt for developers to make exclusive games for Stadia, and one of the company's producers had worked at Irrational with Forrest Dowling. It was a good fit: Google needed games; Dowling needed money.

Dowling met with Google's executives and pitched *Drake Hollow*.[7] They were interested. Dowling flew home feeling optimistic, and not long afterward, Google got back to The Molasses Flood saying it wanted to come to terms. In the ensuing months, the two companies went back and forth on what the arrangement would look like—"The bigger the company, the more there'll be to negotiate," said Dowling. "What kind of insurance to carry. Really boring stuff"—and eventually they finalized a deal. They had finally found funding. After years of treading water, The Molasses Flood could finally get back on the raft.

Yet Gwen Frey couldn't help but feel restless. Back when they'd all gone part-time, she'd started messing around with her own video game, and even when they went back to working at The Molasses Flood full-time, she was spending nights and weekends on the project. *Kine*, as she called it, was a spatial puzzle game, set on a large map full of floating platforms. You'd play as three musically inclined robots who wanted to get together and start a band, and you'd need to maneuver each robot around platforms and obstacles in a series of challenging levels. Frey had pitched the idea to the rest of the team, but they weren't feeling it. ("It didn't feel like what we wanted to do as a studio," Dowling said.) Plus, she knew a musical narrative puzzle game would be a risky business proposition, at odds with the pragmatism that had driven The Molasses Flood since they'd started. So *Kine* became her side project.

---

7 Dowling would not tell me the game's publisher or confirm it was Google, for reasons that will be clear pretty soon. I found that out from other sources.

At first Frey thought she'd work on *Kine* for a few months and then put it online for free, but the more time she put into the game, the more she obsessed over it. It occupied her thoughts while she showered and cooked dinner. Whenever she grew emotionally exhausted from her life's stresses or hearing about Donald Trump's latest tweet, she'd tune everything out and work on *Kine*. For many people, playing video games is a good way to escape reality; for Frey, making a video game was even better. "I'd just go home and work on this, and I was happy," she said. Soon she was starting to feel more passionate about *Kine* than any of the work she was doing at The Molasses Flood. "I just never fell in love with [*Drake Hollow*], and I don't know why," she said. "I felt bad about it."

At the end of 2017, before Google entered the picture, Frey had been operating under the assumption that The Molasses Flood would run out of money, and she was getting ready to dive full-time into *Kine*. "I always had this backup plan: okay, we're probably going to fold, and then from the ashes I will go do this solo dev thing," Frey said. "I reached this really weird point where we didn't fold and I was kind of mad about it, because mentally I'd prepared to go work on this other project." In March 2018, when the Google deal started coming together, Frey pulled her colleagues aside and told them she wanted to leave. "I was just so in love with what I was making," she said. "There was no world where I could stay and make *Kine*."

Dowling was crushed. Here they were in the midst of negotiations for a deal that could save the company, and their technical animator wanted to leave? Not only was Frey a talented artist and an integral part of their team, but Dowling was also worried that her departure might destroy their chance at funding. "Part of my fear at that point was that we were on the cusp of finding a deal," Dowling said. "We were signing a deal as a team of four people—and it's funny to think about it in these terms because it's such a small staff—but if a publisher is signing a deal with a developer, and the developer says, 'Well, 25 percent of our workforce just gave notice,' the publisher might say, 'Uhhh, never mind. Nice chatting. Good luck.'"

In order to keep the split as amicable as possible, Frey agreed to stay on part-time until the deal was completely finished. It wound up taking months. As The Molasses Flood went back and forth with Google, bartering over terms, Frey stuck around to help train a new animator and off-load her work to others on the team. Still, the feelings were raw. "There was one conversation where Forrest said, 'Gwen, you're leaving at the worst possible time,'" Frey recalled. "I said, 'Forrest, if I left anytime before this, the company would've folded. Objectively, am I leaving at the worst possible time?' He said, 'No, objectively you're leaving at the best possible time. But I don't want you to leave.'"

At the same time, Frey was haunted by the idea that she might be giving up a massive payday. "You have no idea how stressful it was to leave," she said, "because I was looking at what they're doing, and I thought, 'They're going to get bought, and they're all going to be millionaires, and I own as much of the company as them, and I could be a millionaire, but I'm leaving to make some dumb shit. I'm an idiot.'" But going completely independent was the only way for Frey to feel creatively satisfied. "The last several years have been so stressful," Frey said. "Having this thing that I love that makes me happy is just priceless."

Not long after leaving, Frey started talking to publishers about potential landing spots for *Kine*. She came close to accepting a lucrative offer from a big company, but when they started talking about using their internal art team to overhaul the game and give it more mass-market appeal, she changed her mind. Instead, she started talking to Epic Games, the company that's today best known for *Fortnite* but has made the bulk of its fortune off the Unreal Engine, a ubiquitous tool used by video game developers both big and small. Epic had just launched its own distribution platform on the PC, the Epic Games Store, and was willing to pay Frey to make *Kine* an Epic Games Store exclusive. The deal would allow Frey to hire a musician and other contractors to help with art and technical work. By the end of 2018, she had turned what was once a hobby project into a big, ambitious puzzle game, and she'd officially started her own independent company. She called it Chump Squad.

▪ ▪ ▪

It's always tempting to believe, when you sign your first big deal or get that contract you've been praying for, that now you've got it made. That stability is within your grasp. That you can finally feel secure. But in the video game industry, there's no such thing as security. And there are no sure things.

By September 2018, the Google deal was official. *Drake Hollow* would be a Google Stadia exclusive, launching alongside the platform the following fall. The Molasses Flood now had a publishing contract with one of the biggest companies in the world, which meant they didn't have to worry about money for a while. Two months later, they moved into a sleek new office on the first floor of an industrial building in Newton, Massachusetts, and by 2019 they'd expanded from four to eleven people, even bringing back Damian Isla, the cofounder who had quit back when the studio was at its lowest point. Isla would go on to be creative director on a second, top secret new project at The Molasses Flood. "We wanted to get something started so we've got something we can move folks onto when the current project is winding down," said Forrest Dowling.

This was the type of move that people had expected from Irrational—a way to ensure that when a game was finished, there was still work for everyone to do. Often in the video game industry, layoffs happened when a company hired hundreds of new staff to ship a project, then found itself paying them all to do nothing once the game was done. By keeping multiple games in different stages of production, The Molasses Flood wouldn't have to face that dilemma.

For a while, things were good. But after four years of financial instability, Dowling still felt a gnawing sense of anxiety about the state of the company. New people meant new mouths to feed, new families to think about. He found himself empathizing with Ken Levine, understanding why his old boss was so stressed leading a team of hundreds. "There's no way to be in this industry and feel utterly comfortable," Dowling said. At Irrational, at least they had felt stable—after all, they were the people behind *BioShock*. Now, they were just another indie game developer. "Having been at two studios that closed and then [having] run my own for five years now," Dowling said, "we'll say the general level of need for antacids has been much greater in the last five years than it has in the ten preceding it."

He had good reason to be anxious. By the spring of 2019, fissures were erupting between The Molasses Flood and Google. By the summer, the two companies began to face what Dowling described as "a deviation of vision." *Drake Hollow* still resembled the initial pitches they'd made, and Dowling thought development was going well, despite a few hiccups in playtesting. Still, the publisher's excitement seemed to wane. "I think what happens when you're working with an external partner and they're potentially in the process of adding middle management and approval layers into their hierarchy," Dowling said, "there might be someone who gets added in who straight up is not into something that's in the portfolio....I can only speculate. But I think we stayed the course."

During one project deadline in September 2019, The Molasses Flood sent a build of *Drake Hollow* to Google and, weirdly, didn't get any responses. A few days later, Dowling got a call from their agent with some rough news: Google was pulling out. "Essentially it was, 'We don't feel we're good partners on this particular project, so it's probably best to sever this relationship,'" Dowling said. "It was a very kind process. It wasn't fraught, it wasn't cold, or anything like that."

Once again, The Molasses Flood found itself on a downward leg of the video game industry roller coaster. This time, Dowling wasn't quite as worried. They were financially secure and didn't need to find a new publisher—The Molasses Flood had built up enough savings to finish the game even without Google—and the timing was actually a little convenient. Dowling already had a flight booked to California, where he and Damian Isla planned to pitch their other project to all the big video game publishers. "All of a sudden we're like, 'Oh, well, we've got two games to show,'" said Dowling. Out of these meetings came a marketing deal with Microsoft, which led to *Drake Hollow* being publicly announced at an Xbox conference on November 14, 2019. A cute multiplayer game about protecting little vegetable monsters wasn't quite what people expected from the makers of *The Flame in the Flood*, but it sure did look fun. *Drake Hollow* came out on June 19, 2020, to mostly good reviews, and Dowling later described sales as "Okay, if not amazing."

Though Forrest Dowling and Gwen Frey no longer work together, they remain friends. They regularly go out drinking and hang out at meetups for Boston game developers. And they now both have a unique perspective on what it's like to run a studio. "I've been really, really fortunate that the two shutdowns I was part of, they had the money to give us severance, had the ability to do it right," said Frey, who wound up releasing *Kine* in October 2019 and, she says, almost immediately making a profit. "Now that I'm somebody who owns a business, and I was CFO [of The Molasses Flood], I know how close you get to being in the red. Right before you get those million-dollar deals, you go to negative money."

Today, The Molasses Flood appears to be stable—or at least as stable as an independent studio can be—thanks to a combination of talent, perseverance, and luck. But another studio that spawned from Irrational Games had a far less fortunate path. In fact, this studio remains one of the most bizarre stories in gaming—a mystery worthy of an Agatha Christie novel. It's a studio that simply vanished.

CHAPTER 4

THE CASE OF THE MISSING STUDIO

When Junction Point and Irrational closed their doors, the video game industry swiftly reacted. Recruiters flew out to Texas and Massachusetts to participate in job fairs. Catchy hashtags like #IrrationalJobs trended on Twitter. Video game websites published articles cataloging each company's history and speculating about what had gone wrong. Friends and colleagues reached out with sympathies.

What happens, then, when a video game studio closes and nobody knows about it? And when its parent company acts like the shutdown didn't even happen?

On October 17, 2013, inside a renovated airplane hangar in Novato, California, the game studio 2K Marin, a subsidiary of the publisher 2K, disappeared. After six years of operation and two games, the development label simply ceased to exist. In the morning, the developers who worked there were split into two rooms, as if they were the winning and losing contestants on some sort of twisted game show. Anyone in the first room was told they still had a job, at a new studio the company had been quietly building that would later be called Hangar 13. In the second room, an HR person stood in front and informed the unlucky contestants that they were all being laid off—and would they kindly stay in the room while everyone was processed?

The word "closure" was never used, much to the consternation of those who had worked there. That same day, when the video game websites Polygon and Rock Paper Shotgun reported that 2K Marin had gone through mass layoffs and might have even shut down, 2K's PR team sent out a statement that seemed to dispute their reports. "We can confirm staff reductions at 2K Marin," the statement read. "While these were difficult decisions, we regularly evaluate our development efforts and have decided to reallocate creative resources.[1] Our goal to create world-class video game titles remains unchanged."

Maybe it was a matter of semantics—after all, the people in the first room would get to keep working at 2K's offices—or maybe the publisher simply wanted to avoid bad press. Whatever the reason, the executives' public position made a huge difference to the people who had worked at 2K Marin. Studio shutdowns always led to an outpouring of support from fans and industry colleagues. If there was a silver lining to your company suddenly shuttering, it was getting to see how much the world appreciated the work you had done. In the same way that a celebrity's death causes a flood of tweets and YouTube videos, a studio's closure can lead to newfound appreciation—and job opportunities—for everyone who worked there. To the people who worked for 2K Marin, their studio wasn't a faceless brand; it was a collection of formidably talented people who wanted to make great games. "That's actually one of the 2K Marin

---

1   Is there anything more ghoulish in corporate America than referring to taking people's jobs away as "reallocating creative resources"?

alumni's serious gripes, that the studio never got officially shut down," said Scott LaGrasta, one of 2K Marin's earliest employees. "They've never said it's a closure. They said it was a realignment of resources. 'Oh, we had to lay some people off.'"

A few months later, at an investors conference in New York, someone asked Strauss Zelnick, the CEO of 2K parent company Take-Two, what was going on with *BioShock*.[2] It was May 2014, and Irrational Games had just shut down—did that mean *BioShock* was dead too? No, he said. *BioShock* would continue as one of their tentpole franchises, and it would be "something 2K Marin will be responsible for shepherding going forward."

This was baffling. 2K Marin had lost all of its staff seven months earlier. Observers wondered: Was it a slip of the tongue? Did the CEO of their company not know that 2K Marin was gone? Perhaps he was referring to the publishing team at 2K's offices in Novato, which would actually go on to oversee a new *BioShock*?[3] Or was he just playing the PR game? Up through June 2015, press releases from 2K included language about 2K Marin, despite the fact that the studio no longer existed.[4] Today, the publisher no longer acts as if 2K Marin is still around, but has never acknowledged the studio's closure. Representatives for 2K still won't even discuss it.

To executives at 2K, the name likely didn't matter. There were still people in the Novato office working on 2K's games—why

---

2   The remarks were reported by the video game website GameSpot, whose reporter Eddie Makuch attended the conference.

3   This fourth *BioShock* game, code-named *Parkside*, first entered development at a company in Texas called Certain Affinity. That version was later canceled and brought back to Novato, where it was taken over by a studio that would eventually be called Cloud Chamber.

4   From a press release on June 1, 2015, nearly two years after 2K Marin closed: "The 2K label has some of the most talented development studios in the world today, including Firaxis Games, Visual Concepts, 2K Marin, 2K Czech, 2K Australia, Cat Daddy Games and 2K China."

should they make a whole fuss about whether "2K Marin" still existed? But to the people who once worked there, these semantics meant something. They didn't see themselves as just another tentacle of the 2K publishing octopus. They thought they were building something special.

■ ■ ■

How do you follow up a game like *BioShock*? In the summer of 2007, after the developers at Irrational Games released their seminal title, Ken Levine first decided he wouldn't even try. But 2K demanded more *BioShock* games, so a handful of Irrational staff moved from Massachusetts to the San Francisco Bay Area to start a new studio that would be responsible for *BioShock 2*.

Under the leadership of Alyssa Finley, a well-respected producer who had helped get the first game out the door, this new team set up shop at 2K's headquarters, a renovated hangar inside an old Air Force base in Novato, California. They called their new studio 2K Marin—after the county—and began developing the sequel to one of the greatest games of all time. Like its predecessor, *BioShock 2* would take place within the underwater city of Rapture. This time, you'd play as one of the menacing Big Daddies that were so prevalent in the first game, getting to see a different perspective of the objectivist dystopia that had haunted the dreams of so many players.

The writer and director of *BioShock 2* was Jordan Thomas, a fast-talker with narrow cheeks and perpetually messy hair. Thomas was a disciple of Warren Spector, having worked with him at Ion Storm in the early 2000s, and he had a similar sensibility for video game storytelling. He loved horror, and one of his first jobs, on the Ion Storm game *Thief: Deadly Shadows*, was designing a haunting mission called "Robbing the Cradle" that took place in an abandoned asylum. The magazine *PC Gamer* would call this mission "one of the most brilliant and disturbing levels ever committed to PC," much to Thomas's delight. When Ion Storm shut down in 2005, he spent some time on a start-up that went nowhere, then connected with an old friend at 2K, who asked if he might be interested in moving to Massachusetts and working with a studio called Irrational Games on a spiritual successor to *System Shock 2*. Of course he was interested. No game was more formative to his career. "I went out, met with the team, and pretty much instantly clicked with them," Thomas said. "They were the cousins of the culture that taught me to make things. It felt like meeting family out of nowhere."

Thomas spent the next year in Boston, helping Irrational complete *BioShock* during its rough final year of production ("I made up for lost time with lack of sleep"). Again he became responsible for the most beloved level in a video game, this time with "Fort Frolic," a neon playground that had been warped into a horror show by a sociopathic artist. It was full of plaster statues of humans that at first seemed like part of the background until suddenly you turned around and one of them was standing there, trying to kill you. When Thomas was done with *BioShock*, he spent a few months at 2K's studio in Canberra, Australia, helping develop an early version of a project that would later cast a great shadow over his life. Then, in 2008, he got a call from Alyssa Finley, asking if he wanted to come out to San Francisco and be the director of *BioShock 2*.

Development of *BioShock 2* was tough, by all accounts, with the rapidly expanding team at 2K Marin putting in extensive hours to finish the game in two years, a tight window for any game of this scale. Throughout 2009, as Thomas and crew realized they would need more people than the few dozen they'd hired in Novato, the *BioShock 2* team did what the first *BioShock*'s developers had done—they borrowed people from 2K Australia, asking them to drop what they were working on and come help make *BioShock 2* instead. This was a common practice at major video game publishers like 2K, where studios and developers were seen as interchangeable resources, to be shuffled and assigned to whichever game needed to come out next. When the people in charge of 2K Australia complained about this, the executives made them a promise: After *BioShock 2*, the next project would be 2K Australia's to lead, and 2K Marin would have to help them out. "There was this clearly communicated sense that we'd have to pay the piper," said *BioShock 2* lead level designer JP LeBreton. "We'd have to pay them back."

For Jordan Thomas, *BioShock 2* became a hard lesson in creative leadership. He'd come to the game with arrogance and a healthy ego, high on the praise he'd received for "Robbing the Cradle" and "Fort Frolic." After a year of working for Ken Levine, he felt like it was his turn to be the auteur, to watch his grand creative vision unfold on the screen. But the story he envisioned, in which players would explore the manifestations of *BioShock* characters' psyches (sort of like the classic platformer *Psychonauts*), was too ambitious. They had to reboot it late in development, leading to a delay and a whole lot of stress.

Throughout this whole process Thomas was terrified, overwhelmed by the pressure of following up on one of the most beloved games in history. For a long time, he believed that the only way to do that was to emulate his predecessor, demanding that everyone else execute on his specific vision. "I absolutely thought that one could not make a *BioShock* without essentially echoing the method that brought the first one to be, and that was very auteur-driven," Thomas said. "A small group of geniuses working for an extra-big genius made this amazing thing. There was a lot of talk early on with *BioShock 2*, that the way a *Bioshock* is made is this. . . . I think we needed to find a method that worked for us, and it was more egalitarian. It came at incredible cost to get to that point."

That cost, Thomas said, was his relationships with other members of the team—people in design, in art, in production. "A couple of people came to me crying, or came to coleads crying about encounters with me," Thomas said. "I think people who worked with me had come to the conclusion that I was a zealot and that I cared far more about the art than the people, and there was no way to reverse that." Over the course of *BioShock 2*'s development, as 2K Marin tried to build and enforce a culture of collaboration and compromise rather than conflict and deference to a single leader, Thomas learned some hard lessons. "It's short-term versus long-term thinking," he said. "Do you care more about art than people? If you're lucky, maybe it's your first instinct to fall on the side of people. But [if not], long-term, you start to realize that burning people for the sake of art is not good for the work, and not good for your soul."

BioShock 2 came out on February 9, 2010, to plenty of adulation, with reviewers mostly agreeing that it might not have been as groundbreaking as the first game, but it was still a worthy sequel. Despite the stresses they'd faced during development, the team at 2K Marin felt energized. They'd put together two of the things that any studio needs to be successful: talent and momentum. Now they just needed to figure out what was next.

Four of the studio's top designers and artists—Jordan Thomas, Zak McClendon, Hogarth de la Plante, and Jeff Weir—began huddling together and brainstorming. After all those negative experiences on *BioShock 2*, Thomas wanted to do away with creative auteurship. This time, all four of them would have equal say. They came up with a few pitches to show 2K leadership, and the executives picked their favorite of the bunch, giving the four developers the green light to work on it for a while. They called the project *Richmond*, after a neighborhood in San Francisco, and spent day after day imagining what it could look like.

Richmond, according to design documents and people who worked on it, was envisioned as an online role-playing game in which you'd team up with friends. It would be a multiplayer immersive sim, full of choices to make and secrets to discover. The developers pitched it as a cross between *Fallout* and *The Truman Show*. Each player would start off in a big dome in which their actions were monitored by some enigmatic alien force. They'd escape the dome to find an unexplored wilderness full of mysterious technology. As they played, they'd meet different factions, explore other domes, rack up quests, collect loot, and interact with other players.

The directors dreamed up all sorts of wild ideas for *Richmond*, knowing that they'd probably cut half of them once they actually started making the game. You could befriend and betray factions. Enemies would remember you if they survived an encounter. You could retire your character, start a new one, and then visit the old character to see how they were doing. *Richmond* was ambitious and exciting, as is typical for games in preproduction, before the cold reality of production sets in. When whispers of the game reached the rest of the studio, people grew excited to start working on it.

But it wasn't time for that just yet. After 2K Marin finished *BioShock 2*, a small team started working on the game's big downloadable expansion, *Minerva's Den*. Jordan Thomas and his group kept daydreaming about *Richmond*. And everyone else at 2K Marin moved to a project that had been in development for years but now, in 2010, finally seemed to be ready for proper production. It was time for them to pay the piper.

▪ ▪ ▪

The word "XCOM" reads like an acronym, but it's actually an abbreviation, for "Extraterrestrial Combat," the secretive paramilitary group charged with defending earth from aliens in the long-running video game series of the same name. The first *XCOM* game, in which you'd battle a variety of colorful alien soldiers in a sequence of turn-based missions, was made by a small team helmed by a British designer named Julian Gollop. It was an instant critical and commercial success when it launched in 1994, selling so well that publisher MicroProse put out a string of sequels and spin-offs. From 1994 through 2001, six different *XCOM* games came out, some better than others. Then the series went unused for a while, thanks to financial struggles and ownership ping-pong. MicroProse was sold to Hasbro, which then became Atari, and soon enough none of those companies were making many video games anymore. The *XCOM* franchise remained dormant until 2005, when 2K Games bought the rights in hopes of reinvigorating it for a modern generation of gamers.

Ken Levine launched a new *XCOM* project that same year at Irrational's second office in Canberra, Australia, while the Massachusetts office was focused on *BioShock*. The developers planned to reenvision the concept of *XCOM* entirely, transforming it from a strategy game into a first-person shooter, in which the main character's eyes served as the camera. Aliens had invaded the earth, and the player would have to take them out, juggling weapons and managing resources along the way. One of the Australia team's first prototypes was set in a gas station swarming with aliens that the player would have to outmaneuver and gun down, like an extraterrestrial take on *Call of Duty*. Another prototype put the player in charge of a flying *XCOM* base that they could pilot around the earth's atmosphere. From there, the player could get into a dropship and plummet right into the center of an alien battle, as if they were storming the beach in *Saving Private Ryan*.

From Boston, Ken Levine served as creative director on *XCOM*, although his attention waned in the coming months as development intensified on *BioShock*. By 2006, the Boston team was dragooning people from Australia to help them finish, leaving *XCOM* with a team too small to get much done. After *BioShock* launched in the summer of 2007, Levine put his eyes back on *XCOM*, telling Irrational that it would be their next big game—the one that Chad LaClair was hired to help make. When Levine saw what the team in Australia had done, he asked them to change everything. "Ken comes on, says, 'This is what I want to do,'" said one 2K Australia developer. "It had nothing to do with what we had done, so we threw that out."

Around the same time, 2K went through an organizational restructure, splitting Irrational's two offices into two separate entities, which would now be called 2K Boston and 2K Australia. 2K Boston would seize back the name Irrational a few years later, but its former sister studio remained 2K Australia. Then, in 2008, Levine and the Massachusetts team ditched *XCOM* for what would become *BioShock Infinite*, giving the project back to their Australian colleagues. At this point, internal politics and squabbles—including many between Levine and 2K's executives—were haunting the entire company. Rumors swirled about the animosity between Levine and Christoph Hartmann, the president of 2K, and the political consequences trickled down to developers at all of 2K's studios. "We got told the entire studio was no longer allowed to talk to Boston for some period," said one member of the Australia team. One common theory was that 2K's executives had intentionally given all the studios monotonous names—2K Boston, 2K Australia, 2K

Marin—so that none of them could develop its own identity. They were all just cogs in 2K's video game production machine.

What was particularly frustrating for the developers at 2K Australia was that every time they tried to make progress on their own game, their bosses would demand that they drop everything and help someone else. That finally changed at the beginning of 2010, when *BioShock 2* was finished and *XCOM* became the next project for the developers in both Australia and Marin. But whereas on *BioShock 2* the designers and artists in Australia had to follow 2K Marin's direction, the roles were now reversed. 2K Marin would be the support studio on *XCOM*. 2K Australia would take the lead.

This led to some grumbles at 2K Marin, where many of the staff saw themselves as too talented to be doing grunt work, although they took comfort in one thing: this wouldn't last very long. Once they'd all finished *XCOM*, hopefully by 2011, they'd get to move on to *Richmond*, which had been building buzz around the office. Nobody really knew why an *XCOM* shooter even existed—wasn't *XCOM* supposed to be a strategy game?—let alone why the Marin team had to work on it when they had so many of their own promising ideas, but the arrangement made sense. The 2K Marin people just had to help get *XCOM* out the door, and then they could work on the game they actually wanted to make. "*Richmond* was our dream project," said Scott LaGrasta, the early 2K Marin employee. "The *XCOM* game was going to be our side job. We'd help them out with it, then go on to *Richmond*."

The executives who ran 2K had certain expectations for the *XCOM* game: namely, that it had to have both a full-fledged single-player campaign and a multiplayer mode, so that people wouldn't just play it once and then trade it in at GameStop. The Australia team, comprising around thirty people, was too small to make a game like that on their own. Instead, they'd design the single-player.

The Marin team—which was by now close to eighty people—would work on the multiplayer mode for a while, then move on to *Richmond*. It seemed like an elegant arrangement.

Of course, you know what they say about the best-laid plans of mice and video game developers. By the spring of 2010, it became clear that even with both the Marin and the Australia studios working together, they didn't have the manpower to make both single- and multiplayer modes, so 2K scrapped the latter. "They were not willing to expand either studio enough to do what they needed," said JP LeBreton, the 2K Marin designer, "and so that's what resulted in the multiplayer we had been working on for a few months getting canned."

Now, instead of 2K Marin and 2K Australia each developing separate components of *XCOM*, the two studios were both responsible for single-player, which meant they had to collaborate closely. Problems that might have previously been surmountable, like the fact that they were nineteen time zones apart, were suddenly catastrophic. It was hard enough to schedule a single Skype call between Novato, California, and Canberra, Australia, let alone communicate as frequently as the two teams would require in order to make a game as complicated as *XCOM*.

Tensions that had already been simmering over the past few months were now boiling over. To the brash, confident 2K Marin team, the 2K Australia team didn't know what they were doing. To the weary, resentful 2K Australia team, the 2K California team was egocentric and clearly didn't want to be working on this game. The design leads in Australia felt like they were being undermined constantly, while the design leads in California felt like they'd just made a great game in *BioShock 2* and deserved better than to be workhorses for people an ocean away. "The relationship was for a long time really antagonistic," said Chris Proctor, a designer at

2K Australia. "Leadership didn't get along at all. Some of it got really nasty."

With one careless move, 2K's executives somehow managed to make things worse. On April 14, 2010, 2K put out a press release announcing that an *XCOM* first-person shooter was in development. Buried at the bottom was a strange line:

> With sister studios in Novato, California, and Canberra, Australia, 2K Marin is a 2K development studio focused on creating new IP and expanding proven franchises for 2K Games.

In other words, the Australia office, which had first been called Irrational Australia, then 2K Australia, was now part of 2K Marin. It was a semantic change, but, like all of 2K's semantic changes, it carried big implications. The developers in Canberra, some of whom already felt like second-class citizens within the company, now didn't even have their own *name*. Technically, they were "the Canberra, Australia office of 2K Marin." A charitable interpretation was that 2K wanted to unify the two teams at a time where there was clear tension, but the move angered the Marin people and mortified the Australia people. "It was devastating," said one person who worked in Canberra. "It was gut-wrenching."

Throughout it all, the *XCOM* project kept changing, like a video game version of Telephone. Today, even those who have worked on the game can't remember all the forms it's taken. At one point it was an asymmetrical multiplayer game that let players take the roles of both humans and aliens. Another iteration revolved around investigating mysteries and taking photographs of aliens without getting caught. There were prototypes with a first-person view, in which you'd see through the main character's eyes, and prototypes with a third-person view, in which the camera would hover over the main character's shoulders. By the summer of 2010, as the project started to go awry, few people at either studio were clear on what the game was actually going to look like. "That was when things went from shaky to absolutely miserable," said JP LeBreton. "The overall design direction that they were trying to represent to us was really floundering."

In less than a year, all of the chemistry and collaborative culture that 2K Marin had tried to build during *BioShock 2* had fizzled. Christoph Hartmann and his team of executives had figured that the combination of staff at 2K Marin and 2K Australia would equate to the manpower they needed, but the two companies weren't interchangeable parts. They were all strong-minded creative people, with egos and ambitions and cultures that couldn't just be jammed into the same machine. "They thought if they had two halves of a game development team, they could staple them together and pretend it was a full enough development team to get this big, ambitious game done," said LeBreton. "It's like a band—there has to be chemistry there."

Meanwhile, Jordan Thomas and the other leads on *Richmond* had been soaking in the creative bliss of preproduction, writing design documents and sketching concept art for what they thought might be their dream game. Thomas felt pangs of guilt every time he heard the latest *XCOM* gossip from his coworkers, but he'd been happy to stay away from the drama. Then 2K's executives came calling, and Thomas realized that his fantasy camp was over. "The team that was working on the new IP was told, 'You have to fix this,'" Thomas said, "and so creative control of it moved once again back to the core Marin shop in hopes that morale could be restored." Somehow, *XCOM* had transformed from a temporary support job into 2K Marin's next big project.

2K's executives had created a lose-lose situation. The Marin people didn't want to be in charge of *XCOM*. Most of them didn't even want to make it. "By that point there was so much already built, and so many series of contradictory decisions in the design," said Thomas, "it was an emergency from the moment we got it." At the same time, the Canberra people had just watched their corporate bosses strip away their autonomy, first by taking away their name, and then by transforming them back into a support studio when this was supposed to be their big chance to lead. Canberra's design director Ed Orman and art director Andrew James resigned, with more following in the ensuing weeks.

A few months later, 2K reorganized again. "We had a meeting invitation sent out to us late one night," said Chris Proctor, the designer in Australia. "'Everybody meet in the car park at 10:00 a.m.'" When he arrived at work the next morning, one of the executives started reading names off a list. This person, go downstairs. That person, upstairs. Proctor was told to go to the downstairs group, which he soon discovered was bad news. It turned out that 2K was pulling the *XCOM* project from the Australia studio entirely, leaving their staff with nothing to do but support Irrational on the next *BioShock* game. "The upstairs group were to stay and continue working on *BioShock Infinite*," Proctor said. "And the downstairs group was laid off." As Proctor sat there in a daze, one of 2K's executives pulled him and a few other designers aside and told them that, actually, they could retain their jobs and keep working on *XCOM*, but there was a catch: they'd have to move to San Francisco. "I was really steamed about that," Proctor said.

Proctor thought about it for a while. Leaving his friends and family behind would be tough, but like many of his game development peers, he'd grown accustomed to moving around the world. Born and raised in Melbourne, Australia, Proctor had worked as a designer at a number of development studios across the country and been laid off several times without shipping anything ("I had so many games canceled out from under me—it was a pretty bad run") until he moved to Oslo, Norway, for a job at Funcom, the company behind an online spy game called *The Secret World*. After getting caught up in another round of layoffs there, he flew back to Australia and considered leaving the video game industry. "I thought: 'You know what, this is way too unstable, and I can't be moving cross-country or between countries all the time,'" Proctor said.

That was when a friend from a previous job suggested he join 2K Australia in Canberra. Enticed by the idea of continuing to make games in his home country, Proctor spent a few months at 2K Australia working on *XCOM* before he was called into that downstairs room for the bad news. Now he had to make yet another tough decision. "I talked a lot to my friends and family about it, and everyone said, 'Oh, you should totally take the opportunity to go to the US,'" Proctor said. 2K paid for his relocation costs and helped him find temporary housing in San Francisco while he searched for a new apartment, and he wound up growing fond of the United States. "It ended up being a really good choice," Proctor said.

Now it was official: 2K Australia was done with *XCOM*. Those who remained would help Irrational finish off *BioShock Infinite* while 2K Marin took full ownership over the *XCOM* shooter. Yet again, nobody was left happy. The Australian studio was decimated, while the developers in Marin were saddled with a game that was constantly changing thanks to reboots and executive mandates— a game that they hadn't wanted to make in the first place.[5] Plus,

---

5   The Australia team would later get to lead its own project with *Borderlands: The Pre-Sequel*, a new entry in the looter-shooter series from Gearbox Software. That game came out in October 2014. Six months later, 2K Australia was permanently shut down.

there was another *XCOM* project in development that fans actually *wanted*—Firaxis, the studio behind *Civilization*, was making a turn-based strategy game more akin to the original *XCOM*. It was a disconcerting feeling, working on a game when you weren't even sure why it existed.

The public trailers for 2K Marin's *XCOM*, shown at trade shows in 2010 and 2011, were brash and explosive, revealing a first-person shooter in which you'd gun down aliens in an alternate-reality version of the 1960s United States. Internally, the game looked much different. As 2K Marin took over, the game went through more reboots, transforming from first-person to third-person. *XCOM* was delayed from March 2012 to early 2013, and then again to the summer of 2013. What had been initially pitched to 2K Marin's staff as a stopgap project was now occupying years of their lives. "The morale on the team was so low," said James Clarendon, a senior systems designer on the game. "Nobody thought we were actually going to ship anything."

To this day, many who worked on the *XCOM* shooter still wonder why it wasn't canceled. Why didn't 2K's executives, namely Christoph Hartmann, cut their losses and move on to something else? The project had been, as journalist Chris Plante described in a detailed report for the video game website Polygon, a "financial sinkhole." Few people wanted to play it, and even fewer wanted to keep working on it. "Having a game canceled hurts very badly, but sitting on a game that is confused and actively robbing you of your capacity for creative thought is not good either," said Jordan Thomas. "It's sort of a slow radiation poisoning."

Thomas wound up leaving midway through development, when Ken Levine called and asked him to come back to Irrational to help finish *BioShock Infinite*. Throughout 2012 and 2013, a number of other veterans also quit 2K Marin, fed up with the state of the *XCOM* project. Some felt like there was no possible positive outcome for the studio. A handful of designers kept working on *Richmond* even after the leads moved to *XCOM*, but by 2012, they'd all either left or been dragged onto *XCOM* as well, leaving the *Richmond* project to quietly die. Many of 2K Marin's frustrated developers had joined the studio to make immersive sims like *BioShock*, full of environmental storytelling and experimental powers. They didn't want to put more years of their lives into an *XCOM* shooter. "'Say yes to the player' was this big thing we foisted on *BioShock 2*," said Scott LaGrasta. "With *XCOM* it was, 'Nope, you're going to sit down and get a story in your eyes. Hope you enjoy cover shooters.'"

David Pittman, a lead AI programmer at 2K Marin, was one of those disgruntled veterans. He quit in March 2013, a few months before the game shipped, out of unhappiness with the state of the game and the studio. "It was such a difficult project for so many reasons," Pittman said. "The direction kept changing. The leadership kept changing." Like many of his veteran colleagues, Pittman had stayed at 2K Marin in hopes of one day working on *Richmond*, but by 2013 it became clear that the project was dead. "I stuck around longer than I probably should have because I wanted to make that game," Pittman said. "Then I started to realize, this game I'm holding up hope to make some day is probably never going to happen."

Attrition wasn't the only bad omen. In 2013, during the final months of development on *XCOM*, the staff of 2K Marin were moved to one of the other hangars at Hamilton Airfield. James Clarendon remembers it being swelteringly hot. "Morale was low, and the conspiracy theories started—that they were trying to sweat us out, that they didn't care about us," Clarendon said. "We were finding giant spiders. Black widows." The office perks they'd grown accustomed to enjoying, like catered lunch and espresso machines, now required a walk back to their old hangar. "It was very clear we were becoming second-class citizens," said LaGrasta.

Soon, rumors began to spread that 2K was actually planning to start another studio in their old hangar, which was being renovated and improved. Then it became official: 2K brought over Rod Fergusson, who had just helped finish *BioShock Infinite* at Irrational Games, to start a brand-new game development label.[6] In the coming weeks, Fergusson started quietly interviewing the developers at 2K Marin to see who might be a good fit for the studio that would eventually become known as Hangar 13.[7]

On August 20, 2013, the *XCOM* shooter finally released, under the unwieldy name *The Bureau: XCOM Declassified*. It got middling reviews and sold poorly, leading many outside observers to wonder why it even existed, especially when Firaxis's *XCOM* strategy game, which had come out in 2012 to solid sales and critical acclaim, was so good. (Firaxis would continue making *XCOM* sequels and spin-offs for years to come.) Of course, people at 2K had been asking that same question for years. "Morale was pretty low at the studio after the game launched," said Chris Proctor. "We were working on DLC, but it felt more and more pointless because it was clear no one really wanted it."

In the coming weeks, the remaining staff of 2K Marin tried to find out what their next project was going to be, but getting a straight answer proved elusive. It felt like they were in video game purgatory, waiting to see whether their next destination would be the good place or the bad place. Some developers started designing prototypes and pitches in hopes that they could convince 2K to

---

6   Fergusson would actually leave before the studio even officially started. A former LucasArts director named Haden Blackman took his place in 2014.

7   The name was a wry joke for everyone who worked at the Hamilton Airfield, where there were only ten hangars, none of them named 13.

green-light something new. Others just sat at their desks, updating their LinkedIn profiles and applying for jobs at other companies. To say it was a strange time would be a profound understatement. "Everybody was just looking for work during business hours," said Proctor. "Leadership seemed fine with that."

■ ■ ■

October 17, 2013, should have been a good day for Scott LaGrasta. For months he and his wife had been trying to buy a house, but they kept getting beaten by all-cash offers from Silicon Valley engineers with bulging wallets. Now, finally, a deal was coming together. Or at least it had been, until 2K Marin split everyone into two rooms for a company meeting. LaGrasta was called into the bad room, where he and his colleagues were informed by 2K's HR people that they were being laid off. "I'm getting messages from my wife: 'They accepted the offer; we're going to get the house,'" LaGrasta said. "I texted her, 'No, we can't take the offer. I'm losing my job right now.'"

LaGrasta had enough video game industry experience to have sniffed out what was coming. He'd joined 2K Marin in 2008, after getting laid off from the Activision subsidiary High Moon Studios down in San Diego. (That layoff had even happened in the same fashion—there was a good room and a bad room.) He had loved being a designer on *BioShock 2*, but *XCOM* was another story. "It was tough," LaGrasta said. "You do the best you can. No, I'm not making the game I want to make, but can I carve off a chunk that is what I want it to be?" Early in *XCOM*'s development, he was enjoying working on the tense, horror-filled levels they'd originally envisioned. "Then we had these direction shifts from 2K corporate," LaGrasta said. "You just get to this point where you're like, 'Tell me what to do and I'll do it. You obviously don't want my creative input, you just want me to execute on your vision.' Then you check out. And that's when it becomes less fun." Eventually he started developing a small game after work, funneling his unspent creative energy into his own project.

Between *XCOM*'s tepid reception, the lack of a new project, and the now-no-longer-secret new studio that was growing next door, LaGrasta had suspected that layoffs were coming. What made it brutal was that wasting three years on *XCOM* hadn't been the developers' decision. It would have been one thing if the studio was closing because they'd taken a big risk and failed, or if they'd made a game that was great but didn't sell well. Then it would still be sad, but at least they could walk away with pride. *XCOM* had been an unwanted assignment—the vestiges of a project that 2K's bean counters just didn't want to kill—which made it all the more miserable that it was the studio's last hurrah.

LaGrasta didn't wind up buying a house. In the years after 2K Marin's closure, he bounced between a few video game jobs in the Bay Area before landing at Telltale, a studio that made narrative adventure games based on big franchises like *Game of Thrones* and *The Walking Dead*. He grew miserable there too. "It was just constant firefighting," LaGrasta said. "I would work eight hours at the office, and come home, then my kid would go to sleep and then I'd see if there were any fires I needed to deal with at work." As he looked for new jobs, he sat down with his wife to confront the reality that if he wanted to stay in games, they might have to move to yet another city. "I think it was my wife who just said, 'Can we go to Europe or something?'" LaGrasta recalled. "I turned to her and said, 'Are you serious? Because yeah.'"

By the fall of 2017, LaGrasta and his wife were packing up all of their things and moving to Malmö, Sweden, where he took a job at the Ubisoft studio Massive Entertainment to work on a game based on James Cameron's *Avatar* movies. For an American who had spent the last decade living in San Francisco, this was a major culture shock. The Swedish lifestyle was very different in many ways. Salaries were significantly lower, for example. When LaGrasta was negotiating for his job, he proposed a number based on his pay history and was told that it'd be more appropriate for a studio lead. At the same time, the Swedish government provided benefits that would seem unfathomable to any American—subsidized health care, education, and a whopping 480 days of paid leave for new parents. Sweden's unioncentric culture made for a sharp contrast to that of the United States, where no video game companies were unionized.

"Ubisoft in general is very good about not having major layoffs," said LaGrasta. "So it feels like a place I could stay." The benefits, combined with the increasingly dystopian reality of Donald Trump's government in the United States, drove LaGrasta to stay in Sweden. "You have to adjust your center of living," he said. "I feel more like lower-middle-class compared to living in California just because I can afford fewer luxuries." Yet, perhaps most important, living in Malmö meant being free from the anxieties spawned by the United States' broken health-care system. "I know that if I get hit by a bus, it's fine," LaGrasta said. "In the Bay Area, in the US, almost everybody is one bad accident away from just being bankrupt."

■ ■ ■

It's become something of a cliché to suggest after a studio closes its doors that it was full of exceptionally talented people. But some clichés are clichés for good reason. As people trickled out of 2K Marin over the years, many of them gave up their AAA salaries in favor of going indie, boosted by the support of friends or family, and created some impressive games. The most notable was *Gone Home*, developed by Steve Gaynor, Johnnemann Nordhagen, and Karla Zimonja, who had all worked together on *BioShock 2*'s expansion. *Gone Home* was a short but poignant game in which a teenage girl returns to her family's empty house and tries to figure out where everyone went. The story was told entirely through the environment: a calendar on the fridge, recorded messages on the answering machine, discarded letters and journal entries. It was *BioShock* minus the shooting. When it came out on August 15, 2013 (just days before *XCOM*), *Gone Home* was critically acclaimed and had an immediate cultural impact, inspiring a number of 2K Marin developers to forge their own indie development paths.

Other independently funded games to emerge from the studio's wreckage included the narrative adventure game *The Novelist* (directed by former 2K Marin lead designer Kent Hudson); an exploration game set in the Himalayas called *The Wild Eternal* (led by former QA tester Casey Goodrow); and a bleak American folktale called *Where the Water Tastes Like Wine* (also by Nordhagen, who went solo following *Gone Home*). Across the world in Australia, *BioShock* development director Jonathan Chey directed a card-based strategy game called *Card Hunter* and then a sci-fi roguelike called *Void Bastards*; while Ed Orman and Andrew James, who had resigned halfway through the *XCOM* project, started an indie studio to develop *Submerged*, a postapocalyptic exploration game.

David Pittman, the programmer who had left 2K Marin in early 2013 after finally accepting that *Richmond* was dead, went on to develop games on his own. With his savings and a substantial bonus that his wife had received from her own gaming job, he figured he'd be okay through the end of the year. "I'd been wanting to make indie games for a long time," Pittman said. "I thought, 'I've got some savings, I could make a thing in eight or nine months.' Worst thing that happens is I take a nine-month vacation, spend it doing something I enjoy."

Over the next few months, Pittman created *Eldritch*, a first-person shooter with blocky, *Minecraft*-like graphics and a setting inspired by H. P. Lovecraft's Cthulhu universe. It was a short but challenging game, with randomly generated levels and a suite of abilities inspired by immersive sims—you could find spells that let you turn invisible, teleport, or hypnotize enemies, allowing you to deal with encounters in a variety of ways. After the tortured development of *XCOM*, working on a small, solo game felt freeing and cathartic for Pittman. He released *Eldritch* in October 2013, just as his former studio was shutting down, and it was received fairly well. "It made back the investment I had put into it, and it funded the next two games," Pittman said.

Those next two games—a political stealth game called *Neon Struct* and a *Buffy*-inspired vampire shooter called *Slayer Shock*—were less successful, and by 2016, Pittman needed to find a more stable job, not just to feed himself but also because he missed collaborating with other people. He occasionally teamed up with his twin brother J. Kyle Pittman, also a game developer, but it wasn't quite the same.

Pittman applied for a few jobs at big-budget companies, but after years of living the indie life, the thought of working on another massive AAA project made his anxiety spike. He took an interview at Hangar 13, the studio that emerged from 2K Marin's ashes. Just walking into the office gave him the sweats. "I already felt so burnt out and exhausted by being in that environment again just for a few hours," Pittman said. "After getting to experience the full breadth of creative work being a solo indie developer, the idea of going back to the kind of minutiae I'd do as an AAA developer just felt really stressful to me." What Pittman really wanted to do, he thought, was reunite with an old colleague.

Jordan Thomas, the director of *BioShock 2*, had been watching his former colleagues' indie adventures with envy. In 2013, as he was in Massachusetts finishing up *BioShock Infinite*, he saw what old coworkers like Pittman and the *Gone Home* team had done and decided that he would also take a stab at independent development. He started talking to Stephen Alexander, another *BioShock* artist with whom he'd grown close over the years, about teaming up to start something new once they'd finished *BioShock Infinite*. "We all felt tired by the AAA machine," Thomas said. "We had a position of privilege where we both had partners who were financially set up and well-supported. So the idea of going indie for us at our age at the time was a little less scary than it would be for a student."

That was the secret sauce—financial support from elsewhere meant a level of freedom that many of the people who were impacted by the 2K Marin catastrophe didn't have. By the summer of 2013, both Thomas and Alexander had quit Irrational, working out of Alexander's parents' house as they brainstormed ideas. Thomas, with his love for brutal horror, made a few dark pitches, but Alexander wasn't feeling them; after all those years in the world of *BioShock*, he wanted something a little lighter. Then an image popped into Thomas's brain: two game developers arguing over some decision or another, with the camera not pointed at them but at the whiteboard they were using, their voices arguing as ideas were scribbled and crossed out with markers.

From this vision, Thomas and Alexander eventually came up with a surreal, fourth-wall-breaking game called *The Magic Circle*, in which you played as the tester of an abandoned, unfinished video game. Your goal would be to escape the game, using the tools that the developers had left behind to alter reality as you went, designing levels and reprogramming enemies' AI behaviors. As you played, you'd witness argument after argument between the game's disgruntled executive producer, Maze Evelyn, and the obsessive, egocentric creative director, Ishmael Gilder, described by Thomas as a reflection of both himself and other auteurs under whom he'd worked. (Says Gilder at one point in the game: "I find the right people, I lock them in a room. The only word for what emerges...is a miracle. Or we kill each other. Either way, problem solved.")

Two years later, thanks to their hardworking spouses and a loan from Alexander's parents, Thomas and his small team released *The Magic Circle*. It made back the money it took to produce (allowing them to pay back the loan—with interest), but didn't generate enough revenue to fund a new game, leaving Thomas and Alexander in a tough spot. They wanted to stay indie, but they needed an investment to keep going. As they reached out to industry contacts and put out feelers, they had one particularly intriguing discussion about the possibility of making *System Shock 3*, but the project fell through (and would ultimately be snagged by Warren Spector). Later, Thomas began chatting with a colleague of his who just happened to be worth hundreds of millions of dollars: Matt Stone, the cocreator of *South Park*. Thomas had done some consulting work on the *South Park* role-playing game, helping bridge the gap between the TV people and the developers, and he'd gotten to know Stone and fellow *South Park* cocreator Trey Parker along the way. Thomas mentioned that they were looking for financing to make a new video game, and Stone made the type of suggestion that you always love to hear from your millionaire friends: What if he and Parker funded it?

Thomas and his team put together a pitch for what they called *The Blackout Club*, an online horror game with a twist that nobody had seen before. Thanks to Stone and Parker, the crew had enough money in 2017 to hire a bunch of other developers including David Pittman, who had been waiting months for the chance to join Thomas after his adventures in solo game development. It was like a mini–2K Marin reunion. "I had to wait for them to come up with the budget," Pittman said. "What they were working on sounded exciting."

The Blackout Club came out in the summer of 2019. Set in a town that had been infected with an enigmatic disease that made everyone sleepwalk at night, the game put you in the shoes of a teenager trying to figure out why the adults in town were all lying about the apparent epidemic and its supernatural origins. Over a series of missions, you'd team up with other players to gather information and try to avoid the monsters haunting the town.

It was a fun game to play, but what really made *The Blackout Club* special was the twist: as you played, real people might suddenly take control of the creatures in your game. The developers had hired a team of actors who would log into *The Blackout Club* at certain hours of the night and randomly join players' missions, showing up as mysterious gods with names like DANCE-FOR-US and SPEAK-AS-ONE. Whenever you played *The Blackout Club*, there was a chance you'd have a surreal encounter with one of these actors or get a creepy text message from one of the developers. It was like interactive theater inside of a video game. "The moment people realize what we're doing, they're overjoyed in a way I've never seen before," Thomas said. "Nothing I've ever worked on has caused people to react like that."

Looking back at all of these innovative games—*Gone Home*, *Eldritch*, *The Blackout Club*—makes one wonder what might have been if 2K Marin hadn't been saddled with a game as disastrous and draining as *The Bureau: XCOM Declassified*. People who worked at 2K Marin, wistful for an alternate reality in which they didn't have to spend years on a game they didn't want to make, still lament what *Richmond* might have been. If 2K's management had made savvier decisions, would 2K Marin be making games as creative as *The Blackout Club* today? If the studio hadn't suddenly vanished as if it were caught up in the rapture, would *Richmond* be as beloved an immersive sim as *Deus Ex* or *BioShock*?

Then again, there's another way of looking at this. If 2K Marin hadn't failed, all of those developers would have been stuck in the morass of AAA development, where the projects are too expensive and the stakes are too high for developers to take bizarre experiments like adding interactive theater to their games. It's easy to imagine an executive looking at a game like *Gone Home* and demanding that its creators add more explosions, or suggesting that *The Blackout Club*'s interactive theater would be unfair to the players who weren't lucky enough to get gods in their game. When there are hundreds of jobs and tens of millions of dollars at stake, the people in charge tend to go with the formulas that they already know—and they tend to force you to make a multiplayer mode.

In the end, David Pittman and Jordan Thomas were the lucky ones. Not everyone had access to financial support from families, partners, or multimillionaire media moguls. Most people weren't free to pursue their creative dreams after 2K Marin shut down. Some left for other big studios in the area, moved to other cities, or struggled to find new jobs.

Kenneth Reyna, a level designer who had been working in the games industry for over a decade when 2K Marin showed him the door, found himself unemployed for nearly six months after the studio closed. He found a contract gig working on *Call of Duty* down in San Mateo, but the two-hour commute was too much for him. By the end of 2014, he had left the video game industry. Between the volatility, the crunch, and the lack of pay, gaming no longer seemed like a feasible career for him. "A person doing a similar job outside of the games industry is going to be paid more," Reyna said. "Going back to being level designer 54 on some giant franchise, it's too much of a pain in the butt to deal with. You're leaving money on the table if you are going back and working at a game company."

Brain drain isn't a video game industry phenomenon you'll often see mentioned on earnings calls or message boards, but sentiments like Reyna's aren't uncommon, especially in the San Francisco Bay Area. Once you've worked in the video game industry for more than a decade and shipped a few games, it might start to become painfully clear that you're being mistreated. Especially when the guy in the office next to you happens to make $35 million a year.

CHAPTER 5

WORKAHOLICS

Zach Mumbach's entry into the video game industry came through what he calls "the stupidest story ever." He grew up a punk rock kid in San Jose, California, skateboarding and dreaming about one day becoming a professional game developer. During high school he dabbled in game design, taking the first-person shooter *Duke Nukem 3D* and customizing it with mods to re-arrange the layouts of levels or replace everyone with *Star Wars* creatures. Success as a modder convinced him that game development might be a feasible career, and in the summer of 2000, right after graduating high school, Mumbach went online and looked up the address for one of his favorite game companies, Electronic Arts (EA).

These days, the name EA might evoke images of stagnant sequels and endless microtransactions, but for a long time, the massive publisher was well-respected and loved by people who played video games. Throughout the 1980s and 1990s, EA built a lucrative monopoly of sports video game franchises (*Madden*, *FIFA*) and made smart investments in teams led by creative geniuses like

Will Wright (*SimCity*); Peter Molyneux (*Theme Park*); and, of course, Richard Garriott and Warren Spector.

Many of Zach Mumbach's favorite games were developed and published by EA. And the company's main campus was in Redwood Shores, just a half-hour drive from his house. "I put on my nicest collared shirt—I had like one—and drove down there," he said. "I walked in the front door and walked up to the security desk, and said, 'Hey, I'm here for a job.'" Then, by Mumbach's recollection, the guard sent him into a room full of people. By sheer coincidence, it was new hire day at Electronic Arts. As the HR reps in attendance handed out packets of paperwork, one of them looked at Mumbach and asked who he was. "I said, 'Oh, I'm Zach Mumbach,'" he recalled. "They said, 'We don't have you on the list. Sorry about that.' And they put me on the list and give me the paperwork—I shit you not, dude—and I fill out the paperwork, and that day I was working in QA as a tester. I rolled in accidentally. It's the stupidest story ever, but this is exactly what happened." [1]

Even if the EA bosses had learned that he wasn't supposed to be there, they probably wouldn't have cared. QA, or quality assurance, was the department of a video game company dedicated to finding glitches, bugs, and errors. To outside observers it was often perceived as the perfect job—play video games all day!—but in reality, it could be a slog. Testers never played games the way normal people did. Sometimes they had to complete the same level over and over for weeks on end; other times they had to spend hours

---

[1] Luke Harrington, who worked on the team, remembered Mumbach's unorthodox hiring. "Zach showed up without the normal HR screening," said Harrington. "Apparently he just walked in the door and enough people said, 'Yeah, give him a shot.'"

repeating a mundane activity like swinging around the camera or running headfirst into walls. At EA in 2000, it didn't take much experience to become a game tester, nor did the job pay very well.[2] One person who worked there called EA's QA department "a total frat house back then." Walk-ins who had just graduated high school would fit in just fine.

Mumbach was elated. This was his big break. He and the other new hires were placed in front of a console loaded up with an old version of *Road Rash: Jailbreak*, an EA racing game that had come out a few months earlier. The old build was full of glitches and bugs that the team had already caught. Now, the bosses wanted to see if Mumbach and the other aspiring testers could catch them too. For the next two weeks, the applicants had to track down as many bugs as they could, repeating the process each day as they received newer builds of the game.

Not everyone made it through to the end of these testing sessions. Some of the new hires were poor communicators, while others couldn't find enough bugs to make the cut. Those who did succeed were moved into EA's testing department, where they'd spend a year working as contractors before EA eventually hired them full-time. Mumbach survived the two-week period, then worked his way up to proper employment. "I'm not religious, but I felt like fate or something was looking out for me," he said. "Or this was meant to be."

Like many aspiring game developers, Mumbach saw QA as a stepping-stone that would eventually lead him into other parts of game development. He felt like he had gotten a job that thousands

---

2   Even today, at many large video game companies in the United States, QA testers make close to minimum wage and are treated like a lower caste, often given fewer benefits and told not to speak to other developers.

of people wanted, and that this was his pathway into making video games for a living. So he embraced the role, putting extra hours into his work testing game after game, from shooters to sports, from *007: The World Is Not Enough* to *Knockout Kings 2001*. Mumbach didn't care about many of these games, but he'd stay late at the office every night nonetheless, tracking down glitches big and small. He figured the best way to stand out at EA would be to prove that he was the hardest worker, and that if he stood out, he'd get to move from testing to making games.

Mumbach also had a good reason to spend more time at the office—he couldn't go anywhere else. During high school, he had been an accomplice to larceny, driving out to pick up a friend who had broken into a skateboard shop after-hours. "I basically made up an alibi for him," Mumbach said. "I said he was with me the whole night when he wasn't. And then he confessed." The police charged Mumbach for obstruction, and when his case finally made it into a courtroom, just a few weeks after he'd started at EA, he pleaded guilty.

The verdict was three months of house arrest. As Mumbach left the court, a monitor strapped to his ankle, he was told he could spend his time in two places: work and home. Mumbach didn't have a great relationship with his parents, so EA's Redwood Shores campus became his new residence. "I basically lived at EA for the first three months I worked there," he said. "I'd be there at nine in the morning and I wouldn't leave until like one in the morning. I'd go home to sleep, then just come right back."

Even when his house arrest was over, Mumbach kept working as many hours as possible, charming his bosses with his charisma and tenacity. By 2001 he'd been promoted to lead tester on Maxis's *Sim Golf*, a simulation game in which players would design and play on their own golf courses.[3] He relocated to Maxis's offices in Walnut Creek, fifty miles north, and spent the next few years helping test out games with titles like *The Sims: Bustin' Out* and *The Sims 2: Glamour Life Stuff*. Then he moved back to the Redwood Shores studio as part of an EA restructuring that gave Mumbach a big promotion.

At Maxis, Mumbach had worked closely with the production department—the people responsible for scheduling, budgeting, and other logistical duties. In layman's terms, a producer was best described as the person who made sure everything happened. Production was better-paying and more glamorous than testing—plus, it was where pivotal development decisions happened—and Mumbach had already been doing some of those organizational tasks as part of his job as a lead. After nearly five years as a QA tester, he was ready for the job. "They said, 'Hey, we need producers, and you've been doing production as a QA guy,'" Mumbach recalled. "'Do you want to just be a producer now?'"

Mumbach's first game as a producer was *The Simpsons Game*, which came out in 2007. It was a silly game that shattered conventions and regularly broke the fourth wall; by the end, you'd have encounters with in-game versions of Will Wright and Matt Groening, the show's creator, then challenge God to a match of *Dance Dance Revolution*. The writing was solid, but the critical reception was a resounding meh. "*The Simpsons Game* has everything a fan

---

3   *Sim Golf*, which came out in January 2002, emerged from the failure of legendary designer Sid Meier. For years, Meier had been trying to make a game about dinosaurs, but his prototypes never clicked. One day, by colleague Jake Solomon's recollection, Meier said he was giving up on the dinosaurs and disappeared from the office for two weeks. When he got back, he told everyone that he'd come up with their next game, and showed them a prototype in which you could design golf courses. EA was sold immediately. "Anyone who saw it thought that it was pretty awesome," Solomon told me.

could want," wrote a critic for the magazine *Game Informer*, "but not everything it needs to be a fun, interesting game."

EA's Redwood Shores development studio just couldn't seem to find a breakout hit—or an identity. Across the video game industry, other studios had become renowned for their biggest franchises. Maxis was beloved for *SimCity* and *The Sims*. BioWare was known for role-playing games like *Mass Effect*. Irrational had just commanded the world's attention with *BioShock*. Bigger companies like Blizzard and Nintendo experimented with multiple genres and franchises, but they polished their products to glossy perfection. If you bought a game like *Diablo II* or *The Legend of Zelda: The Wind Waker*, you knew you were getting something incredible.[4]

Nobody associated EA Redwood Shores with much of anything. It was an eclectic game studio, developing whatever EA's executives demanded in any given fiscal quarter, be it a *Tiger Woods* golf game or a *Lord of the Rings* movie tie-in. Most games developed at EA Redwood Shores were tied to external licenses, like *James Bond* and *The Godfather*. Developers there seemed to the outside world less like a team of artists and more like a group of mercenaries, taking on whatever jobs would generate the most revenue for EA. The studio didn't even have a proper name.

In 2008, the company's fortunes changed. A team at EA Redwood Shores led by two men, Michael Condrey and Glen Schofield, designed a sci-fi horror game in which you'd play as a scientist named Isaac Clarke, sent to answer a distress call from a

---

4   It might have been more astute for video game connoisseurs to associate each game with the people behind it, rather than the brand, but (a) video game teams usually consisted of dozens if not hundreds of people; (b) game studios liked to keep their inner workings opaque; and (c) it was easier to remember the name of a company than the names of the creative director, lead artist, programmers, and so on. Hence the power of brands.

crashed spaceship. Aboard, he'd discover that the ship's crew had been ravaged by an alien virus that brought corpses back to life as mutated abominations. Equipped with old mining tools and improvised flamethrowers, Clarke would have to battle his way through these creatures, fighting off disturbing hallucinations as he progressed. *Dead Space*, as they called it, launched in October 2008 to rave reviews. It wasn't a smash hit—EA would later say it sold about a million copies in its first few months, which failed to meet the publisher's lofty expectations—but people loved it. After years of making games based on other people's properties, EA Redwood Shores finally had a critical hit to call its own.

The next year, EA's executives rebranded EA Redwood Shores, calling it Visceral Games and announcing that it would be expanding into two new locations: Visceral Montreal, in Canada; and Visceral Melbourne, in Australia.[5] It was a semantic change, but just like 2K's various brand changes, it had a big impact on the people who worked there. By rebranding from EA Redwood Shores to something unique, the studio was declaring its identity. This was Visceral. They made third-person action-adventure games. They had an empire of subsidiaries all over the world.

They would also get to make a *Dead Space* sequel, which EA's executives hoped would perform better thanks to the first game's critical acclaim and strong word of mouth. While creating the first *Dead Space*, the developers at Visceral had learned a lot about linear horror games and how to make them. Now, they hoped, they could do even better. Zach Mumbach hadn't worked on the first *Dead Space*—he'd been helping produce a bizarre video game adaptation

---

5   The word "visceral" generally refers to something that you can feel deep down in your gut. As anyone who has sat through an E3 press conference can attest, it's also one of the most overused pieces of jargon in video games—up there with "immersive" and "teraflops."

of *Dante's Inferno*—but he was thrilled to become an associate producer on *Dead Space 2*.

People who made *Dead Space 2* say development was an idyllic experience—one of the best projects they've worked on. Yara Khoury, who was a production intern on *Dead Space 2* in the summer of 2010, loved being at Visceral so much she asked for an extension to her internship that eventually turned into a full-time job. "To this day, I think if you ask anybody, they'll all tell you *Dead Space 2* was one of the highlights of their career," Khoury said. "The organization at large was very supportive of the project. Autonomy on the team was really high. There was a sense of empowerment and ownership which really boosted everybody's morale."

Dead Space 2 came out in January 2011 to more fantastic reviews, and EA would go on to say in a call with shareholders a few weeks later that it was outselling the first game "two-to-one." It seemed in many ways like a success. But success was relative. As Warren Spector had learned years earlier, publicly traded game publishers like EA weren't content hitting singles and doubles; they demanded home runs. Executives at EA needed to show shareholders that their profits were growing exponentially every year. "It's the worst part about EA," said Mumbach. "This idea that if I made $10 million this year, I'm successful, but if next year I make $10 million, I'm not. My stock goes down. I'm not showing growth."

In 2011, the video game marketplace was changing radically. Games were growing more and more expensive to make, especially in the San Francisco Bay Area, where the cost of living had exploded thanks to the glut of tech companies. Linear, single-player games were starting to feel like a high-risk, low-reward proposition, which was why publishers like 2K tried to shoehorn multiplayer into games like *The Bureau: XCOM Declassified* and *BioShock Infinite*. One industry bogeyman was the used-game marketplace, which was largely facilitated by GameStop, the biggest chain of video game retailers in North America. GameStop was happy to sell you a game for $60, let you trade it in a week later for $30, and then turn around and sell your used copy back to customers for $55. That meant pure profit for their stores, and it infuriated a whole lot of video game executives, who saw the whole cycle as tantamount to piracy. When you bought a used copy of *Dead Space 2* from GameStop, EA didn't see a penny.

The rise of digital distribution a few years later would help solve this problem, but during the *Dead Space 2* days, GameStop had a monopoly on video game retail. EA and other megapublishers couldn't prevent GameStop from buying and selling used games, no matter how nicely they asked, and boycotting the biggest video game chain on the planet wasn't an option. So they came up with another strategy: make used games less valuable. Maybe fewer people would buy used games if they got more for their money by buying new.

One of the more devious schemes, popularized by EA in 2010, was the "online pass." When you cracked open a new game, right next to the disc and whatever other promo materials had moseyed into the case, you'd find a small slip of paper with a unique code on it. Load up the game and enter that code and you'd be able to access something cool. Maybe you'd get some extra downloadable content, or maybe you'd be able to access the game's multiplayer mode. The catch was, it was one time only. If you used your code and then sold your game back to GameStop, whoever bought your used copy would have to spend roughly $10 for their own online pass. *Dead Space 2* was one of the first games to use this model. The first *Dead Space* had been single-player-only, but *Dead Space 2* came with a four-versus-four competitive multiplayer mode that EA hoped would keep people playing long after they'd bought it. To play that multiplayer mode, you needed the online pass.

Morale was high at Visceral after the launch of *Dead Space 2*, even if the series still wasn't as massive as EA had hoped it would be. That didn't matter as much to the developers, who were delighted to learn that they'd get to make a *Dead Space 3*. This time, in hopes that they'd really crack the mainstream market, EA took the multiplayer mandate even further, telling Visceral that they had to make the entire campaign playable with two people. *Dead Space 3* was set on an icy planet called Tau Volantis, and while you'd still go around dismembering aliens with the scientist Isaac Clarke, this time you could do it with a friend, who would play as the hulking Sergeant John Carver, a new addition to the series. You could play the whole game either by yourself or with a buddy, but playing cooperatively would give you access to some extra stuff. All you needed was that pesky online pass. "Co-op did not come from the team," said Mumbach. "Co-op came from publishing. Publishing said, 'You need to make this game co-op for it to be viable.'"

Executives at EA also pushed Visceral to tone down the horror and ramp up the action in hopes of making *Dead Space 3* appeal to a wider audience than its predecessors. At E3 in June 2012, midway through development of *Dead Space 3*, EA executive Frank Gibeau suggested in an interview with the gaming website CVG that they had lofty expectations for this one. "We're thinking about how we make this a more broadly appealing franchise, because ultimately you need to get to audience sizes of around five million to really continue to invest in an IP like *Dead Space*," he said.

At the same time, visions of a multinational Visceral empire hadn't panned out. In 2011, EA had shut down Visceral Melbourne. Zach Mumbach briefly worked on a sequel to *Dante's Inferno*, but that was canceled, and in 2012 he went up to Visceral's Montreal office to help finish a shooter game called *Army of Two: The Devil's Cartel*. What he thought would be a two- or three-week trip turned into an entire year. Then, in February 2013, less than a month before

Army of Two: The Devil's Cartel even came out, EA closed Visceral Montreal.

That same month, *Dead Space 3* launched. It did not sell five million copies. Visceral staff say it did just fine, but at this point they'd released three games that all failed to live up to EA's huge forecasts. "My understanding is that *Dead Space* made a little money, just not a lot," said Mumbach. "And then the same thing with *Dead Space 2*, and then the same thing again with *Dead Space 3*, so it's like, 'Okay, this isn't catching.'" From EA's point of view, if *Dead Space* wasn't growing exponentially, then it must be niche, and if it was niche, then EA wanted nothing to do with it, even if it was profitable. "At some point the expectation is, if you sell three million units, then you're gonna sell five, and then you're gonna sell ten," said Mumbach. "You're going to grow."

Shortly after the release of *Dead Space 3*, word came down from above that EA was putting the franchise on ice. It cost too much and didn't make enough for the executives to justify investing in a *Dead Space 4*. Plus, thanks to titanic tech companies like Facebook and Google, the San Francisco Bay Area was becoming an increasingly untenable place to work. Engineers were hard to keep, rents were astronomical, and by one former Visceral employee's estimate, the company's costs hovered around $16,000 a person per month, a number that included salary and other expenses. At that estimate, a staff of one hundred people would cost more than $19 million a year. Visceral's office was right next door to the EA executive suite, so it felt like their bosses were constantly watching them, waiting for them to justify their existence. Of course, as Visceral's staff were well aware, the salaries of just two or three of those bosses could fund the entire studio. (In 2012, EA chief executive officer John Riccitiello made $9.5 million while Frank Gibeau made $9.8 million, according to SEC filings.)

Things seemed grim, but at least Visceral had another shot to prove itself. Throughout 2012, a small team of developers had been working on the next game in the *Battlefield* franchise, a hugely popular series of first-person shooter games. What materialized was *Battlefield Hardline*, a game starring cops and criminals in modern-day Miami and Los Angeles. In 2013, after finishing *Dead Space 3*, the bulk of Visceral's developers were moved to *Battlefield Hardline*. The hope was that this new shooter would be a mainstream commercial success, leading to long-term stability and giving their staff the freedom to pursue more original ideas in the future, like an open-world pirate game that a small group of Visceral staff was also prototyping on the side. *Battlefield Hardline* seemed like an easy win for a studio that desperately needed one.

The problem was, a lot of Visceral's staff didn't want to make a multiplayer shooter. Visceral had established itself as the *Dead Space* studio, and many of their newer developers had joined so they could make games like *Dead Space*. Their talent and expertise were in action-adventure games, not shooters. Even something as ostensibly simple as a switch from the third-person perspective of *Dead Space* to the first-person perspective of *Battlefield* would require a massive shift in design mentality. It'd be like a film director moving from a wide camera angle to a close-up—when crafting levels and encounters, you'd have to adjust your brain accordingly. Not everyone at Visceral wanted to make that transition, and throughout 2013, many of them left the studio, not unlike their neighbors up north at 2K Marin, who were facing a similar identity problem. "Some of us said, 'Cool, I like making different stuff. It's a change of pace,'" said Mumbach, who was now a producer for *Battlefield Hardline*'s multiplayer mode. "But no doubt about it, we lost a ton of great people."

At this point, Mumbach had been working at EA for more than

thirteen years. His workaholic mentality had never gone away, even when he met and began dating Lisa Johansen, the woman he would eventually marry. "They needed bodies in chairs and he was always willing to do it," Lisa said. "I remember one time he was working fourteen- or sixteen-hour days, and we'd meet for his lunch at 5:00 p.m. at the Wendy's across the freeway from EA. Those were the only times I saw him for a couple months." Lisa was accustomed to being around workaholics; her mom was an attorney and her dad was a consultant, and they'd both worked nights and weekends when she was growing up. Plus, it felt like everyone in San Francisco was working endless hours to start new companies or impress their bosses. "It's an epidemic issue," she said. "I was really used to it, even if I didn't love it."

In March 2014, as *Battlefield Hardline* was entering its final year of development, Zach and Lisa Mumbach had a son. They were in the middle of remodeling their house, so they were living with Lisa's parents, which itself presented a number of sociological challenges. Zach took a week of vacation after the kid was born, then went back to work on *Battlefield Hardline*, which desperately needed the manpower. "Being in the last eight weeks of a remodel, being a first-time parent, living with my parents, and him crunching was not an ideal situation," Lisa said.

For Zach Mumbach, the crunch never seemed to end. He found it tough to shake the work-first attitude that had served him so well during his early days at EA. Most nights, he'd come home from the office, have dinner with his family, and then drive right back to work. "No one was telling me to stay late at EA on *Hardline*," Mumbach said. "I was just there because I was obsessed with that game and I'd lose track of time, or I'd prioritize that over other parts of my life, including my family, which I'm not saying was a good thing, but I was doing it. I got to this point at EA where I was given responsibilities: 'Hey, you're in charge of *Battlefield Hardline* multiplayer.' And I took that extremely seriously."

This workaholism had been creeping into Zach Mumbach's brain since those early days of house arrest, and now it was getting worse. When he drove home at night, he was pondering the number of maps and guns *Battlefield Hardline* should have. When he sat at the kitchen table talking to his wife, he was debating how many seconds it should take before a player could respawn once they'd died. Whenever he tried to watch movies or play other video games, his mind just kept drifting back to *Battlefield Hardline*. "I think there's a lot of people who are wired that way, and I'm one of them," Mumbach said. "We're a huge part of the problem."

Mumbach's workaholism spread across the studio like a viral infection. For other Visceral employees who respected and looked up to Mumbach, seeing him at work all the time made them feel guilty for leaving. "You're going to feel like, 'Oh shit, I'm not pulling my weight. Look at all these guys who are here all the time,'" said Mumbach. "It creates this social pressure to also do that." That sort of insidious crunch culture was common in the video game industry; it was how many companies drew extra work out of their employees without even having to ask. "If you're a really smart executive, you just hire people that are wired that way and put them in high-up positions," said Mumbach. "Then you don't have to demand that people work overtime. You can just turn a blind eye to it."

There was also an underlying sense that people should feel lucky to be there. Mumbach figured that if he wasn't working as much as possible, he'd be replaced. He'd seen a constant cycle of shutdowns and layoffs all across the video game industry. He'd watched closures happen firsthand within EA, and even at Visceral, where he'd watched friends and colleagues lose their jobs during company cost-cutting initiatives. Mumbach figured the best way to make himself layoff-proof was to work harder than everyone else around him. "Zach was always walking super fast through the halls of EA as if he had somewhere to go," said Luke Harrington, who worked with him there. "Running up and down the stairs."

Mumbach often compared the video game industry to professional sports, where the highest achievers were the ones dedicating their lives to their craft. Kobe Bryant, for example, was infamously obsessive in his pursuit of greatness. He was the first one to go to the gym every morning and the last one to leave. Teammates would find him running shooting drills while injured, in the dark, just because he could. When he wasn't practicing, he was watching game film.

Of course, Kobe Bryant was paid $25 million a year for those hours.

"I never even thought about that part," Mumbach said. "I just thought about the demand for the job, and then the fact that people are going to push that hard. You can either try to keep up or not." Mumbach knew that when it came time for layoffs, bosses were going to prioritize keeping the people who worked twelve hours a day for six days a week over the people who clocked in at 10:00 a.m. and went home at 6:00 p.m. "It's a little bit cutthroat," Mumbach said. "If you have a job on an AAA team, there are people that want your job. There are people that are gunning for your job, and you feel that pressure, especially as you start to get a little older, get married, have kids, start having a life."

Battlefield Hardline came out in March 2015, following three tough years of production, and it sold well enough to keep the EA executives satisfied. When they'd finished the game, the developers at Visceral split into two groups. One group moved to their next project, which was code-named *Ragtag*, while the other group started working on multiplayer expansions for *Battlefield Hardline*. Mumbach was happy to be on the latter team. *Battlefield Hardline* wasn't as beloved as *Dead Space*, but it had a consistent base of people who played every day, and Mumbach would frequently join them, sharing his handle on Twitter so fans could find him for multiplayer matches. He and some others on the *Battlefield Hardline* team spent a few months coming up with pitches and prototypes for follow-ups, but EA turned them down. By 2016, Visceral needed all hands on deck for *Ragtag*. After all, it was the biggest and most exciting project they'd ever had.

■ ■ ■

In April 2013, around the time Zach Mumbach started working on *Battlefield Hardline*, Frank Gibeau and the other EA executives next door were negotiating a monumental deal. Disney had just purchased Lucasfilm, and the megapopular *Star Wars* franchise along with it, fundamentally shifting the media landscape. Disney had subsequently shut down the iconic video game studio LucasArts, laying off 150 people and canceling all of the projects they'd been working on. (This came just months after the closure of Junction Point.) One of those LucasArts projects, *Star Wars 1313*, had stolen the show at E3 less than a year earlier. There were conversations about EA taking over production of the game—conversations so serious that a squad of *Star Wars 1313* developers even drove down to Visceral to show off what they'd made—but those fell through. *Star Wars 1313* was canceled.[6]

Instead, EA's bosses struck a deal for the exclusive rights to

---

6   You can read the whole story of *Star Wars 1313* in my last book, *Blood, Sweat, and Pixels*. Sorry for the gratuitous plug. Okay, fine, I'm not that sorry.

Star Wars console games, which they officially announced on May 6, 2013. Other companies could play around with social or mobile *Star Wars* games, but EA would be the only publisher allowed to make *Star Wars* games for "core" audiences, according to the announcement. As part of the press release, EA announced that three studios would be working in the world of *Star Wars*: DICE, BioWare, and Visceral.

This was a coup for the long-running game studio. While the bulk of Visceral worked on *Battlefield Hardline*, a second small team was now working on their very own *Star Wars* game. It changed forms and code names a couple of times before they hired Amy Hennig, best known for directing the popular *Uncharted* games, to come lead the project. By the time Zach Mumbach finished his work on *Battlefield* and joined the *Star Wars* team, in the spring of 2016, it had become a third-person action-adventure game just like *Dead Space*. It was a heist story—*Oceans Eleven* set in a galaxy far, far away—with multiple protagonists including a Han Solo–esque, mustachioed rogue named Dodger and his gunslinging partner, Robie. They made for a motley gang, so the team gave the project the code name *Ragtag*.

Most video game developers would have been thrilled at the idea of working on a game like *Ragtag*. But Mumbach found himself disappointed. Sure, he was a big *Star Wars* fan, like just about every-one else in the video game industry—after all, he'd gotten started by making *Star Wars* mods for *Duke Nukem*—but he wanted to play *Star Wars* games, not make them. Mumbach wanted to work on a sequel to *Battlefield Hardline*, and he felt like it was a shame to let go of *Battlefield* before they really had a chance to see what they could do with it.

At least now they had security. After *Dead Space 3* had failed to live up to EA's expectations, there were plenty of people at Visceral who worried that the executives might glance next door and wonder why they were still paying for such an expensive studio. Now, though, Visceral was making a game in one of the biggest franchises on the planet, and EA had been very public about that fact. If anyone in the video game industry was protected from layoffs and studio closures, surely it was the people who were working on *Star Wars*. "Honestly," said Mumbach. "I felt like we were the safest we'd been in a long time."

But the production of *Ragtag* was growing turbulent. Visceral was short-staffed compared to other studios working on projects of a similar scale. There were technical issues with Frostbite, the video game engine that Visceral used to build the game.[7] There were conflicts between Hennig and other staff at Visceral. There were heated battles between the game's directors and EA executives, who fought over everything from gameplay innovations to *Star Wars* references. The development team wanted this to be a gritty take on *Star Wars*, with no Jedi or furry monsters, but EA's market research suggested that fans associated *Star Wars* with specific characters, leading executives to ask the team questions like, "Where's Chewbacca?"

There were battles over monetization, as EA's bosses pushed for a multiplayer component on *Ragtag*, just like they had on *Dead Space 3*. "Where's your *FIFA* Ultimate Team?" executives would ask,

---

7   A video game engine is a suite of reusable code and technology that's used to make development more efficient. Throughout the 2010s, EA strongly encouraged all of its studios to use a single engine: Frostbite. On paper this was a smart move, as using one engine would allow all of EA's subsidiaries to share technology and save the company millions of dollars in licensing costs to third-party engine companies. However, Frostbite was designed by DICE to make first-person shooters. Trying to use it for other genres could cause all sorts of headaches, as it did for Visceral's staff and, most infamously, for BioWare, whose games *Dragon Age: Inquisition*; *Mass Effect: Andromeda*; and *Anthem* were all severely hampered by Frostbite's quirks. Put another way, as a BioWare developer once told me: "Frostbite is full of razor blades."

referring to the card-collecting mode in EA's soccer franchise that brought in hundreds of millions of dollars in revenue per year. Those old online passes had been so unpopular that EA was forced to kill them in 2013, but the company's priority was still to ensure that all of its games were both protected from the used-game market and generating as many dollars as possible. EA wanted games that could keep making money long after release. (The popular term was "games as a service.")

Once again, Visceral was facing an identity crisis. For years, the studio had stuck to licensed games before finally carving out something of its own with the *Dead Space* trilogy. Then came *Battlefield Hardline*, which drove away a number of Visceral developers who wanted to make third-person action-adventure games. To make that game, Visceral recruited new people with experience on first-person shooters. Now, three years later, Visceral was a studio full of people who knew how to make first-person shooters but were assigned to make a third-person action-adventure game. "The people we had three years ago would've been perfect for this," said Mumbach. "But we decided to become a multiplayer shooter studio. So we rebuilt ourselves to do that. And now you're asking us to rebuild ourselves again. At some point that's not going to work."

By 2017, it was clear to everyone that *Ragtag* was in trouble. EA had assigned a team from its Vancouver office to join the project, and it became apparent to Visceral staff that EA's plan was actually to have the Vancouver team take over production. The two studios clashed immediately, squabbling over processes and design decisions, and as they built levels and demos for the game, progress moved slowly. Mumbach, like many of his coworkers, felt like something was going to give. He thought that maybe Amy Hennig would quit, that EA would move the project to Vancouver, or that maybe another support team would come to help out. What few people expected was what was actually about to occur. "It literally came out of nowhere," said a different Visceral developer. "I had no idea that anything like that was going to happen."

■ ■ ■

Early in the morning on Sunday, October 15, 2017, Zach and Lisa Mumbach had their second son. The next day, as they were driving home from the hospital, a high-ranking EA executive reached out and said he wanted to chat. *Sure*, said a giddy, sleep-deprived Mumbach. *Come on by.* When the executive arrived, he greeted the couple and smiled at their new baby. Then he pulled them aside and delivered some crushing news: Visceral was shutting down. *Ragtag* was canceled. The company would be holding a meeting on Tuesday to tell the whole staff.

The EA executive kept talking, offering explanations about how the game was behind schedule and how operational costs in San Francisco were just too high, but Mumbach wasn't paying much attention. His mind was occupied by thoughts of his one-day-old child, and his old company, and the fact that suddenly the people he'd worked with for years would no longer be in an office with him every day. Mumbach wasn't concerned about finding new employment—the executive had assured him that there were other spots open at EA—but he was worried that some of his coworkers might not be as lucky. "The game, I let that one go really easy," Mumbach said. "It sucks to not get to make that game, but the studio getting shut down part of it, that's brutal."

On October 17, 2017, Mumbach walked into the Visceral office in Redwood Shores, California, for what he knew would be the studio's final all-hands meeting. The rest of Visceral's staff had no idea what was coming, and some were surprised to see him—wasn't he supposed to be on paternity leave? Why was he at work? "My presence there alerted some people that something bad was going to happen," Mumbach said. "Other people were oblivious. This one guy I love runs up to me as we're going to the meeting room and gives me a big hug because he's stoked, knows I just had a kid. He says, 'Congratulations!'"

Crammed together in the first few rows of the theater on EA's campus, the Visceral staff sat in stunned silence as executives Patrick Söderlund and Jade Raymond told them that the studio was shutting down. There were a lot of factors, the executives said. The video game market had changed, and EA no longer wanted to spend big money on linear, single-player games that a person would only play through once before selling them back to GameStop. The executives talked about the new mega-popular battle royale game *PlayerUnknown's Battlegrounds*, which they were looking to emulate, and they praised Visceral's staff, offering platitudes about how talented the team was and how hard they'd all worked. Then they told everyone how to get their severance packages.

Once the meeting ended and dozens of employees filed out of the theater, reality began to set in. They would all have to find new jobs, either within EA or at other companies. Some of them would have to move to new cities, uprooting their families if they wanted to work at big-budget studios with Visceral's pedigree. They all had a financial cushion—the severance was generous—but they also knew their lives had just irrevocably changed. "People were super bummed," said Mumbach. "Everybody reacted differently. Some people were angry; some people were just sad. Some people were just fed up: 'Yeah, fuck it, burn this place down.'" Mumbach's reaction was simply to go home. "I'm out of here. I'm on paternity leave. I disengaged immediately."

In public messaging, EA suggested that the decision to shut down Visceral was spurred by *Ragtag*'s creative challenges, writing on their website that the project was "shaping up to be a story-based, linear adventure game" and that they planned to transform it into "a broader experience that allows for more variety and player agency"—in other words, less *Uncharted*, more open-world. "Throughout the development process, we have been testing the game concept with players, listening to the feedback about what and how they want to play, and closely tracking fundamental shifts in the marketplace," wrote EA executive Patrick Söderlund in the blog post announcing the closure. "It has become clear that to deliver an experience that players will want to come back to and enjoy for a long time to come, we needed to pivot the design."[8]

These comments led to endless speculation and theories about the death of Visceral Games. What did this mean for the video game industry? Were single-player games dead? Was EA planning on pivoting exclusively to games as a service—video games that were designed to be played indefinitely—and giving up on franchises like *Dead Space* for good?

A few weeks after Visceral shut down, another theory emerged. On November 9, 2017, EA announced that it had purchased the game studio Respawn for more than $400 million. Respawn, which had formed in 2010 following a mass exodus of staff from *Call of Duty: Modern Warfare* studio Infinity Ward, had worked with EA on two other games, *Titanfall* and *Titanfall 2*. At the time, EA was expecting a third *Titanfall*.[9] EA had also signed a deal with Respawn

---

8   The project moved to EA Vancouver, where it was rebooted as an open-world *Star Wars* game code-named *Orca*, which lasted for around a year before it was canceled. The developers then went on to launch a new *Star Wars* project, a *Battlefront* spin-off code-named *Viking*. That, too, was canceled.

9   The planned *Titanfall 3* eventually transformed into a battle royale game called *Apex Legends*, which was an immediate success for EA when it launched in February 2019, living up to EA's hope for a game that emulated *PlayerUnknown's Battlegrounds*.

for another game—a third-person action-adventure game set in the *Star Wars* universe. That game, which would later become known as *Star Wars Jedi: Fallen Order*, was very different from what Visceral had envisioned for *Ragtag*, focusing on a lightsaber-wielding Jedi hero rather than a gang of misfits and scoundrels, but it led to some obvious questions about whether both games could really fit in EA's portfolio.

Were Visceral's shutdown and Respawn's acquisition connected? EA won't say, but there's a lot to support the theory. A week before the purchase, the video game website Kotaku obtained documents revealing that the Korean publisher Nexon had made an offer to purchase Respawn that summer. Respawn's publishing agreement gave EA the first right of refusal on acquisitions, so EA's executives were stuck with a tough decision: either lose the money they'd poured into the *Titanfall* franchise, which Respawn owned and would therefore become Nexon's property, or come up with enough cash to make a counteroffer.

They chose the latter. Perhaps as a result, Visceral was no more.

■ ■ ■

In the weeks and months after Visceral closed, the studio's former employees mourned and tried to figure out their next moves. Some stayed within EA, taking jobs at *The Sims* studio Maxis or moving to other cities, like Vancouver, where EA had a huge campus. Others got jobs at different game studios both in and out of the Bay Area or left the video game industry entirely, taking lucrative offers at nearby tech companies like Facebook and Apple.

For Zach and Lisa Mumbach, the first few days after the shutdown were frantic. Having a new baby was difficult enough in the best of situations—after a job loss, it was terrifying. Not only did the

Mumbachs have to worry about bringing in a paycheck and health insurance for their three-year-old and their newborn, but their entire social sphere had suddenly shattered. The staff of Visceral, some of whom had known one another for more than a decade, would now be splitting up for good. "It was pretty overwhelming, especially with a brand-new baby," said Lisa. "We felt very comfortable there. Most of our friends were through EA....Our whole network came through there, so it was the end of an era, really." They had gone to EA holiday parties every year. They would take their kids to the annual EA summer fair. It was hard to imagine what their lives would look like without that infrastructure.

The good news was that Zach Mumbach had a lot of options. Shortly after Visceral's closure, Mumbach got on the phone with Scot Amos, an old friend of his from the days of *The Simpsons Game.* Amos was now running the show at the nearby studio Crystal Dynamics, which was developing a game based on *The Avengers.* "He offered me a job on the spot," said Mumbach. "He said, 'We'll work out the details, but I want you to know you have a place to land.'"

Visceral was paying out severance until January, so Mumbach spent the next two months hanging out with his family, which gave him a lot of time to think. For seventeen years he'd given his life to EA, and while they'd treated him well, it was hard not to think about the wealth disparity between the developers at Visceral and the executives who worked next door. EA chief executive officer Andrew Wilson had made over $35 million in the 2018 fiscal year (April 2017 through March 2018), according to SEC filings. Patrick Söderlund could have made over $48 million thanks to a stock retention bonus that EA had given him to stick with the company—he didn't stick with the company, but still walked away with millions.

While Mumbach and his colleagues had crunched on games like

Battlefield Hardline, he'd watched those EA executives leave the office at 5:00 p.m. every day. He'd always thought he needed to put in extra hours to be the elite of the elite—to be Kobe Bryant—but the people who actually got paid like superstar athletes were working forty-hour weeks. The people who had crunched at Visceral were now looking for new jobs.

Even a top salary like $100,000/year wouldn't go very far in San Francisco. "I'm tired of working eighty-hour weeks so that people like Patrick Söderlund can get a new car," said Mumbach. "You're making a salary and it's a good salary, but it's not like people are thriving. People are surviving." Among Mumbach's peers, developers were treading water—they could afford to pay their rent and bills, but they weren't making much more than that. The thought of home ownership was a pipe dream to most of them. "You work so hard, two to three years go by, and then you get what, a twenty- or thirty-thousand-dollar bonus?" said Mumbach. "It's public information what the executives of EA and Activision are making. They're not the ones making the games. There's a major disparity there."

Mumbach now had a lot of time to think about corporate politics and executive machinations. He'd watched EA shut down not just Visceral, but a dozen studios including Visceral's other offices in Montreal and Australia as well as iconic companies like Bullfrog (*Dungeon Keeper*); Origin (*Ultima*); Westwood (*Command & Conquer*); and many more. To EA's executives, who prioritized investors and fiscal quarters, it seemed like people's lives were just numbers on a spreadsheet. "It doesn't even matter if they keep their jobs," Mumbach said. "One year, a $20 million bonus, I'm set for the rest of my life. So if I can make a decision to triple the stock today knowing in two years it's going to tank, what the hell do I care?" In Mumbach's view, the people who ran EA seemed to care less about making great video games and more about maximizing profits as quickly as possible. "It feels like these guys are playing games," Mumbach said. "They're playing games with budgets; they're playing games with revenue; they're playing games with overhead. They cut people just to hire people back because it looks good for this quarter or that quarter."

And then there was his newborn. While helping out his wife with his second baby in the months after Visceral closed, Mumbach realized that he had really missed out the first time around. For the first few months of his older son's life, he'd been crunching on *Battlefield Hardline*. Now he was actually seeing how much work his wife had to put into feedings, diaper changes, and all of the other delightful little burdens that came with a new baby. "You realize, 'Oh shit, I really fucked up the last one,'" Mumbach said. "I was not around. This is really brutal on my wife, and she was getting no help."

Now he could actually help out. Now he actually had the time to be around his kids. "He was spending so much time with the family day to day," Lisa Mumbach said. "Once you're part of that, it's hard to let go."

■ ■ ■

Three months after Visceral closed, in January 2018, Zach Mumbach walked into Crystal Dynamics as a brand-new producer. Within his first few days at the office, he began feeling uneasy. The *Avengers* game was exciting, but did he really want to go through the grind of video game production again? Mumbach had taken the job in a panicked state, worried about providing for his kids and keeping his family on health insurance, but now he was starting to wonder if he'd made the wrong decision. Working at Crystal Dynamics didn't feel much different from working at Visceral. "They weren't making me crunch," Mumbach said. "But I'd go there and think, man, this team is so excited about the game they're making, and they're working superhard, and I'm going home every day at 6:00 p.m. and feeling bad about it." He started to feel those same familiar guilt pangs that he had felt while working on *Ragtag* and *Battlefield Hardline* and all of Visceral's other games. While sitting at dinner or putting his kids to bed, Mumbach would zone out, thinking about Thor's hammer animations or how the game's cooperative missions would function. He started getting the urge to go back to the office at night, when he knew the other developers at Crystal Dynamics would still be there, working on the game.

Mumbach started feeling grumpy and depressed, like his body was being yanked in multiple directions at the same time. He felt like he couldn't commit fully to his work, nor could he be completely devoted to his family. Every day at the office, he'd ask himself just what he was doing there. When he'd started at EA back in 2000, Mumbach was always the youngest person in the office. Now he was thirty-six. "I look around and I don't see a lot of people older than me," Mumbach said. "When I started, everyone was older than me. That was eighteen years ago. The guys that were thirty or twenty-eight then, where the fuck are they now?"

The answer to that question was becoming more obvious every day.

In February, just a month after he'd started at Crystal Dynamics, Zach Mumbach told studio head Scot Amos that he was quitting. Amos said he understood and asked Mumbach to stay a couple more months while they found a replacement. Mumbach's last day would be April 4, 2018, three months after he'd started. "I'm a hypocrite too," said Mumbach, "because I've had conversations with people at work—I believe that once you're on a game, you shouldn't leave that game. You should get the game done." Once you'd become a cog in the great machine that is game development, leaving a project meant creating extra work for all the people around you. "It's better to never join at all than to join a team for six months and then bounce," said Mumbach. "But it just came to, well, it's my family or this."

Over the next few months, Mumbach and his wife decided to make big changes. They gave up on the Bay Area, selling their house in San Mateo and moving up to Bainbridge Island, Washington, just outside Seattle. Through an old EA connection, Mumbach got an office job at an architectural firm. In the following months, he found himself working a more normal schedule. He'd leave the office every day and have dinner with his family. He'd play with his kids every night before they went to bed. Slowly but surely, Zach Mumbach was able to separate his work life from his home life, training himself out of the bad habits he had picked up over eighteen years of game development. "It's engaging and interesting, but not the thing I dreamed of as a kid," Mumbach said. "So it's not the thing that's occupying my mind at all times."

The lifestyle difference was monumental. Instead of driving into bumper-to-bumper traffic every day, Mumbach would take a ferry from Bainbridge Island to Seattle, then bike to his office downtown. Instead of living in a San Francisco house where they could see their neighbors through the kitchen window, they now lived in the middle of the woods, surrounded by nature and tranquillity. All they could see were trees. "We're very happy here," said Lisa Mumbach. "The change has been really good for us. The downside is leaving friends and family, but the pace of life is so different. It's very woodsy, very naturey. There's no traffic. It's great."

But there was still something missing in Zach Mumbach's life. In daily conversations and on his Twitter profile, Mumbach kept identifying himself as a game developer. When he met new people and they asked what he did for a living, Mumbach had a hard time answering that he worked in architecture. "It's shocking how it stings, how it hurts my ego," he said. "It's a pride thing. I worked so hard to be an AAA video game maker. That was my dream since I was fourteen years old. It's really hard on the ego to say, 'Oh, I'm not a game maker anymore.'"

At the same time, Mumbach had been watching with awe as one of his old friends from Visceral, Ben Wander, developed and released *A Case of Distrust*, a detective game set in California during the Prohibition era. It wasn't as massive or hyped as an EA game, but it was an impressive project, with sleek, hand-painted silhouettes and a twisty, hard-boiled story about 1920s bootleggers. Wander also spent his spare time traveling the world, and he was in the process of figuring out his next project with a few other ex-Visceral staff. "We'd been making a demo," Wander said. "We sent it to friends for feedback. 'Hey, is this good enough? What do you think?'"

One of those friends was Zach Mumbach, who started asking them questions about their project and what the past few years had been like for them. Then he started making pitches. "Initially I said, 'Hey, can I invest? I believe in you guys. I have a little extra money. I'm sure you guys need money. Can I invest in the game?'" said Mumbach. "And so they said, 'Well what does that mean? What do you want for your investment?' I said, 'I don't want anything. I just want to help you guys.'"

Of course, Mumbach didn't actually want to be an investor. What he really wanted was to reclaim his identity. What he was really asking was if he could be a game developer again. Ben Wander's next project, *Airborne Kingdom*, was a strategy game in which you'd manage and operate a flying city, and Mumbach desperately wanted to help them make it. "Zach seemed absolutely stoked from the beginning," said Wander. "All he wanted to do was be part of it in some way." Wander also desperately needed a producer, and

Mumbach was happy to oblige, even if it meant not getting paid. "We were barely getting by on our own," Wander said. "We didn't have the budget to pay somebody else."

Mumbach began developing a routine. He'd go to work to pay the bills, then come home and spend time with his family. At night, when the kids went to bed, he'd put in a few extra hours to help produce and market *Airborne Kingdom*. There was certainly a risk that he would burn out again, but Mumbach needed the creative outlet. "I felt like he made this huge sacrifice in taking a job he's not passionate about in order to have a better quality of life," Lisa Mumbach said. "I was very concerned about him giving up the dream. Once this opportunity with Ben came up, it seemed like the best-case scenario. He could exercise that passion while also being a part of our lives."

By the summer of 2020, Wander had found enough funding for *Airborne Kingdom* to hire Mumbach properly, and he was able to end his two-year hiatus to once again become a full-time game developer. Yet Zach Mumbach still vows that he'll "never work for an AAA publisher again." Leaving the big-budget video game industry has served him well. "When you're doing it, it feels like the most important thing in the world," Mumbach said. "What I'm doing is so important. I'm making this big AAA game." With some distance, and in the wake of a newborn child and a studio shutdown, it became clear that other things in his life meant far more to him. He no longer wanted to work for executives whose salaries were exponentially higher than his, and he no longer wanted to have to worry about the sustainability of companies like EA. "Independent is the way to go," Mumbach said, "and in the end, independents are going to make better games."

Before it was shut down, one of Visceral's biggest problems was that it had no identity. Between staff shake-ups and genre whiplash, this was a studio that never quite made a name for itself, which ultimately helped lead to its demise. But in the video game industry, as evidenced by Junction Point and Irrational, even studios with strong identities can wind up shutting down with no warning. The tornado of volatility can hit at any time, for any reason. Even when your company is owned by a legendary baseball player worth tens of millions of dollars.

CHAPTER 6

BLOODY SOCKS

What blew Thom Ang away were the perks. Ang had been a professional video game artist for over a decade, first at Disney working on licensed games like *The Lion King* and *Toy Story* for the Super Nintendo and Sega Genesis, and then at Sony, EA, and THQ. Those had all been good jobs, but none of them were as luxurious as 38 Studios.

38 Studios was the type of company a teenager might dream up when fantasizing about what it'd be like to make games for a living. Located in a historic former mill in Maynard, Massachusetts, with red-bricked walls, a looming clock tower, and picturesque views of the nearby Assabet River, the company appeared to be flush with cash. Its executives acted like they ran a Silicon Valley tech unicorn that had just received a billion-dollar valuation. Employees received top-notch health benefits and gym memberships. They got personalized high-end gaming laptops worth thousands of dollars. There were free meals, lavish travel expenses, and Timbuk2 bags customized with an illustration of the world map for their in-progress video game, which was code-named *Copernicus*.

The man responsible for all of these perks was Curt Schilling, the sandy-haired former professional athlete who founded and ran 38 Studios. Schilling had spent two decades pitching in Major League Baseball, helping win championships for the Arizona Diamondbacks and, most notably, the Boston Red Sox, a team he had led to its first title since 1918. Now retired in Massachusetts, he was a video game CEO unlike any other in the industry. "Curt really took care of people," said Ang. "He recognized that in his field, he's treated as a star. He's a top-level athlete. He was given Cadillac packages for everything. He said, 'That's how I want my team to feel. I'm going to attract the best, and I'm going to treat them as if they're the best.' And he did."

In 2008, when Thom Ang first got a call from a 38 Studios recruiter, he was skeptical. He'd grown up in Southern California and couldn't see himself moving to the East Coast, where the winters were cold and miserable. But he already knew a bunch of 38 Studios employees from his EA days, so he figured he'd let the company fly him out to Massachusetts just to say hi to them. "I went in knowing I'm not going to take the job," Ang said. When he got there, he was awed by the office, the promises, and the swag. Then his former colleagues showed him the art they'd been making for their game. "I said, 'Oh my god, this is gorgeous,'" Ang recalled. "'This is a fantastic-looking game. I want in on this.'"

When Ang accepted the offer, 38 Studios gave him a hefty relocation package, even flying him back out to Boston so he could look for a new place to live. He fell in love with a beautiful three-bedroom ranch on a lake in Acton, Massachusetts. "I've always wanted this," Ang said. "In L.A. you can't get a house on a lake." And in June 2008, Thom Ang officially started work as 38 Studios' art director; he was responsible for managing a team of artists and establishing a visual tone for *Copernicus*. There wasn't a lot done on the game, even though the studio had been operating for two years, but Ang didn't think that was a problem. Throughout his years in the video game industry, he'd seen how slowly things could move at the beginning of a project.

Ang never really worried about 38 Studios' finances or wondered where the money was coming from. After all, he was an artist. He was one of the company's directors, sure, but he wasn't involved with business development or financial planning. The game's timeline did seem a little unrealistic—Schilling would tell people that they were targeting the fall of 2011, which probably wasn't possible based on how little had been done so far—but the man in charge was rich. Mind-bogglingly rich. Curt Schilling had earned in excess of $114 million over the course of two decades in baseball, and he saw video game development as his second career. Schilling wanted to make a *World of Warcraft* killer, and he was willing to spend serious money to make that happen. What could possibly go wrong?

▪ ▪ ▪

Many years earlier, in the fall of 1978, a British university student named Richard Bartle was spending a lot of time thinking about how much the world sucked. Bartle grew up poor in a small town along the coast of England, where he lived in public housing, surrounded by kids with tough family lives. His escape was to play board games and dream up fantasy worlds in his head, and when he was fortunate enough to be admitted into the nearby University of Essex, he was immediately drawn to the campus computer lab. Computers were the one thing that could make his fantasies feel real. "To get into computer science in those days, you had to have a particular worldview," Bartle said. "Computers were a way to empower individuals, to change the world. They were going to make the world so much better than it was." Most of the other kids at the University of Essex came from middle- or upper-class backgrounds, so Bartle was elated to meet another working-class student named Roy Trubshaw. The two grew friendly and began talking about what it'd be like to create a virtual world where class didn't matter—where everyone had equal opportunities to succeed, no matter who their parents were. "I didn't really like the real world," Bartle said. "It sucked. It still sucks."

In October 1978, Trubshaw and Bartle first tested out the technology for a game they'd invented that would be called *Multi-User Dungeon*, or *MUD*, and over the next few years they opened it to the public. The game unfolded entirely through text, describing a virtual world using expressive sentences ("There is a fire burning merrily in the grate") and allowing you to interact with that world using simple commands like "Go west." You'd get to role-play a character, fighting monsters and casting magical spells, but unlike other text-based adventures of the era, *MUD* would let you play with other people. It ran on the ARPANET, an early online network that would become the foundation for the internet, and went through various iterations during the 1980s and 1990s, growing popular among other young geeks with access to computers.

Trubshaw and Bartle released the source code for *MUD* to the public for free, destroying any shot they might have had at getting rich but triggering a surge in popularity as programmers across the world built their own games on top of *MUD*'s code. In the years that followed, a number of spin-offs and successors popped up across the fledgling internet, with the name *MUD* evolving into shorthand for an online text adventure. The most notable new game was *DikuMUD*, released in 1991 by a group of Danish students who wanted to play an online game like *Dungeons & Dragons*, complete with in-depth stats and tense dungeon crawling. Unlike many other

MUD code bases, *DikuMUD* worked right out of the box—you just needed a server and some basic programming knowledge to get it running. Since it was all text, the game was easy to customize. If you wanted to turn the weapons into rubber chickens or replace all the enemies with *Rugrats* characters, you just needed to swap some words. Throughout the 1990s, people used code bases like *DikuMUD* to make online games based on just about every popular franchise, from *Harry Potter* to *Dragon Ball Z*. If you liked it, there was probably a virtual world for it. (Needless to say, there were plenty of *MUD*s featuring erotic role-playing.)

Every copy of *DikuMUD*'s source code came with a massive disclaimer: Nobody could use it to make money. At all. If you wanted to make a game based on *DikuMUD*, you couldn't sell copies, ask for subscriptions, or charge for in-game items. So in the 1990s, when the people behind burgeoning big companies like Electronic Arts looked over at these popular virtual worlds and tried to figure out how to profit, they realized they needed to start from scratch. For EA, Richard Garriott turned his famous *Ultima* franchise into a virtual world in 1997 with *Ultima Online*, which was heavily inspired by *DikuMUD*. In 1999, Sony Online Entertainment released a massively popular online game called *EverQuest*—essentially *DikuMUD* with graphics.[1]

Both *Ultima Online* and *EverQuest* were addictive in ways that the video game industry hadn't seen before. By combining the compulsive leveling loops of a traditional RPG with online social dynamics, these newly monikered massive multiplayer online role-playing games (MMORPGs) could hook people into forgetting to

---

1   This led to a brief controversy when one of its developers said during a conference that *EverQuest* was based on *DikuMUD*, but since the creators of *EverQuest* had not actually used *DikuMUD*'s code—only its ideas—they were in the clear.

eat or sleep. Players would befriend like-minded players from all across the world. Then they'd feel obligated to continue playing in order to maintain those relationships and keep their levels up. *EverQuest* became known as "EverCrack," often said in a tone more resigned than comedic.

For video game companies, this level of engagement meant tremendous profits. Both *Ultima Online* and *EverQuest* charged people a monthly subscription to keep playing, which meant a revenue stream of millions of dollars that would continue for as long as those players stayed addicted. By the turn of the century, every company in video games wanted its own MMORPG. Richard Bartle's vision of a virtual world had come to fruition...and the monkey's paw curled. With these new online games, anyone could escape their real lives to a place where they'd all be on the same playing field, no matter where they were born or who their parents were—as long as they could afford to keep paying $10 a month.

Ultima Online and *EverQuest* were both successful, bringing in hundreds of thousands of subscribers, but it would take another few years for MMORPGs to become truly mainstream. On November 23, 2004, Blizzard Entertainment, the rapidly growing video game company behind masterpieces like *StarCraft* and *Diablo*, released a game called *World of Warcraft*. Based on the *Warcraft* strategy game series that had put Blizzard on the map back in the 1990s, *World of Warcraft* took place in a fantasy land full of elves, gnomes, and dwarves. You'd play as a member of one of two factions—the human-led Alliance or the orc-driven Horde—as you'd go on quests, battle through dungeons, mine for resources, and slowly level up your character from peon to powerhouse. You could join a guild and participate in forty-person raids like the Molten Core, a volcanic dungeon full of bosses that required precise collaboration to overcome. Triumphing over this raid would give your character unique gear that you could

"The people were top-notch, top talent in the industry. And I was prepared to just live there the rest of my life, to work there the rest of my career."

But to anyone who looked closely, One Empire Plaza wasn't as stable as it seemed. Between the constant flow of new hires, the free swag, and all those mortgage payments, 38 Studios was chewing through millions of dollars a month. They also had to start paying back the Rhode Island loan right away, before the company had released any games or generated a single dollar in revenue. Throughout 2011, reports later suggested, 38 Studios had a burn rate of more than $4 million a month, a whopping sum that would eat through their entire loan in a year. Court documents later revealed that 38 Studios had received only around $49 million of the $75 million that Rhode Island had earmarked for the loan. The banks kept the rest, much to Curt Schilling's dismay.

To keep the company going, Schilling needed more money. As 38 Studios continued working on two games—*Kingdoms of Amalur: Reckoning* at Big Huge Games in Maryland, and *Copernicus* in Rhode Island—Schilling kept hunting for new investors. After years of failing to convince anyone to put substantial funds into his company, his quest may have now seemed quixotic, but Schilling still believed that if he put his heart into something, he could simply will it into existence. The investors might not have been there yet, but they would be. "That's the way I'm built," Schilling told *Boston* magazine when asked about this attitude. "I think it's one of the reasons I was able to do what I did playing baseball. And it's not fake. I've been around situations where you can make people believe something they don't believe."

It never occurred to Schilling to rein in his spending. After all, he saw his 38 Studios employees as family. *Family.* That was a word he used frequently in meetings with staff. In Schilling's mind, all-star treatment was the only way to keep his employees from leaving for other clubhouses. "We did everything we could do to make sure they understand they'd never work for someone that cared more about them than we did," Schilling later said on a Boston WEEI-FM radio show. "That was the only way we could build the team we built."

When Jennifer Mills first arrived at 38 Studios, three months before the Rhode Island move, she was awed. It was her first job out of college, and she was entranced by what she saw of the game and the company. On her first day, she went around to introduce herself to her new coworkers and was warned that not all video game studios treated their employees this well. Not all video game studios recruited so many great artists or offered so many great perks. "Everyone shook my hand and said, 'Wow, this is your first job? You're really spoiled. It's never going to be as good as this again,'" Mills said. "I was blown away by the talent there."

The game looked gorgeous, full of sleek medieval castles and vivid environments—humongous waterfalls, ancient statues, craggy mountains, menacing underground cities lit with sickly shades of neon green. Mills was a texture artist, which meant that her job was to paint 3-D models and environments. She'd spend her days coloring in grass, trees, rocks, and all the architecture that made *Copernicus*'s levels look so pretty. She was 38's first environment texture artist, and within a few months, she wound up in charge of an intern, then a few interns, and then more artists. Before Mills had been there a year she'd been promoted to lead—a title usually reserved for people with far more experience. Later, when the press began to descend and whispers began to circulate about 38 Studios, one common rumor was that promotions had been handed out willy-nilly, but Mills was a talented artist who felt she deserved the bump. "At least on my team, that was not the case,"

Mills said. "If you got promoted, you earned it. I did a badass job at what I did."

Problem was, Mills didn't get the pay raise that was supposed to accompany the title. In early 2012, when she was promoted, she was told that there were no salary increases being approved. "We went into a hiring freeze, and what that also meant was a freeze on spending more money at all," Mills said. "I just remember thinking that, financially, they're trying to keep things a little closer to the chest." What she didn't realize was that hiring freezes were almost always a harbinger of worse things to come. "That being my first job," Mills said, "it might have been naïveté that I didn't see that as being something worse than it appeared to be."

Like a beautiful gold texture painted over a drab gray model, the glitz of 38 Studios concealed an ugly reality. It was only a matter of time before the paint came off.

■ ■ ■

On Christmas Day 2011, Andy Johnson and his family packed up all of their things for the long move from Phoenix, Arizona, to Providence, Rhode Island, where he'd just accepted a job at 38 Studios. Johnson had spent the past six years working for the prolific video game publisher THQ, but he was starting to get anxious about the company's shaky finances. Executive shuffling, big stock falls, and constant layoffs were becoming part of his daily routine. "You'd send an email and then you'd get a bounceback from people you were working with for three months," Johnson said. Knowing that his job might be in peril, Johnson applied for a number of new positions and eventually got a call from 38 Studios, who told him they were planning to release their new MMORPG soon and needed to build a localization team—a group that would handle the logistics of getting the game out in multiple languages and countries. Johnson had been working in localization for decades. "I was thinking, 'This is great timing, because I'm about to be laid off anyway,'" he said. "But it was definitely out of the frying pan into the fire."

When Johnson arrived at One Empire Plaza in January 2012, he went around introducing himself to the executives and developers at 38 Studios. They wanted him to start hiring staff and getting the localization pipeline in place for *Copernicus* to launch in the fall. "I started talking to designers, and asking them questions about the size and the state of the game," Johnson said, "and it was pretty clear that they didn't really have a grasp on where the game was at." Then he put together an estimated schedule based on the number of words each of the game's zones would require. "It put them a year over where they were at," Johnson said. Even his most conservative estimate showed that there would be no way for *Copernicus* to come out in 2012.

The following week, Johnson brought the schedule to one of 38's vice presidents, who shut the door and asked him who else had seen it. "After that point, on the Monday of my second week, everything started cascading into lunacy," Johnson said. Word spread among the other vice presidents and executives, who would barge into Johnson's office, wondering about this schedule he had created. "I started getting visits from people to my room saying, 'What's this file, what's this thing, who have you shown it to, show me,'" Johnson said. "I was like, 'Oh crap.' I had just done my due diligence of trying to figure out sizing, scope, estimate time for all this stuff. I felt like I'd uncovered some big secret."

That was when Andy Johnson started to panic. Had he just left one sinking ship for another? He didn't yet know that 38 Studios was running dangerously low on money, but he soon started to feel like the layer of people just below Curt Schilling had grown dysfunctional. As the developers happily worked on the game, receiving great perks and salaries and growing close to their coworkers, the executives above them had been re-creating *Game of Thrones*. Many of those executives were responsible for operations that didn't exist yet, like physical merchandise and external licensing for the imagined Amalur universe, and they often battled over these territories. "There were teams not talking to each other, lots of suspicion," said Johnson. "It was not a cohesive environment. It was very fractured." Vice presidents at 38 Studios would often engage in what Johnson called "empire-building," fighting over the sizes of their teams and the breadth of their territories. And they all wanted to make sure that Curt Schilling saw them succeeding, because making him mad could have consequences. A *Boston* magazine report suggested that the former pitcher could be vindictive, freezing out lieutenants who got on his bad side or told him news he didn't want to hear. "They didn't work well together," Schilling later admitted to the magazine. "I was amazed at the turf-building and protecting that went on."

Then the hiring freeze started, which left Johnson unable to do his job. "Other people who'd been brought on at my level to build support teams said, 'I'm just going to sit in my office and work on spreadsheets and plan out as if something's going to happen,' or 'I'm going to start looking for jobs,' and then they'd just lock themselves in their rooms," Johnson said. Bored, he went to visit the other departments, asking if anyone needed help. He eventually joined the website support team as a senior producer, changing jobs after less than a month at 38 Studios.

At the same time, *Copernicus* was making progress. The developers, who were mostly unaware of the executive politicking, just kept working on the game. The design team had some trouble nailing down the combat system—Schilling would often lament that the game wasn't fun to play—but there was still time to get things right.[5] Some of the ideas they were exploring were revolutionary for online games in 2012. Players could change the outcome of the world based on how well they performed—if one server full of players defeated the evil dragon, their world would enter a celebratory state. Another server might fare worse, failing to beat the dragon and watching it destroy their cities with molten lava. Unlike *World of Warcraft*, the *Copernicus* MMORPG was designed to be finite, with a story that would progress over time and eventually end, leading into expansions and sequels.

But in the years since Schilling had started 38 Studios, the world of MMORPGs had changed. In 2012, fewer players wanted to shell out $10 or $15 a month, and pundits believed that the future of online gaming was free-to-play, a model that eschewed subscriptions in favor of microtransactions—items like weapons and costumes that were sold for small fees. 38 Studios hired some consultants to put together financial models for *Copernicus* as a free-to-play game. It wasn't immediately clear to the developers which route they'd follow, but if they did go free-to-play, that would require them to make big changes to the design and structure of the game. That would take even more time, which would burn through even more cash.

With dysfunction infesting the company's upper levels, money dwindling, and *Copernicus* progressing slowly, 38 Studios might have been close to danger. But at least there was finally a game to release. On February 7, 2012, 38 Studios put out *Kingdoms of*

---

5   Later, one 38 Studios developer would reach out to Kotaku to dispute Schilling's public comments that *Copernicus* wasn't fun to play. "The last playtest of the company, literally two days before this debacle happened, was immensely fun," they wrote. "It was the first time [player vs. player combat] was in the game and many of us did not want to stop playing."

Amalur: Reckoning, the single-player RPG that Big Huge Games had been developing for the past few years. The timing wasn't ideal—Bethesda's revolutionary *The Elder Scrolls V: Skyrim* had come out three months earlier—but *Kingdoms of Amalur: Reckoning* was a solid game with beautiful art direction and excellent combat. A reviewer for the *Guardian*, Mike Anderiesz, wrote: *"Kingdoms of Amalur: Reckoning is a triumph that makes the prospect of a future MMO based on the same world and engine all the more enticing."* It sold well, moving 1.3 million copies and beating EA's projections, although it came in below 38's lofty expectations and didn't immediately recoup its production costs. What that meant was that 38 Studios would get no revenue from the game yet—bad news for a company that was nearly out of money.

In March 2012, unbeknownst to most of the staff, 38 Studios stopped paying many of its external vendors.[6] Jennifer MacLean, the chief executive officer, stepped down. It had been less than a year since they'd moved to Rhode Island, but 38 Studios had already churned through nearly all of the $49 million they'd received. Still, Curt Schilling believed that he could find new investments, and he was in conversations with game publishers to fund a sequel to *Kingdoms of Amalur: Reckoning*. He was also pitching the Chinese megacorporation Tencent and the Korean game publisher Nexon on investing in 38 Studios—deals that Schilling thought might come together soon. They just needed a little more time, even if they had to neglect a few bills while they waited.

▪ ▪ ▪

---

6   The company's coffee supplier, Donald R. Barbeau, later told the *Providence Journal* that he was out over $7,000 thanks to unpaid bills from 38 Studios.

On May 15, 2012, 38 Studios designer Heather Conover was walking to One Empire Plaza when she ran into one of her colleagues from the design department. She greeted him and they started walking together. Then he turned to her and asked if she had been paid. She wasn't sure, she said, but she would check. When they arrived at the office, Conover logged in to her checking account. There was no deposit. "We all sort of had this sinking feeling as it started spreading," Conover said. "'Did you get paid? Did you get paid? No, I didn't. Oh my god, me neither. What does this mean? What's going on?'"

Conover had first started at 38 Studios in the summer of 2010, back when they were in Massachusetts, as an intern on the quality assurance team. She'd loved it so much that as soon as she had the chance, in 2011, she returned to work as a designer at the Rhode Island office. She built zones, quests, puzzles, and creatures, teaming up with other designers and artists on *Copernicus* to try to develop engaging tasks and challenges for players. "It was a really fun mix of creative pursuits," she said. "Content design in and of itself is really multifaceted and requires a bit of generalist skills, which I really appreciated."

One lesson Conover had learned, for example, was that subtlety in an MMORPG was hard to pull off. For one starter zone—an ice village full of elves—she'd designed a quest in which the player would meet a man whose wife was missing. The village wizard, who had become renowned for making beautiful ice sculptures, would try to convince the player that nothing had gone awry, saying the guy's wife must have left because she was unhappy. But if the player pieced together enough hints, they'd figure out what really happened. "It turned out the village wizard was freezing people and turning them into ice so he could have the glory of being this wonderful artist," Conover said. "The concept of trying to lead the player to put together these clues without being super explicit was challenging." In a single-player RPG she might have been able to stick with subtlety, but for an MMORPG, in which you'd be surrounded by other players and often chatting with your buddies while playing, it was important to give straightforward instructions.

These types of design challenges were fuel for Conover, who loved every day she got to spend at 38 Studios—at least until the day her paycheck didn't show up. "That was the kickoff of the shitstorm," Conover said. Suddenly, stories started swirling around the studio. The caterers weren't getting paid. Local journalists were calling people's homes and showing up at the office. One developer's pregnant wife was at a doctor's appointment when she learned that the 38 Studios health insurance plan was no longer active.

Conover and her coworkers wouldn't get the full picture until much later. On May 1, 2012, 38 Studios had failed to make one of its bank loan repayments, putting the loan into default and triggering the ire of Lincoln Chafee, who was now the governor of Rhode Island. Since taking office, Chafee had backtracked a bit on his earlier public criticism of 38 Studios, perhaps recognizing that he was stuck with the deal and had to make peace with it. In 2011, when Schilling and crew moved to Rhode Island, Chafee took a tour of the new offices and said he'd do his best to support the company. But he'd largely stayed silent since then. 38 Studios missing a loan payment was the political bullet Chafee needed to start firing.

On May 14, 2012, Lincoln Chafee told reporters that his goal was "keeping 38 Studios solvent." Those four words echoed across the industry and spooked all of the potential investors that had been talking to Schilling, including Tencent and Nexon. "The conversations ended immediately," Schilling later said on a Boston radio show. "I knew then that we were in a world of hurt." And on

May 15, all 379 of the company's employees in Rhode Island and Maryland learned that they weren't getting paid. "We'd gone over the cliff at that point," said Andy Johnson, "and we were just in free fall waiting to hit the ground."

The next few days were chaos—a blur of angry all-hands meetings and frazzled employees who still hadn't received their paychecks. Management asked them to keep coming in and working, saying that 38 Studios was a family, and that they needed to stick together to get through this. If nobody came to work, they'd get bad press, which could destroy any chance of the company saving itself, the executives said. Reporters with cameras and microphones camped outside the office, approaching employees as they entered and exited. Some developers didn't bother showing up. Others tried to bring home the office equipment. "People were picking up desktops and monitors, saying, 'Screw this, I'm taking this, that's my payment,'" Johnson said. "Security were on overload trying to stop people from taking stuff out of the office."

Curt Schilling, their leader, stayed uncharacteristically quiet as he tried to make a miracle happen, working with his lieutenants and lawyers to try to salvage the company. He'd put up his prized collection of gold coins as collateral for a different bank loan, but that wasn't nearly enough. One elaborate plan involved getting tax credits from Rhode Island and then leveraging them for investments, but Chafee held up that deal. The governor, who saw this debacle as a political opportunity, was now attacking 38 Studios every other day in the press, even calling Kingdoms of Amalur: Reckoning an "abject failure," which was, by any metric, false. (For a brand-new franchise, it had actually performed pretty well.)

Soon, Chafee was publicly revealing what 38 Studios saw as proprietary information, like Copernicus's projected release date (by now, June 2013), and regularly attacking the company's freewheeling spending. It turned out he had grander ambitions—he'd try to run for president as a Democrat in 2016 and then again as a Libertarian in 2020—and going after 38 Studios seemed like an easy political win. In a scathing newspaper editorial a few years later, Schilling pinned the blame for his studio's failure on Chafee's behavior. "Mr. Chafee is a liar and a phony," Schilling wrote. "He was unqualified to be governor. He lacked the skills to insert himself into and influence a business deal that was way over his subpar ability to understand. What he did, and did not do, for the people of Rhode Island, and especially for the employees of 38 Studios, is something I will not let people forget."

Through the end of May, many 38 Studios staff kept going to work, even though the paychecks never came. A few people put together a two-minute trailer zooming through *Copernicus*'s gorgeous environments and released it on YouTube, partly as a last-ditch effort to try to convince some video game publisher to snap them up, but also to ensure that even if the game never came out, their work would still be seen by the world.

But by now, the earth had been scorched. New reports were coming out every day about the turbulence at 38 Studios. Big video game publishers, always risk-averse, wouldn't dare jump into business with a company that had been getting this much bad press. Yet some of 38 Studios' employees still believed Curt Schilling would find a way to keep the company afloat. "I kept thinking, 'They're going to pull a rabbit out of their hat,'" said Thom Ang. "'They're going to work something out.'"

After all, belief in Schilling was what had gotten them this far. He was still their captain, their leader, the guy who had won the pennant in bloody socks. "I love that man for what he did in that company," Ang said. But Schilling's last-ditch efforts hadn't worked, and negotiations with Chafee and the state of Rhode Island were going nowhere. "I remember we had a mandatory all-hands meeting," said Jennifer Mills. "A couple of the highest-ups and Curt came walking in, and Curt just sat down in front of everyone and just put his head in his hands. I think everyone's hearts dropped when they saw that, because we knew how much he wanted this to work."

On May 24, 2012, an email went out to everyone who worked for 38 Studios. Written by Bill Thomas, the kindly chief operating officer and Curt Schilling's wife's uncle, the email was bizarrely cold:

> The Company is experiencing an economic downturn. To avoid further losses and possibility of retrenchment, the Company has decided that a company-wide lay off is absolutely necessary. These layoffs are non-voluntary and non-disciplinary. This is your official notice of lay off, effective today, Thursday, May 24th, 2012.

There was no severance. Employees would not be paid the money they were owed from their final paychecks. Their health care was gone. Bankruptcy filings later showed that 38 Studios was $150 million in debt, with millions owed to loans, vendors, and insurers, not to mention all of the employees.

In the coming days, Curt Schilling would say in interviews that he had put $50 million of his own money into the company and was now "tapped out." He told reporters and radio interviewers a few times that he hadn't taken a penny from the company, but that wasn't entirely true. Although Schilling did not receive a salary, bankruptcy filings later revealed that he had spent close to $40,000 of company funds on travel since June 2011 and that he was on the company's health-care plan, amounting to nearly $1,500 a month. C-suite executives at 38 Studios also did well for themselves, including Bill Thomas, who received $421,678 in total compensation from

38 Studios in its final year of operations, according to the filings. That sum included a $129,857 payment for relocation, over $50,000 in travel expenses, and a consulting fee of over $10,000 for Thomas's work shutting down the studio—even as the rest of the 38 Studios employees hadn't been paid. Schilling had liked to talk about his employees as family, but at the end of things, it was his real family that benefited the most.[7]

Staff at 38 Studios had known that Schilling liked to spend extravagantly. What they wouldn't realize until later was that many of his executives were getting huge salaries, and that the company was spending more money than it actually had. Until May 14, there had been few indications that 38 Studios was struggling. When *Kingdoms of Amalur: Reckoning* launched in February, everyone on staff had received an expensive statue of one of the game's hulking trolls.

The developers had believed they were thriving and that the Rhode Island loan guarantee would at least let them finish and release *Copernicus*. They'd believed in Schilling's promise of complete transparency—a promise on which they'd all thought he had been delivering. "The employees got blindsided," Schilling later said in a radio interview. "One of the many mistakes that was made, or that I made, or that we made as a leadership team, was that this came out of nowhere for them."

Later, when lawsuits were filed and pundits tried to figure out who was to blame for the 38 Studios catastrophe, fingers pointed in all directions. Schilling and many of his former developers pinned the blame squarely on Lincoln Chafee. Some members of the executive layer accused Schilling of ineptitude, saying that he knew

---

7   Heather Conover said she now sees the word "family" as a red flag. "Curt would often talk about us like a family," she said. "That actually is a little bit triggering for me now. Anytime anyone at a studio talks about us being a family, I'm just like: No; that's not reality; that's not true."

they had failed to pay their bills but did nothing to cut costs, inform employees, or wrangle the situation under control. It was like he was a baseball manager watching a struggling pitcher throw hit after hit—everyone knew a change needed to be made, but Schilling refused to put someone new on the mound.

Thom Ang was still reeling when he got a letter from MoveTrek Mobility, the company that 38 Studios had hired to sell his old lake house in Massachusetts. Turns out it hadn't sold. And somewhere in the fine print of his contract, Ang had agreed that if 38 Studios ever faced financial trouble and stopped paying the mortgage, the obligation would fall back to him. He was now once again the owner of a Massachusetts house he thought had been sold a year ago. Panicked, Ang called up MoveTrek Mobility and asked what was going on. "They said, 'It means you have to pay the bank on the loan,'" Ang said.

Now, Ang didn't have a job or a paycheck, but he did owe rent in Rhode Island and a mortgage in Massachusetts. And he was one of the lucky ones—his home had regained some value. Six other 38 Studios employees were also stuck with Massachusetts houses that hadn't been sold, and some of their mortgages were tens of thousands of dollars more than the values of their homes. Two former 38 Studios employees each faced a net loss of over a hundred thousand dollars, according to company bankruptcy documents.

It also turned out that 38 Studios still owed money to the moving company it used to relocate employees. Andy Johnson, who had shipped his family from Arizona to Rhode Island just five months earlier, received a bill for $10,000 from the movers. "I was in panic mode," he said. Johnson was unemployed, his family was stuck in a city they barely knew, and he couldn't even afford the rent. "I had to dip into all of my retirement to cover us because it was six months that I was out of work," Johnson said. "On my fortieth birthday, a particularly proud moment—and when I say proud, I mean low—of my life, my mom in England was paying our rent." (He never wound up paying the moving bill.)

Curt Schilling's gamble had failed. His belief that he could just keep pitching through the injuries—that with sheer persistence and willpower, things would be okay—hadn't come to fruition. And hundreds of people's lives were torn apart as a result.

■ ■ ■

In the weeks following the 38 Studios shutdown, the video game industry came together to try to help out the displaced employees. Recruiters promoted social media hashtags like #38jobs and flew out to Providence for a job fair. Rhode Island sent representatives to One Empire Plaza so that people could file for unemployment at the office, while some 38 staffers brought in canned food to help struggling coworkers. Everyone got together to drink and lament the way it had all ended. For some of the developers, even those who had worked in the video game industry for years, 38 Studios had been one of the best experiences of their lives.

Heather Conover, who had found out they weren't getting paid on her walk to work, wound up talking to a company called Carbine at the job fair and falling in love with their online game, *WildStar*. After a moment of trepidation about leaving New England, where she'd lived her whole life, she accepted the job and moved out to Southern California. It wasn't too hard a sell, Conover recalled. "They said, 'Heather, it's going to be sunny literally every day.'" She spent four years at Carbine, using and honing the MMORPG design lessons she'd learned at 38 Studios, before losing her job in another layoff. Then she relocated to Seattle, Washington, for a job at ArenaNet helping design the online game *Guild Wars 2*. Seattle was a hub for the video game industry, the home of massive companies like Microsoft and Nintendo, which was one of the reasons she took the job—if things didn't work out at ArenaNet, there were other options. For Conover, being in the game industry has meant sacrificing her life's goals. "One of my dreams is owning a house, and it just doesn't really totally make sense working in games," Conover said. "When everything happened with 38 Studios, it was like a rude awakening—'Oh, well, you should never feel secure enough to own a house.'"

Pete Paquette, the animator who had started a year before the shutdown, found a new job just a few miles north of Providence—at a company called Irrational Games. Two years later, he was in the same position. "At first I was in shock, because I was like, 'Oh crap, here we go again,'" Paquette said. "'I can't seem to keep a job longer than two years.'" He wound up going freelance, doing remote animation work for companies like Riot and Blizzard. "I could look back on both situations and have a sour grapes attitude," Paquette said, "but working for those two companies has opened up a massive amount of opportunity for me that by itself is worth its weight in gold."

Jennifer Mills, the lead environment texture artist, had braced herself for potential layoffs before she'd even started. "I was always of the mentality that I'll probably end up being kinda nomadic the first part of my career," Mills said. "I remember saying to myself, 'Okay, I'll probably get laid off at some point.' But I didn't expect it at my first job. I didn't expect something of this scale to occur at my very first studio." In the years after 38 Studios, she moved back to Boston (where she was laid off), then to Texas (where she was laid off), and then to Seattle for a dream job—art director at Wizards of the Coast, the company behind *Dungeons & Dragons*, which was making big investments in video games. Mills loved her new job, but the trauma lingered. "Even at this amazing company, within days, I still started to feel, 'Oh my god, when's the other shoe going to drop?'" Mills said. "I just felt this looming doom." It helped to talk it through with her coworkers, many of whom had been through similar career roller coasters. Just about everyone who worked in video games had a story like hers.

That was the common thread: volatility. While the 38 Studios shutdown was wild and unusual—no other video game studio in history has received a $75 million loan guarantee from a US state— it had the same results as any other big layoff. Hundreds of people were left stranded in Rhode Island, where there were no other video game companies or jobs. Those who wanted to stay in the video game industry had to again uproot their lives and move to new cities.

Today, former employees of 38 Studios speak fondly of their time there, lauding both the team and the game. Many say they still keep in touch with their old coworkers and speak fondly about what could have been—if only they'd gotten more time; if only Lincoln Chafee hadn't made those awful comments; if only Curt Schilling hadn't burned through so much money.

Opinions are mixed on Schilling himself. Some still speak wistfully about their former captain, while others blame his arrogance for everything that happened. Maybe *Copernicus* wouldn't have been the *World of Warcraft* killer that Schilling imagined it would be. Maybe it wouldn't have been a megafranchise generating billions of dollars off merchandise and TV deals. Maybe today it'd be in the bargain bin—yet another game that tried to make money off Richard Bartle's vision for a virtual world. What's heartbreaking for the team, even years later, is that they didn't even get a chance to try.

After the demise of 38 Studios, Curt Schilling turned into something of an internet troll, advocating for Donald Trump and sharing conservative memes on Facebook and Twitter, where he spent a great deal of time attacking liberal politicians, progressive causes like Black Lives Matter, and just about every news organization that wasn't named Fox. In 2015, he was suspended from his job as an ESPN analyst for posting images comparing extremist Muslims to Nazis. A year later, ESPN fired him for sharing transphobic memes on social media. Later, he hosted a radio show for Breitbart and said he was thinking about running for Congress.[8]

Many former 38 Studios developers today find Schilling's behavior appalling, although they said he had never spoken or acted like that in the office. The Curt Schilling who led 38 Studios was many things, but by all accounts he was gentle and kind to his employees. Years later, some who worked with him describe him as a great leader—someone who fundamentally cared about his staff and their families—even if his financial gambits failed. It's tough for many to reconcile their firsthand experiences of Curt Schilling in 2008 with the Curt Schilling of 2015 and beyond. Then again, as one former 38 Studios employee acknowledged, maybe they didn't really know him.

There's no doubt that the events of 38 Studios had an outsize impact on the legendary baseball player. At the same time that he was attacking Democrats and sharing nasty memes, Schilling was giving depositions and watching a bankruptcy auction sell off his company's assets. In 2016, following a complicated web of lawsuits, the US Securities and Exchange Commission charged the Rhode Island Economic Development Corporation and the Wells Fargo Bank with defrauding investors by failing to disclose that 38 Studios

---

8   On August 13, 2019, Donald Trump tweeted: "Curt Schilling, a great pitcher and patriot, is considering a run for Congress in Arizona. Terrific!" Schilling did not run for Congress in Arizona, although he did continue promoting Trump.

didn't actually receive the entire loan it needed. Said the complaint: "We allege that the RIEDC and Wells Fargo knew that 38 Studios needed an additional $25 million to fund the project yet failed to pass that material information along to bond investors, who were denied a complete financial picture."

The 38 Studios debacle became a national news story for months following the shutdown, bringing attention to Rhode Island and its risky deal with a superstar athlete. Four hundred miles southwest, however, dozens of people were also victims of Curt Schilling's catastrophe. Their story didn't get nearly as much attention, which was tragic and a little ironic. After all, they were the ones who had actually finished a game.

CHAPTER 7

BIG HUGE PROBLEMS

Tuesday, May 15, 2012, was *Diablo* day at Big Huge Games. The people in charge of the Maryland video game studio, recognizing that the launch of the long-anticipated *Diablo III* might take a bite out of productivity, told employees to come in and play at work. It'd be, uh, *competitive research.*

Really, this was a good month to relax. Big Huge Games had just released a new game, *Kingdoms of Amalur: Reckoning,* followed by two expansions, and the studio's leadership team was close to signing a deal to develop a sequel. "We decided to take a *Diablo* research day," said Ian Frazier, a lead designer at the studio. "Go play *Diablo III* all day. It's going to be fun." But *Diablo III* was on few people's minds as they filed into work and the questions started. *Have you been paid yet? No, have you?*

There had already been a few rumors of financial turmoil at their parent company, 38 Studios. The night before, Rhode Island governor Lincoln Chafee had made those notorious comments about how he was working to keep 38 Studios solvent, and some Big Huge Games staff were hearing whispers of catastrophe. Joe

Quadara, who ran the combat team at Big Huge Games, had heard on Monday night that the company no longer had enough money to pay its staff. Tuesday was payday, and if the rumors were true, that was when they'd find out for sure. "I woke up and first thing I do is check my direct deposit," Quadara said. "I don't see anything there. I'm like, 'Oh shit, here we go.'"

Justin Perez, one of the combat designers, had taken the day off. He and three coworkers had decided weeks earlier that they'd get together and play *Diablo III* all day, lugging their desktops to one guy's house so they could all be in the same room. Even when they found out that they could just come in and play *Diablo* at the office, Perez and crew had stuck to their original plans. They were going to spend the entire day thinking about nothing but Blizzard Entertainment's new game, tuning out the rest of the world as they click-click-clicked their way through goatmen and demons. It'd be like an old-school LAN party.

At least that was the plan until their phones started ringing. "Some of our friends at the office called," Perez said. "They said, 'Hey, maybe you guys want to come in.' So we went in." What they found was an office in confused panic. *Kingdoms of Amalur: Reckoning* had sold well, and the team had been brainstorming all sorts of ideas for building on that momentum with a sequel. Most of them had no clue that Big Huge Games or 38 Studios might be in financial trouble. After all, Curt Schilling had just received a $75 million loan guarantee from the state of Rhode Island. How could the company miss payroll? "I remember it being a shock," Perez said. "But also, this was the first time I'd ever been through anything like this, so I had no sense of whether it was normal. Does this just happen sometimes? Or is this a big deal?"

That afternoon, the staff of Big Huge Games got on a video

conference call with the executives at 38 in Rhode Island, who asked them to be patient. "The messaging was very much, 'Oh, we hit a snag, but we're figuring it out; don't worry about it,'" said Perez. "'We'll figure it out tomorrow, or this week. But we're working on it, so don't be too concerned.'" Over the next few days, that was the continued promise. *Don't worry about it. We'll figure it out.* Every day for the next week and a half, Big Huge Games employees checked their bank accounts for a direct deposit. It was never there. On May 24, they were all officially laid off.

In the hours after it went live, *Diablo III* was plagued by server crashes and glitches that came coupled with a vague, frustrating message: "Error 37." It sucked. But what the staff of Big Huge Games really had to worry about, they would soon realize, were the errors of 38.

■ ■ ■

Funnily enough, Ian Frazier's video game career had started with *Diablo*. He'd grown up reading choose-your-own-adventure books and daydreaming about designing his own games, encouraged by his dad, who had majored in engineering, to explore game development as a career. In 2003 he graduated from college with a degree in computer graphics technology, then began applying for jobs at big video game studios. Nobody bit. The only companies even willing to give him an interview were those hiring for QA testing positions, which would pay minimum wage—not nearly enough to justify moving to a big city like Los Angeles or Seattle.

Frazier wound up taking a logistics job at a Walmart distribution center out in the Smoky Mountains of Tennessee, where he built up his savings while continuing to apply to video game companies. Eventually he discovered Iron Lore Entertainment, a new studio near Boston that was looking to make its own version of *Diablo*. The most recent entry in the series, *Diablo II*, had come out in 2000, and few games were as addictive or as globally appealing. Playing as a sorceress, paladin, or one of a handful of other fantasy characters, you'd blast your way through hordes of monsters and demons, chasing top-tier equipment along the way. The trick to *Diablo*'s success lay in random numbers—the maps, weapons, and armor were all generated procedurally by computer algorithms, ensuring that every new game felt slightly different to play.

Now, studios like Iron Lore were trying to emulate *Diablo II*'s success, which Frazier thought could be his big break into the video game industry. "I thought, 'Hey, these guys are a brand-new studio; maybe they don't know what they're doing,'" said Frazier. "'Unlike all these established studios that are shutting me down, maybe they'll accept my résumé. Because they don't know any better.'"

Frazier applied for an entry-level designer position at Iron Lore. No response. So he looked up the studio's website and found that they'd made a critical error—along with their staff names and bios, they listed their office's phone number. He called them up, found the general manager's voice-mail box, and left a message. "'Hi,'" he recalled saying. "'My name's Ian Frazier. I'm sure you've already rejected my application because I'm a rookie and nobody wants to hire rookies, but I've made this awesome mod....'" He went on to explain that for the past four years he'd been working on a project called *Lazarus*, a complete remake of Richard Garriott's 1988 fantasy role-playing game *Ultima V*. In 2000, when Frazier was starting college, *Ultima V* was looking and feeling dated, with rudimentary graphics and actions that mostly unfolded through scrolling text on your screen ("Giant Spider missed!"). Frazier had loved the game as a kid, and he figured it'd be fun, and probably good for his career, to spend his spare time working on a remake.

By 2004, when Frazier applied to Iron Lore, he had recruited a small team of fellow *Ultima* fans who were all collaborating on *Lazarus*. It was ambitious, with 3-D graphics and gameplay that felt more modern and accessible than the original *Ultima V*. The *Lazarus* project impressed the leads at Iron Lore, who flew Frazier out to Massachusetts to interview and take a design test. "They sit you in a room with their proprietary level editor," he said, "and they say, 'Okay, make us a level, make it awesome, and let us know when you're done.'" Frazier hammered at this level for a few hours, then started to panic. Nothing he was putting together seemed to be working. This was his shot to get into the video game industry—maybe the only one he'd get—and he was blowing it. "I almost got up, took my bag, and just walked out of the building without saying anything," Frazier said. Instead, he wiped it all and started a new level from scratch. By 10:00 or 11:00 p.m., as the final straggler in Iron Lore's office walked up to Frazier and said it was time to lock up and get out of there, Frazier had finally made something he felt comfortable showing. It was good enough to get him the job.

Ian Frazier moved from Tennessee to Massachusetts in February 2005, helping develop and release Iron Lore's *Titan Quest*, which took the basic hack-and-slash gameplay of *Diablo* and spruced it up with monsters and settings from Greek and Egyptian mythology. The game sold well, as did its two expansions, but by 2007 the studio was struggling to find a publisher for a *Titan Quest* sequel and burning money quickly, with forty mouths to feed. In a last-ditch effort to save the company, Iron Lore's management started hunting for work-for-hire jobs, and Frazier put together a pitch to make an expansion to *Dawn of War*, a popular real-time strategy series based on the *Warhammer* tabletop games. They won the contract, and Frazier became lead designer on what became known as *Dawn of War: Soulstorm*. But a year later, when *Soulstorm* was finished, they were in the same tough position: unable to find a new deal and running out of money fast.

One day in early 2008, Iron Lore president Jeff Goodsill called the whole company into a room and said that they were going to run out of funds soon. It didn't look like they could pull any rabbits out of their hats this time, he said, so they were going to start winding down the studio. "Rather than run us up to the very last day of money and then have us be screwed, he wanted to give us all at least a tiny bit of severance," Frazier said.

Then, Goodsill pulled Frazier aside and told him he'd be getting one last pay bump. Frazier had been paid far below average for his title, lead designer, because Iron Lore couldn't afford to pay him what a lead would typically make. "He gave me a significant raise in my final paycheck, just so when I went to the next company I could say, 'Look, this is what I was making before,'" said Frazier. "It's the sort of thing people don't tend to think about. It was really kind."

When Iron Lore's shutdown was public, the recruiters came calling, and soon Frazier was moving to Baltimore, Maryland, for a job as a designer at Big Huge Games, a cheekily named studio with ambitious goals. Founded in 2000 by four former Firaxis employees who had worked under Sid Meier, the legendary designer of *Civilization*, Big Huge Games was known for a series of popular strategy games called *Rise of Nations*. In the *Rise of Nations* games, you'd battle opponents over control of territory using armies that evolved through different eras of technology. Each player would pick a civilization (from England and France to Inca and Maya) and compete against all the others. *Rise of Nations* was never quite as popular as its biggest rival, *Age of Empires*, but it held its own, allowing Big Huge Games to thrive and even expand over the years.

After seven years of strategy games, the leadership of Big Huge Games decided to pivot. In February 2007, they made a splashy hire: Ken Rolston, the lead designer of the groundbreaking RPGs *The Elder Scrolls III: Morrowind* and *The Elder Scrolls IV: Oblivion*. At Big Huge Games, Rolston was put in charge of designing a new open-world RPG—the studio's attempt to branch out of the strategy genre. By May they had announced a publishing deal with THQ, and soon the two companies were discussing taking their relationship to the next level. THQ, which generated huge profits by cranking out licensed games with companies like Nickelodeon and World Wrestling Entertainment, had been gobbling up other game studios like Pac-Man pellets. In January 2008, the deal was finalized and announced: THQ had purchased Big Huge Games.

Frazier joined Big Huge Games a few weeks after this acquisition, signing on to be the lead systems designer on Rolston's new RPG, which was code-named *Crucible*. "A lot of it was super exciting," he said. They hoped to mix the combat of the popular action game *God of War* with the scope and exploration of *The Elder Scrolls* games, which took place in massive fantasy worlds full of people to meet and cities to explore. "There's a lot to love in that fusion," Frazier said.

But the staff of Big Huge Games had spent the past decade making strategy games, not RPGs. As Visceral and many other studios would come to learn, pivoting to a brand-new genre could be a hefty challenge. It took the developers at Big Huge Games a long time to envision what *Crucible* was and how they would make it. "You can spend months or years trying to figure out what the game is," said Frazier. "You're building up the technological infrastructure to be able to figure it out. On *Crucible* there was a lot of trying to figure it out while building the technical underpinnings, and that can be stressful."

The nice thing about being owned by a big publisher like THQ was that they didn't have to worry about running out of cash. They were stable. Whereas Iron Lore had to seek out a new source of funding every time it finished a project, leaving its staff in a constant state of uncertainty, Big Huge Games was now part of a big, publicly traded company. Throughout 2008, as the development team struggled to define *Crucible*'s vision, THQ executives assured the team leads that they had plenty of time. "The message we kept getting was, 'You have effectively infinite money, keep figuring it out,'" said Frazier. "I've learned now: don't ever believe that phrase 'We have infinite money.' At the time, it seemed believable."

It didn't take long for it to become clear that, actually, THQ's money was very, very finite.

■ ■ ■

Joe Quadara had always been a competitive person. Growing up with six younger siblings, he spent a lot of days battling over who got to play the Nintendo. Throughout the 1980s he was part of the San Francisco arcade scene, hunting for quarters under machines and competing with strangers over fighting games like *Street Fighter.* Over time, he befriended some of the other arcade junkies, including a group of guys who would show up at one of his favorite haunts, Sunnyvale Golfland, every Wednesday night. Word started floating around that these weren't just arcade players—they were actual game developers, from companies like Sony and Crystal Dynamics—and eventually Quadara asked one of them how they got into the video game industry. "He said, 'Oh, we all got in through testing,'" Quadara said. Testing meant hammering away at a video game in order to find all the bugs and glitches, which was something Quadara already did for fun at the arcade, hunting for every possible competitive edge. The developer looked at him. "'You know, come to think of it, you'd be pretty good too.'"

A few interviews later, Quadara was working at Crystal Dynamics as a tester, helping track down bugs in games like *Soul Reaver 2* and *Anachronox* (developed by Crystal Dynamics' sister studio, Ion Storm Dallas—the twin of Warren Spector's Ion Storm Austin). Not long after Quadara started, he saw other developers playing the team shooter *Counter-Strike* at lunch. He had never played *Counter-Strike* before, but his competitive instincts started flaring. "I just jumped right in and got my ass handed to me," he said. "I went home and built a PC just for playing *Counter-Strike* and practiced and practiced until I was the best at the studio." In the coming years, Quadara learned from many of the veterans at Crystal Dynamics, including Zak McClendon (who would later work at 2K Marin on *BioShock 2*, *Richmond*, and *XCOM*). Quadara moved from QA into production and then to design, where he found that he had a knack for making video game combat feel satisfying.

In the fall of 2008, after six years at Crystal Dynamics (broken up by a short stint in Sony QA), Quadara decided to move to Baltimore, Maryland, and join Big Huge Games to be the lead combat designer on their RPG, *Crucible*. "When I got there, I thought I'd been hoodwinked a little bit," he said. "They had shown me a video of the gameplay, and it looked pretty good. When I got there, the character couldn't even move straight." The animations looked janky, buttons wouldn't always work, and the gameplay just felt off to Quadara in a lot of ways. It became clear that they'd need to overhaul their processes if they were going to make *Crucible* work—something Quadara began trying to do, building a team of artists and designers that would be devoted entirely to combat.

At the same time, Quadara realized that THQ was in trouble. Thanks to a number of factors—the global recession of 2008, the decreasing popularity of those Nickelodeon- and WWE-licensed games, and some ill-advised directional pivots including a big bet on gaming tablets—the massive publisher was losing millions of dollars. The words "infinite money" were no longer part of the directive. By November, THQ had shut down five of its game development studios and was telling employees to cut costs. "They had a company-wide blast, and the message we got was that we were tightening our belts," said Ian Frazier. "Don't get the fancy toilet paper, don't take first-class seats, miscellaneous things. It was pretty clear, when we got that message, that we were not in a good place." THQ also canceled a second project that Big Huge Games was trying to get off the ground, a Wii simulation game called *God: The Game*, forcing all of those people to move to *Crucible*.

In March 2009, word came from above that THQ was no longer interested in keeping Big Huge Games around. THQ gave the studio an ultimatum: find a new owner within the next sixty days. If nobody wanted to buy Big Huge Games, THQ would shut it down. The gesture was nice—usually, a big publisher would just shutter studios with no warning—but now they were racing against a ticking clock.

Big Huge Games' leadership team gathered the staff, telling them what THQ had said and warning them all to start polishing their résumés just in case. The timeline was tight, but the executives had faith that they could find a buyer. "We had this half-built RPG, which are hard to build, and the technology was actually quite impressive," said Frazier. "We thought: 'Someone's gonna want this. And the studio alongside it. And the people alongside it.'"

Over the next few weeks, Frazier, Quadara, and the rest of Big Huge Games felt like they were on some surreal version of *American Idol* as different publishers toured the studio. Half a dozen companies sent groups of executives to check out *Crucible* and talk to the developers who worked there. "It was almost like we were performing or being interviewed by all these different groups," said Justin Perez, the designer. For Perez, a big sports fan, it was particularly bizarre when a legendary baseball player showed up at the office. "I remember when Curt Schilling announced he was making a game studio, and the reaction was very much, 'Oh, that's weird,'" Perez said. "We didn't really think about it at all. Then that group showed up and it all seemed to click well together."

It was the perfect fit. Big Huge Games had a role-playing game that needed a more coherent vision, while 38 Studios was oozing with lore and story crafted by the prolific fantasy author R. A. Salvatore, but desperately needed to release a game and start generating revenue. "They were immediately enamored of the idea of taking *Crucible* and rebranding it with the narrative and art direction of the world of Amalur," said Frazier. "We'd come to market first. We'd say, 'Hey everybody, welcome to Amalur; isn't this universe cool; isn't this art direction cool?' And after folks get a taste of it, they'd go to an even bigger experience in the MMO."[1]

---

1   For Ian Frazier, this was a fun and strange coincidence—38 Studios was located in the same Maynard, Massachusetts, plaza as his last job, Iron Lore Entertainment. "The biggest threat to us at Iron Lore from a recruiting standpoint was that once 38 started, they were poaching our artists because all the artists wanted to go work with Todd McFarlane," Frazier said. Now, he had come full circle.

Over the next few weeks, Frazier and the *Crucible* team put together a demo using 38's art assets and ideas to show that they could make their RPG look and feel like what Schilling expected. The deal came down to the wire, and there were layoffs during the process—the *Crucible* team had gotten too big with the absorption of people from *God: The Game*—but eventually pen was put to paper. On May 27, 2009, 38 Studios announced that it had purchased Big Huge Games.

From there, the two companies got to know each other. R. A. Salvatore came down to Baltimore to show his nine-hundred-page lore bible to the staff of Big Huge Games and to talk through the narrative for *Crucible*, which would soon become known as *Kingdoms of Amalur: Reckoning*. They decided to set the game thousands of years before the events of 38's own game, *Copernicus*, so that Big Huge Games would have the freedom to make their own story decisions without having to worry about which events had happened and which characters were killed. By the end of the year, they'd secured a deal with Electronic Arts to fund and publish the game.

At first, 38 Studios seemed like a good parent company. It was privately owned by Schilling and completely independent, which meant it didn't have to fret over investors and fiscal quarters. Yet when the veterans of Big Huge Games saw the state of *Copernicus*, it was hard not to be wary. "There were a lot of good people, but their eyes were bigger than their stomachs," Frazier said. "They were trying to be a *World of Warcraft* killer, which didn't go well for pretty much anybody that tried to be a *World of Warcraft* killer. And the upper leadership of the company for the most part didn't have games experience."

Over the next few months, that lack of experience began translating into problems for Big Huge Games. The biggest problem was one with which the developers at 38 had grown very familiar—meddling from Curt Schilling and other executives. The former pitcher would frequently contact programmers and designers at Big Huge Games with suggestions, much to the chagrin of the studio's leadership. Unhappy with the animation work that Big Huge Games had been producing, one of Schilling's lieutenants tried to replace much of the animation team, which led to some heated disputes. The animations in *Kingdoms of Amalur: Reckoning* weren't quite as sleek as the ones in *Copernicus*, but *Reckoning* actually had deadlines and a publishing deal, while *Copernicus* had a seemingly unlimited budget and a never-ending timeline—another point of contention between the two studios.

The animators wound up staying at the company, but so did the tensions. The developers in Maryland would scoff at their parent company in Massachusetts: Here they were, working their butts off to try to get *Kingdoms of Amalur: Reckoning* out the door in the next two years, while 38 Studios had spent years failing to produce a *World of Warcraft* killer that some suspected might never actually ship. Meanwhile, Schilling seemed to have nothing better to do than email Big Huge Games staff with ideas and suggestions, some of which directly contradicted what the directors of *Kingdoms of Amalur: Reckoning* were telling them.

One weekend during the summer of 2010, Joe Quadara arrived at the office and found the cofounders of Big Huge Games packing up their things. They wouldn't tell anyone what was happening—it turned out they were under heavily restrictive NDAs that prevented them from explaining. What Quadara would learn later was that the cofounders had gone to the leadership team of 38 Studios, sick of the meddling, and asked if they could spin off Big Huge Games as an independent entity. Rumor was, they had threatened to quit if that didn't happen. In response, 38 Studios had fired them. "[The founders] offered to take it back independent," said Ian Frazier. "38 Studios said, '(a) No; and (b) We're done with you.'"[2]

It was a debacle for Big Huge Games. The company was still under contract with EA to make *Kingdoms of Amalur: Reckoning* but no longer had a leadership team. Over the next few months, they hired a new studio manager—a former THQ creative director named Sean Dunn—and they did the only thing they could do: kept working on the game. "We had such a strong culture," said Quadara. "We were able to actually continue sans the founders. And it wasn't that the founders were obsolete or unneeded, it was that they had infused us with a style of working together that continued after they left."

Schilling's meddling grew less frequent after the cofounders departed, but the fractures in the two companies' relationship never healed. As they continued to work on *Kingdoms of Amalur: Reckoning*, some of the developers in Maryland kept wondering: What was 38 Studios going to do when it ran out of money? "I always saw 38 as having questionable odds of success from a business standpoint," said Frazier, who began asking himself a question that would prove to be prescient. "Do we really want to be attached to this entity that might burst into flames at any point?"

▪ ▪ ▪

Most of the rooms in the Baltimore headquarters of Big Huge Games were traditional offices, meant for one or two people. In one corner of the floor, however, the studio had knocked down some walls and created two bigger rooms, each capable of fitting eight to ten developers. One of these big offices belonged to the world

2   The four founders of Big Huge Games all either declined to comment or didn't respond to requests for comment.

design team of *Kingdoms of Amalur: Reckoning*, dedicated to quests and levels. In the other, a small group of designers and artists was focused on one thing and one thing alone: making combat feel as good as possible. They called themselves the combat pit.

This combat pit, led by Joe Quadara, had an unusual makeup. A lot of video game studios had designers who worked primarily on battling systems, but in 2009, few companies had specialty teams made up of both designers and animators, with an intimate enough relationship that they could give each other feedback from their desks. "Our entire workflow was working on little things and then just yelling out to the room, 'Hey, come look at this,'" said Justin Perez, who was part of the combat team. "So we could do things really fast."

The sole goal of the combat pit was to make the process of attacking enemies in *Kingdoms of Amalur: Reckoning* feel tactile and satisfying, whether you were slashing a sword, firing a bow, or using one of the game's more unusual weapons, like the chakrams, a set of razor disks that your character could swing around their body and hurl at enemies. A good combat system was all about what Perez called the three Cs: "How the character moves, how responsive the controls are, and what the camera is doing." All of those mechanics would directly translate to how fun it felt to hack into enemy monsters. Tiny details, like a slight camera shake or a subtle graphical flourish, could have a massive impact on the success of a combat system, which is why it was so useful for the combat pit to be constantly talking and tweaking their work.

Over time, the designers and animators in the combat pit grew close. Like Joe Quadara, they were all competitive-minded people, and they liked to play silly games against one another. Soon, those games turned into an office tournament. "I don't remember how it started," said Perez. "It'd be like Connect 4, or throwing a ball into a bucket. Someone would be doing some stupid thing and then we'd all start to get really competitive: 'Oh, I can do that better.'" The games ranged from silly to serious, from throwing balls into a trash can to heated matches of *Street Fighter*, like Quadara had played as a kid back at those San Francisco arcades.

Soon they'd come up with a scoring system and even bought trophies that would float around the combat pit based on how they'd all performed. "If you won, you got to hold the trophy for a week," said Perez. "If you were last place, you had to have a picture on your desk of the winner holding a trophy.... The group was so close because we did stupid stuff like that." Sometimes it felt like they were part of a frat house—Quadara had to institute a "safety veto" after one designer got a little too creative with a game proposal involving belly-flopping on a giant rubber exercise ball and almost propelled directly into a wall—but the team chemistry helped make *Kingdoms of Amalur* better. Every week, members of the combat pit would sit around a big screen and play a new build of the game with whatever each of them had been working on— a new fireball spell, a heavy sword swing, a special ability—and then they'd discuss it. "Everyone else in the room woud just rip it to shreds, nitpick every little thing," said Perez. "No one took that personally. It was all like, 'Yep, right, let's fix all those things, and the next one will be better.'"

Ensuring that criticism remains constructive can be a tricky needle to thread, but the Big Huge Games combat team made it work. This was a room full of people who liked and trusted one another— the type of department where they'd pass around a trophy based on who could be the best at trash-can basketball. One animator who worked on the team told me it was the best job he'd had in his life. "We were constantly surprising ourselves with just how much fun it was to build this game," said Joe Quadara. "Every month it got more and more fun as we got better at what we were doing."

Development of *Kingdoms of Amalur* had plenty of problems, though. The relationship between Big Huge Games and 38 Studios remained shaky even after the founders left, and Curt Schilling still seemed unable to help himself when it came to meddling with designers. "Curt emailed me at like 2:00 a.m. about something he had seen in a new *God of War* trailer or something," said Quadara. "He said, 'Hey, can we get this?'" Quadara spent a few hours carefully composing an email that tried to tell Schilling, in a gentle way, to back off. Schilling didn't write back, which made Quadara anxious. Was he pissed? Was Quadara going to be fired for pushing back?

A few months later, in March 2011, Quadara was in Boston for the PAX East convention, at which they'd demo *Kingdoms of Amalur: Reckoning* to a room full of excited fans. Schilling got up to introduce the game's leads, including Quadara. "He brought up that email: 'This is a guy who very diplomatically tells me to shut the fuck up, and I trust him, so here's Joe,'" recalled Quadara. "That was the first time we had interacted since that email, and it made me feel really good. I said, 'Okay, cool, he got it.'"

It was easy to see how Schilling had inspired so many people. He had natural charisma, and although he didn't spend a ton of time at Big Huge Games—the MMORPG's development and Rhode Island politics were keeping him busy—Schilling was still a constant presence on *Kingdoms of Amalur: Reckoning*, for better and for worse. Sean McLaughlin, a UI artist who was on the fence about joining Big Huge Games when he got an offer in 2010, made up his mind after getting a personal call from Curt Schilling. "He sold it to me," said McLaughlin. "He felt very passionate about it. I thought it was nice that he reached out. Obviously you get a little starstruck."

Throughout 2011, as 38 Studios moved from Massachusetts to Rhode Island, the developers at Big Huge Games kept working on

Kingdoms of Amalur: Reckoning, which they released on February 7, 2012. The reviews were mixed, but if one thing was universally lauded, it was the combat. "EA was really cool with sharing their metrics," said Quadara. "They go into every review that's written and they highlight every aspect of every game: the levels, the story, the combat. And they will rate it, whether it's positive, negative, or neutral. Combat was 98.6 percent positive and the rest was neutral."

The critical consensus was that for a brand-new franchise, *Amalur* was a very good starting point. Developers at Big Huge Games were hungry to make a sequel—to take the lessons they'd learned from *Amalur* and improve on everything they'd gotten wrong. "There were so many people on that team who had never made a game before," said Quadara. "There was a bit of a letdown for some people in terms of how it was received, but at the same time there was a renewed sense that we can really do this." As Quadara and his combat pit started to brainstorm boss battles and other new ideas for *Amalur 2,* they felt like there was a great deal of potential at the studio. "I was just seeing this leveling up of everybody," Quadara said.

Ian Frazier and other leads at Big Huge Games started talking to EA about a sequel, tossing around ideas for where in the Amalur universe they could set the game and how they could make it better, but EA hesitated. Like Disney, which was shutting down Junction Point and exiting console development entirely, EA's executives were worried that traditional gaming might be on its way out. Plus, they had already made a hefty investment in BioWare's much-anticipated *Dragon Age: Inquisition,* so they weren't sure if their portfolio could handle another big RPG. "They ultimately passed, and because they passed, we could shop it around," said Frazier, who was primed to be the director of *Kingdoms of Amalur: Reckoning 2.*

The publisher most interested was Take-Two, the corporation behind 2K, Rockstar, and Irrational Games. Take-Two executives went back and forth with 38 Studios and Big Huge Games for weeks, listening to pitches for *Kingdoms of Amalur: Reckoning 2* and negotiating contract details, and in May, all three companies struck a verbal agreement. In addition to funding for the game, the developers at Big Huge Games would finally get their independence. Take-Two would publish the sequel to *Kingdoms of Amalur: Reckoning* and start a new studio with the staff of Big Huge Games, spinning them out from 38 Studios and moving them to an office alongside the 2K-owned studio Firaxis, the developer of *Civilization*, which was just down the road. (It was a strange twist, given that Big Huge Games had been started in 2000 by a group of former Firaxis employees.)

On May 14, 2012, executives from Take-Two flew down to Big Huge Games to sign the deal. The contract was finalized. The deal was hours away from being official. Ink was about to be scribbled on paper. Then, Rhode Island governor Lincoln Chafee told press that he was working to keep 38 Studios "solvent"—one small word that had devastating consequences. Suddenly, Take-Two executives called Big Huge Games from the airport and said they had to pull out. If 38 Studios went bankrupt, which appeared imminent, it would lead to the deal falling apart for complicated legal reasons. "All of a sudden, we were this toxic political mess that nobody wanted to touch," Frazier said. "Chafee's announcement made it so not only was 38 doomed, but also Big Huge Games was doomed, because nobody wanted anything to do with this toxic mess that we had suddenly become. Suddenly there wasn't going to be a *Reckoning 2*."

What was particularly infuriating was that if they'd had more warning from Curt Schilling, the staff of Big Huge Games might have been able to sort things out. If they had even the slightest indication that 38 Studios might be in financial trouble, they might have put together the Take-Two deal earlier and potentially saved the studio. As one person involved with negotiations described it: "It was akin to hitting a half-court shot to win the NBA championships and then have it taken away because the clock operator screwed up."

Then came May 15, 2012—*Diablo III* day—and a massive punch right in the gut of the staff of Big Huge Games. Suddenly, they weren't getting paid, and nobody knew what would happen next. "It was really anxiety-inducing," said Quadara. "A lot of families live paycheck to paycheck. Your health benefits are suddenly gone. And you're in Baltimore—it's not like there's a huge game development community." The next few days were a mess of uncertainty as Curt Schilling tried to save his empire, desperately negotiating with the state of Rhode Island over defaulted loan payments and tax credits. Down in Baltimore, meanwhile, most people just kept coming into the office, taking comfort in their coworkers and in the fact that they were all in it together. Every day, executives from 38 Studios held video conferences with the staff of Big Huge Games to assure them that things would be fine, but it was hard not to be skeptical. "We all started using that time to make sure our résumés and portfolios were in order just in case," said Justin Perez.

On May 24, 2012, nine days after the paychecks stopped, the staff of Big Huge Games found out that they were all laid off. 38 Studios was declaring bankruptcy and shutting down all operations in both Rhode Island and Maryland. The studio was done.

What they didn't know was that the catastrophe was just getting started.

■ ■ ■

When a company shuts down, someone has to take care of everything left behind. In the case of Big Huge Games, that someone was Ian Frazier, who was trying to figure out his next career move when he got a call from a colleague at EA. Turns out the Big Huge office still held hundreds of development kits for the PlayStation 3 and Xbox 360—pricey pieces of hardware that EA had leased from Sony and Microsoft for the development of *Kingdoms of Amalur: Reckoning*. And EA didn't even know who to call to get them back. "Our producer on the EA side called me and said, 'Hey, we're kind of hosed,'" said Frazier. "I ended up driving up to our studio, because I was one of the few people who still had a key." He loaded up a cart full of PlayStation and Xbox development kits, drove them to the UPS store, and then shipped off hundreds of thousands of dollars' worth of hardware. "Little wacky things like that were all happening at the end there just to try to take care of people," Frazier said.

But thanks to 38 Studios' neglect, a lot of people weren't getting taken care of. Joe Quadara had filed an expense report for thousands of dollars he'd spent booking *Amalur* press travel on his personal credit card—money that he now realized he'd never see again. The Big Huge Games caterer, who worked on a lower floor of their building, hadn't been paid in months. "We had no idea," said Frazier. "We were just enjoying our bacon, not knowing that they weren't getting paid." One day, the caterer came up to Big Huge Games to ask what was going on, but there was nobody left to ask. Just a handful of people were trickling in and out of the office to see old colleagues and wrap up loose ends. "We were like, 'Hey, just take whatever you can,'" said Quadara. "I think he ended up taking the big TV that was in the lobby."

The caterers weren't the only ones snatching equipment. Some of the former staff of Big Huge Games, knowing that those lost paychecks would never come, decided to take home some of the office's expensive computer gear, much like their colleagues in Rhode Island. Groups of work friends tried to spend as much time together as possible, knowing they'd soon be scattered across the country. By this point, the story of 38 Studios had become national news, and just like in Rhode Island, there were recruiters from other companies reaching out. "It shocked me how much people who were not us cared about this," said Katharine Star, a QA tester at Big Huge Games. Local studios like Bethesda and Firaxis, also in Maryland, put out offers to Star and a few of her former colleagues, which was a nice break—they wouldn't have to pack up and move across the country for their next gig.

At the same time, down in Cary, North Carolina, one man was coming up with a bigger scheme. Mike Capps, the bald, gregarious president of Epic Games, had been on one hell of a run over the past decade. Under his stewardship, Epic had created the massive sci-fi shooter franchise *Gears of War*, made millions of dollars off game development technology called the Unreal Engine, and plunged into iPhone gaming with a popular series called *Infinity Blade* that Capps had gotten to announce on the same stage as Steve Jobs. Now, as Capps heard that nearly one hundred developers were suddenly out of work, he saw an opportunity. He made a few calls, then got in the car with his head of human resources and drove up to Baltimore, where he opened a bar tab and invited the former staff of Big Huge Games to hang out. "Maybe 90 percent of the people in the studio showed up," said Capps. "I don't think that's because of Epic. I think that's because they loved each other and wanted to be together."

Capps told the former Big Huge Games developers that Epic was interested in making some job offers and perhaps even starting a new studio. He couldn't hire them all, he said, but he could at least take some of them through the interview process and see who made the cut. In the coming days, he convinced the former leadership of Big Huge Games to come aboard, including Ian Frazier, who was very close to joining BioWare to work on *Dragon Age: Inquisition*, but chose to stay behind and help out his friends. "Epic made it pretty clear that the leadership team needed to stay together," Frazier said. "That was part of the deal. If we weren't all together, the studio was not going to happen."

Once the Big Huge Games leadership team had signed up, Capps convened with the other executives at Epic and convinced them that this was money worth spending. "I said: 'This is the cheapest, best talent we'll ever find,'" said Capps. "'They're close by, it's not an expensive town, and these folks are as good as we are. We won't get them if we don't move fast.'" Working with Sean Dunn, who had been the general manager of Big Huge Games, Capps put together a list of just under forty people whom Epic Games could hire. "We met with them, we introduced ourselves, talked about what we do, and then they presented the game to us," said Frazier.

"The game" was a project called *Infinity Blade: Dungeons*. Down at Epic, a group of designers and engineers had been playing around with prototypes that they thought might turn into cool video games one day.[3] One of those prototypes was a spin-off of Epic's popular *Infinity Blade* series, which now consisted of three games and had brought in tens of millions of dollars in revenue on iPhones

---

3   Another of those prototypes, a cross between *Left 4 Dead* and *Minecraft*, would later get some attention—a little game called *Fortnite*. Before it became a cultural phenomenon, *Fortnite* was a troubled project that went through significant staff upheaval. "Fun fact," said Ian Frazier. "*Fortnite* was nearly canceled three times during the limited window of time I worked for Epic."

and iPads. Whereas the main *Infinity Blade* games were focused on pure combat, allowing players to battle gargantuan enemies with swords and axes in grueling one-on-one fights, this would be more of a dungeon-crawler. In fact, *Infinity Blade: Dungeons* would be a lot like *Diablo*.

The Epic offer came together at such a rapid speed that to the people involved it seemed too good to be true. After missing out on the chance to make a sequel to *Kingdoms of Amalur: Reckoning* because of Rhode Island politics, then watching their company fall apart due to circumstances beyond their control, now they had a chance to at least keep some of the band together. Epic was able to hire only a third of Big Huge Games' staff, but to those who made the cut, it seemed miraculous. After three years of drama, they were finally free of Curt Schilling and 38 Studios. That summer, they rented out an office and gave themselves a name befitting their circumstances: Impossible Studios.

For the next few months, this new team full of old colleagues worked on *Infinity Blade: Dungeons*, taking the core mechanics that Epic had made and adding more to the game—more dungeons, more classes, more weapons. The game was already fun to play, and finishing it wouldn't take more than a few months. From there, Impossible Studios could work on a new project of their own. The wounds were still raw from what had happened in May, but this was a lifeline. Thanks to the Unreal Engine, Epic Games was one of the most firmly established companies in gaming—almost the polar opposite of 38 Studios. "Epic was working on blueprints to build us a building," said Sean McLaughlin. "They were putting all this money into us. It was feeling really cool."

Yet despite its successes, Epic Games was going through upheaval of its own. Toward the end of 2011, after the launch of *Gears of War 3*, Epic decided to eschew the traditional publisher model in favor of "games as a service"—games it could publish and continually update rather than releasing and selling once. In July 2012, the Chinese megacorporation Tencent (which Curt Schilling had tried to convince to help save 38 Studios) made a massive investment in Epic, buying just under 50 percent of the company. Tencent had previously acquired Riot Games, the company behind the online battling game *League of Legends*, which was completely free to play. Instead of selling the game or offering subscriptions, Riot made its money off optional microtransactions that players could buy, allowing them to acquire new characters or put their old ones in fancy costumes. It was a successful business model that worked particularly well in China, where Tencent was based. Epic CEO Tim Sweeney, predicting that expensive console games were no longer a viable strategy, began preaching that free-to-play was the future.

Soon, Epic Games told the developers at Impossible that they should transform *Infinity Blade: Dungeons* into a free-to-play game. The first three *Infinity Blade* games had been "premium"—you paid once to buy them, and that was the end of it. *Infinity Blade: Dungeons*, however, would be free to download and come with some sort of store that incentivized people to spend money. To Ian Frazier and the rest of the team that had been working on the dungeon-crawler, this was unwelcome news—another dramatic twist in a year that had felt like a lifetime. Switching business models meant overhauling the entire design of the game. "We were a month from content-complete, two months at the most," said Frazier. "We came back and said, 'We can do that, but it wasn't designed to be free-to-play.'"

They wound up devising some new mechanics to help make *Infinity Blade: Dungeons* work as a free game, like a build-your-own-dungeon system reminiscent of the old strategy game *Dungeon*

Keeper. Epic leadership didn't love the pitch, though, which made sense—it had been thrown together in just a few weeks. "To be fair, I didn't like it either," said Frazier.

In November 2012, just before Thanksgiving, Mike Capps resigned from Epic Games. He had a child on the way and knew that continuing to serve as president of the company would make it difficult to find any sort of work-life balance.[4] "It was seventy-five hours a week, three days a week on the road," Capps said. "My dad was a workaholic, and I promised myself I wouldn't have kids and be like that." Capps planned to give six months notice and leave around spring, but when he told Tim Sweeney his plans, Sweeney insisted that he step down right away. Capps would get to keep a seat on the Epic board, but the message was clear: he was no longer in power. Just as things were getting rocky at Impossible Studios, the man who had started the company was no longer there to protect it.

■ ■ ■

One day in the beginning of February 2013, the internet went out at Impossible Studios. This wasn't particularly unusual—the office was still new, and sometimes they had connectivity hiccups. Justin Perez thought nothing of it, although they couldn't access the Perforce servers without internet, so they couldn't get much work done.[5]

---

4   "I hate the part I played in that," said Capps of crunch at the company he helped lead. "Epic was a company that was very successful, and part of our success came from doing more with less. We were very honest about it. *Halo* has 250 folks, we're going to have 70, and we're going to make half as much money, and we're going to share it all. That was the deal, but it meant we worked very hard."

5   Perforce, a version control program, is commonly used across the video game industry to ensure that nobody writes over another's work. It also keeps track of changes over time, allowing developers to do things like create different branches for different platforms. In other words, it's useful!

He asked some colleagues if they wanted to walk to the coffee shop and take a break. They were about to file out into the hallway when one of Impossible's higher-ups stopped them. "Someone said, 'Hey, hang out for a little bit,'" recalled Perez. "'We're going to have a meeting over in the common area.'"

Joe Quadara, who had arrived earlier that morning, had noticed that something was wrong. When he got to work, he saw that someone had closed the door to the office in which Impossible's general manager and executive producer sat. That door was *never* closed. Once the internet went out, Quadara started walking over to the all-hands meeting when he ran into someone from the leadership team. "I made a joke on the way out. I said, 'Do I need to get my résumé ready?' And nobody laughed."

Minutes later, the forty employees of Impossible Studios sat in a meeting, befuddled, as executives from Epic Games told them their studio was closing. Less than a year after forming the studio, Epic had decided to shut it down. The internet was off so nobody could leak anything. "They said, 'Look, Epic has decided to go another way,'" recalled Quadara. "'We're shutting this down effective immediately.'"

People were stunned. This made no sense. It had been only eight months since Impossible Studios opened, and *Infinity Blade: Dungeons* was nearly finished. How could Epic Games do this to them? Ian Frazier, who had found out earlier in the day what was happening, thought it was a joke. "As cynical as I am, I was like, 'Oh come on, not really,'" Frazier said. "'Who would shut us down before shipping the game? That's crazy.'"

Earlier, the Epic board had met to vote on shuttering Impossible Studios, and only one person voted against it: Mike Capps. "The idea of closing that studio months after we just announced we'd saved them, it's horrifying to me," said Capps. "That's not the message we should be sending as Epic, even if you think they're not a good studio. I'd looked them in the face and said, 'You're going to be okay.' I was the sole dissenting voice, I believe, in that discussion. I was removed from the board immediately afterwards."

For the developers, who had now gone through two studio closures in less than a year, this was baffling and infuriating. Messaging from Epic had been that Impossible was doing just fine, even at the studio's top levels. "The week before we were closed, Tim Sweeney told us on a call how important we were to the company and how valuable we were," said one former high-level Impossible Studios staffer.

The staff of Impossible Studios didn't get much of an explanation for the closure, and in public, Epic Games CEO Tim Sweeney was similarly vague. "When former members of Big Huge Games approached Epic last year, we saw the opportunity to help a great group of people while putting them to work on a project that needed a team," Sweeney wrote on Epic's website in a blog post announcing the closure. "It was a bold initiative and the Impossible folks made a gallant effort, but ultimately it wasn't working out for Epic."

At least this time they'd get severance. All of Impossible's employees were told they'd receive three months of pay after the shutdown date. Usually, severance pay would vary based on time served, but for Impossible that wasn't an option—nobody had worked at the company for more than eight months. Some opened their severance packets and found slips of paper telling them they'd been offered jobs down at Epic's main offices in North Carolina. "I don't think any of us took it," Quadara said. "Just because it was a little too weird to lay off all your friends and then offer you a job."

Quadara wound up returning to San Francisco, where he took a job back at Crystal Dynamics and worked on their reboot of *Tomb*

Raider. Ian Frazier, who had come close to moving to Canada to join BioWare's Edmonton office and work on *Dragon Age: Inquisition*, instead moved to a different part of Canada to join a different part of BioWare—BioWare Montreal, at which he'd go on to help make *Mass Effect: Andromeda*. Later, at a different studio in the same location, he'd direct the space combat game *Star Wars: Squadrons*. Justin Perez also spent a few years at BioWare Montreal, but left in 2017 after *Mass Effect* shipped, packing his things (and his dog) and taking a lengthy road trip to Los Angeles, where he got a job at Respawn to work on a different *Star Wars* game—*Star Wars Jedi: Fallen Order*, which would be praised for its challenging and satisfying combat mechanics.

Today, many of those who worked at Big Huge Games still describe it as the best place they've ever worked. They still get frustrated when they talk about how close the company came to finding a new home at 2K and about how Epic Games treated them and their colleagues. One member of the combat pit theorized that they might have followed a path similar to that of CD Projekt Red, the popular Polish developer behind the fantasy RPG series *The Witcher*. If *Kingdoms of Amalur: Reckoning* was their *Witcher 2*, he said, then the sequel could have been their *Witcher 3*—a critically acclaimed breakout hit that put Big Huge Games on the map. If not for a single catastrophic sentence from Rhode Island governor Lincoln Chafee, they might still be making games today.

At the end of it all, as the former staff of Big Huge Games scattered to new cities and countries, there was another twist befitting one of the oddest stories in video game history. Two of the studio's cofounders, Tim Train and Brian Reynolds, started a brand-new company to make a strategy game called *DomiNations* for phones and tablets. Their studio would eventually be purchased by the Korean publisher Nexon, the other company that Curt Schilling had been trying to convince to invest in 38 Studios during those final chaotic months. When they announced their plans, Train and Reynolds explained that they had gone to the 38 Studios bankruptcy auction and purchased the rights to a familiar old trademark. Their studio, founded in 2013 and still thriving in Baltimore as this book is written, had a name that brought everything full circle. They called it Big Huge Games.

CHAPTER 8

GUNGEON KEEPER

The first thing Dave Crooks ever said to Brent Sodman was that their company was about to shut down. They met in an airport in the summer of 2012 as they were both about to fly from Virginia to San Francisco for EA's annual new hire orientation. Sodman had just started as a technical artist at the EA-owned studio Mythic Entertainment, where Crooks was a community manager. Both were in their twenties and new to the video game industry. Sodman was a reserved artist, while Crooks was brash and blunt, the type of person who would introduce himself by predicting that they were both about to lose their jobs. "Dave sat down next to me at the airport," said Sodman. "I think the first words he said to me were, 'You know the studio's going to shut down soon, right?'"

Sodman did not know that. Things were in flux at Mythic Entertainment, sure, but it was a bona fide institution. Founded in the 1990s to make online video games inspired by *MUDs*, Mythic had earned renown in 2001 with *Dark Age of Camelot*, one of the many games that tried to build off Richard Bartle's virtual world. Whereas other top MMORPGs like *Ultima Online* and *EverQuest* took place in traditional fantasy settings full of dragons and wizards, *Dark Age of Camelot* was based on real-world mythology. You'd pick one of three realms—Albion, based on the legends of King Arthur; Hibernia, full of Celtic forklore; or Midgard, a playground of Norse myths—and compete against players who had selected the other two. The game grew popular, bringing in hundreds of thousands of players who paid monthly subscriptions to play, which helped Mythic grow and thrive. In 2006, EA purchased the studio, giving it access to resources it had never had before. Curt Schilling, a big fan of *Dark Age of Camelot*, would stop by from time to time, once leaving them a signed baseball as memorabilia.

Now, in 2012, the popularity of MMORPGs had waned and nobody was sure where the genre was headed, leaving Mythic's projects in flux as their developers tried to figure out how to embrace the latest trends. Still, Crooks's claim seemed a little far-fetched to Sodman. Times were certainly changing, but a studio shutdown? "I had maybe at that point gotten a bit of a negative vibe from people," said Sodman. But he had just joined a few weeks earlier—it seemed absurd that the studio might close now.

Despite the fact that they were both en route to EA orientation, Dave Crooks had already been working at Mythic's office in Fairfax, Virginia, for a year. "There was no real reason for me to go," Crooks said. "I asked because I'd never gotten to go and it was a free trip to California." He was a natural schmoozer, and over the months he'd grown close with the studio's leaders, including Paul Barnett, one of Mythic's top designers. The night before his flight to San Francisco, he'd heard from Barnett that EA's executives were pessimistic about Mythic's future. "There was a target on it," Crooks said. "The missile hadn't been fired, but things were rocky."

EA orientation took place in Redwood Shores, California, on a twenty-two-acre campus full of sprawling lawns and lavish offices.

(A quick walk from where Crooks and Sodman were participating in orientation, Visceral Games was in the thick of development on *Dead Space 3*.) Recruiters would talk up the company and promise employees in attendance that they would have careers at EA for years to come. In the middle of one of those speeches, Crooks decided to speak up. "I raised my hand and said, 'My studio is closing down tomorrow,'" said Crooks. "They pulled me aside and said, 'No, it'll be fine—we'll help you out.'" The next day, the EA people grabbed Crooks again and told him that Mythic wasn't shutting down. In fact, they said, Paul Barnett would be taking over as studio head. "Well that's great news," Crooks recalled saying.

Back in Virginia, as Barnett took control of the studio, he was taking one last gambit to keep the studio alive. For the past few years, Mythic had been struggling to make a profit. They needed to pivot to keep up with modern video game industry trends. To do that, the studio's developers would have to transition to making games for what had quickly become the biggest video game platform on earth: the iPhone. Mythic Entertainment was going to become a mobile studio.

■ ■ ■

Carrie Gouskos started at Mythic Entertainment in 2006, when the company was flying high. She'd moved to Virginia because she loved *Dark Age of Camelot* and wanted to work with the people who had created it. Under EA, Mythic had started developing a second MMORPG called *Warhammer Online*, based on the miniature figurine game, which Gouskos was hired to help develop. But as she rose through the ranks, starting off as a designer and then moving into a producer role on *Warhammer Online*, the industry shifted. Few MMORPGs seemed able to compete with the mighty *World of*

Warcraft, and even those online games that brought new ideas to the table couldn't seem to maintain a steady base of players. When *Warhammer Online* launched in the fall of 2008, it had a strong start but lost subscribers quickly. "Long-term, the MMO business wasn't the future," Gouskos said. "I think that was safe to say."

In 2009, EA had a restructuring—every corporation's favorite buzzword—and folded Mythic into BioWare, the legendary studio behind role-playing games like *Star Wars: Knights of the Old Republic* and *Mass Effect*. Mythic's office would remain in Virginia, but structurally, it would report to BioWare, as EA hoped to put all of its RPGs under the same label. The studio, now called BioWare Mythic, kicked off some new projects, trying to get *Dark Age of Camelot* and *Warhammer Online* running on consoles and even experimenting with a short-lived *Warhammer Online* MOBA, or multiplayer online battle arena, along the lines of *League of Legends*. "It never got out of beta, but I'm so proud of that work," said Gouskos. "I actually thought the game was pretty fun."

One week in 2010, while Gouskos was on vacation in Versailles, France, she got a call from Mythic's studio head. Turned out the studio owed George Mason University, their neighbor in Fairfax, a big favor. George Mason's students kept taking internships at Mythic, using those internships to get job offers, and then dropping out of college. The university had a good relationship with Mythic, but they were sick of losing people, and they were calling in that favor—they had a vacancy and needed a professor as soon as possible. "He said, 'I need you to teach a class on the history of video games starting Tuesday,'" said Gouskos. "It was a Saturday. I said, 'Ummm.'"

Gouskos had never taught students before, but as soon as she started, she fell in love. Being a teacher was a lot like being a video game producer—your job was to convince people to stop talking and just listen to you already. Gouskos stuck with the gig, first teaching video game history and then expanding to a second class on game design. In the design class, she noticed one standout student: a senior named Dave Crooks. "He was very talented, he was very engaged in the class, and he was tenacious," Gouskos said. "Not in the 'keeping the professor after class to be annoying' sense, but in legitimately having questions and asking them."

Crooks had joined the class on a lark. He'd originally studied 3-D art with dreams of making video games for a living, but he grew frustrated with his limitations as an artist. Assuming that he'd never be good enough for a career in games, he switched to an English major with a minor in Japanese cinema. At the beginning of 2011, he was killing time, with plans to move to Japan at the end of the semester, when he saw that George Mason had opened up a game design class. "I had very low expectations," Crooks said. "But I was like, 'Whatever, I've got nothing to do.'" When he found out that his new professor was actually a producer at Mythic Entertainment, his tune changed. "I learned that the first day that I walked in and I thought, 'Oh boy, time to turn on the smooth,'" Crooks said. "So I was the best student ever. I did all the assignments way overboard. I actually read all the texts super seriously."

Crooks and Gouskos grew friendly—they liked talking about *Metal Gear Solid*, which had been a formative experience for both of them—and by the end of the class, he'd left a strong impression on her. That spring, as the school year wound down, Crooks wrote to Gouskos asking if there were any positions open at Mythic. "I sent her an email," he said. "'Hey, I'm about to go to Japan, but I was only doing that because I gave up on my dream of making video games. Is there anything at the studio I could do?'" Crooks added that he was willing to do anything, as long as it meant joining the video game industry.

Gouskos was in the middle of a meeting when she saw the email.

She looked down at her phone and was immediately impressed, first by the formality of the introduction ("Dear Professor Gouskos," Crooks had written) and then by what Crooks had to say. Mythic needed a community manager—someone to run all the websites, collect feedback, and handle the Facebook and Twitter pages. Why not give a chance to this talented kid in her class? "She said nothing for two weeks," said Crooks, "and then I got an email saying, 'You have an interview on Wednesday.'"

In April 2011, Dave Crooks began working at Mythic Entertainment as a community manager, coming in laser-focused with a single goal—to ditch that job and become a video game designer. He had no interest in policing forums or making social media posts. For Crooks, community management was just a means to an end—the first rung on his career ladder. "I'd go over to the games team and pester them," Crooks said. "'Hey, you got any garbage work you don't want to do?'" He slowly started building a pile of tedious tasks, like writing names and descriptions for items, with hopes that if he did the work that none of the real designers wanted, eventually they'd see his value and bring him into their department. "I wasn't secretive about it at all," Crooks said. "Everyone knew immediately."[1]

But Mythic was struggling. Attempts to pivot *Warhammer Online* to a free-to-play model hadn't quite worked out, while their newest project, a remake of *Ultima IV* called *Ultima Forever*, had gone through some reboots and was taking longer than expected.[2]

---

1   Some in the video game industry have worked hard to treat community management as a discipline worth respect, but the job has also long been perceived by many as an entry-level path to game development.

2   *Ultima* came into EA's hands when the megapublisher purchased Origin, where Warren Spector had worked back in the early 1990s. EA shut down Origin in 2004, and Mythic Entertainment acquired a bunch of its old stuff a few years later, including the long-running MMO *Ultima Online*, which Mythic would continue operating until 2014.

Whispers of doom and gloom filled the studio as rumors spread that Mythic was losing money. "I really loved *Warhammer Online*, and I really wanted that to be the future," said Carrie Gouskos. "But times changed. The games industry changed." In the summer of 2012, as Dave Crooks met Brent Sodman and the two flew out to EA's Redwood Shores campus for company orientation, it was easy to think the studio might be sinking—until EA offered them a mobile gaming lifeboat.

No innovation had changed the video game industry more in the previous decade than smartphones, which transformed every professional commuter into a potential gamer. Mobile apps like *Angry Birds* and *Doodle Jump* cost significantly less to make than traditional console games and had profit margins so large you could fly a plane through them. EA executives had marveled at the success of *The Simpsons: Tapped Out*, released earlier in 2012, which raked in cash by letting players build and solve quests in their own virtual versions of Springfield. Now, EA wanted more of its studios making phone games, and Mythic made for the perfect fit.

Paul Barnett, the veteran designer who had been leading *Ultima Forever*, became the boss of a newly refocused Mythic, one that would transform into a "mobile-first" games studio. Some of their games might wind up on other platforms, but their priority would be iPhones and iPads. Mythic would no longer be part of BioWare, instead moving into EA's mobile division, and it would now aim to release *Ultima Forever* on iOS the following year. It was clear to Mythic's employees that the studio wasn't out of danger just yet—they still weren't actually generating a lot of money—but with this new focus, they had a shot at success.

Dave Crooks was elated when one of Barnett's first moves as studio head, in the fall of 2012, was to make him a full-time game designer. Finally, after months of moonlighting design tasks alongside his job as a community manager, Crooks got his wish. "It was the dream come true," he said. "I became a game designer at a studio. My entire identity is built around that, so the moment that happened was—I really can't describe it. It was just the best."

The designers at Mythic who weren't working on *Ultima Forever*, including Crooks, were told to spend time coming up with pitches for other mobile games. "There was a push for prototyping new projects," said Brent Sodman. "Because (a) new projects are fun and revitalizing for a team that's been working on the same thing for a while; and (b) if we can get another project green-lit before *Ultima Forever* is finished, that'd be good for the studio's longevity." The exciting part about this process was that EA gave Mythic permission to comb through its old library. After decades of games and studio acquisitions (many of which had shut down over the years), EA had built up a treasure trove of beloved classic franchises, and Mythic now had access to them all.

Crooks was told to make a prototype for an old game called *Desert Strike*, in which you'd gun down enemies while flying around an Apache helicopter. Crooks had an aptitude for design but wasn't a natural programmer, so he struggled to get some of the basic features working. Not wanting to let down his colleagues or blow his first chance at proper game development, he called up a friend— David Rubel, a savvy engineer who had been a military defense contractor at Lockheed Martin and now spent his time trying to build a robot that could invest in the stock market. Rubel had always been interested in game development; in fact, he and Crooks spent weekends together experimenting with game-making tools and dreaming up indie projects. So when Crooks called Rubel and asked for assistance, Rubel was happy to drop everything and help out.

Rubel spent the next few days coding a version of *Desert Strike* that could function on the touch screen of an iPhone—a challenging but interesting experiment. "We got that to a point where it was feeling really good," Rubel said. "It was fun just flying the helicopter around." When it was ready, Crooks took the prototype to Paul Barnett, who played around for a while and then said he loved it. Crooks confessed that he hadn't actually done most of the work; Rubel had. "I said, 'I did the title screen and my buddy did the movement of the helicopter,'" Crooks recalled. "They said, 'Who's your buddy? He want a job?'"

A few interviews later, Dave Rubel was hired as an engineer at Mythic Entertainment, teaming up with Crooks to work on *Desert Strike* for real. It was certainly an unusual way to start one's video game career. "I was always targeting the games industry," Rubel said. "But I heard it was hard to get in." When he started, on Halloween 2012, Barnett introduced Rubel with a joke: he'd made them a prototype, so now they had to hire him, or else they'd get sued.

Desert Strike never got much further than those early prototypes, but there was another game that stood out in the Mythic offices. Brent Sodman was working on a game that would soon turn into the studio's next big project. Just like *Desert Strike*, it was based on a classic franchise that had been gathering dust in EA's vaults for years. But this prototype was a little bit different. In fact, it would determine the fate of the entire studio.

■ ■ ■

In the 1980s and 1990s, you couldn't shake a stick without hitting a video game inspired by *Dungeons & Dragons*. The world of electronic entertainment was so new and unfamiliar, it made sense for game developers to stick to tropes they knew would resonate with people—intrepid parties of warriors and clerics, plunging into dungeons to fight gibbering goblins and collect shiny gold coins.

Video game developers figured that players wanted to live out a power fantasy—they wanted to be the heroes, the good guys, the saviors of the world. It was with that in mind that a group of snarky British designers at an EA-owned studio called Bullfrog Productions decided to make a video game in which you got to murder those heroes.

Dungeon Keeper, released for computers in 1997, let you play as the unabashedly evil entity in charge of designing and defending one of those dungeons that the good guys explored. Using an army of magical thralls called Imps, you'd dig out dirt, build lairs, and lure in creatures like trolls, orcs, and bile demons—bloated red creatures that could spew poisonous gas at opponents. You'd pay your creatures by mining gold from veins across the map, and you'd keep them happily fed with a hatchery full of live chickens, which your minions would pop into their mouths like gumballs. Then you'd defend your dungeon from gangs of do-gooder adventurers who wanted to steal your treasure and take you down. It was a funny, delightful strategy game that players loved enough for Bullfrog to quickly put out a sequel, *Dungeon Keeper 2*, in 1999. A planned third game was later canceled, and EA shuttered Bullfrog in 2001, putting the series on ice.

A decade later, *Dungeon Keeper* was up for grabs, one of the many classic games on the list that EA's executives had offered to Mythic to revitalize on mobile phones in 2012. It was easy to imagine *Dungeon Keeper* working nicely on iPhones and iPads. The old games unfolded from a top-down perspective, letting you dig map tiles and pick up creatures using an omnipresent, gnarled hand that replaced your cursor. It could feel slick and intuitive on a touch screen, with your finger replacing the mouse. Plus, *Dungeon Keeper* was an easy game to play in short sessions, which was ideal for the mobile audience, many of whom would play games in ten- or twenty-minute bursts while riding the train to work or sitting in the waiting room at their dentist's office.

Brent Sodman and a small team of other developers at Mythic began working on this mobile version of *Dungeon Keeper*. On a basic level, their prototype looked a lot like the old games. It had the same top-down perspective, and it allowed the player to summon evil creatures and dig out squares of dirt. There was one wrinkle, though: every time you dug out a tile, a timer would pop up. In the original *Dungeon Keeper*, you'd click a piece of dirt and wait the few seconds it took for your imps to get there. In this mobile version, a ticking clock would appear, and the dirt would remain in place until the timer ended. The numbers weren't finalized yet, but the implications were clear. "If you had a timer in a mobile game, everybody knew what that meant," said Sodman. "Some of them were going to be really long, and you were going to be able to pay to skip them."

Mobile gaming hadn't just changed the way games were played—it had also changed the way they were sold. When the App Store first launched in 2008, developers started to sell their games at fixed prices like they would on any other platform, but in the subsequent years something strange began to happen: mobile developers found that they could make even more money Trojan horse–style, by giving out games for free and charging for what was inside. By the summer of 2011, free-to-play games on the App Store were generating more money than games sold the traditional way, according to a report by the mobile analytics firm Flurry. Everything people had learned about selling games on the Xbox and PlayStation was upended by this strange new platform, as the developers at Impossible Studios would later learn when Epic made them overhaul *Infinity Blade: Dungeons*.

To designers who came from the world of traditional game

development, where you simply made a game and then sold it for a set price, entering the mobile games industry was like landing on an alien planet. The way to make money on phones was to release your game for free, get players hooked, and then convince them to spend money on in-game microtransactions. Some games were "pay to win"—the more you spent, the higher your chances of taking down opponents. Other games, like the popular *Tiny Tower* and EA's own *The Simpsons: Tapped Out*, pushed you to spend money by making basic tasks take a fixed amount of time, then letting you pay to skip the wait. There was a sort of evil logic to it that might have delighted the demons of *Dungeon Keeper*. Rather than being designed for sheer enjoyment, these games were designed to give you *just* enough enjoyment that you'd spend money to keep playing.

Playing mobile games was sort of like walking into a Vegas casino, complete with flashy graphical effects and joyful clanging sounds. Plopping down a new building in *The Simpsons: Tapped Out* would send an endorphin jolt through your brain, hooking you on the rush and enticing you to keep going. Like casinos, these games wouldn't take money directly. Instead, you could buy "premium currency" like gems (or, in *The Simpsons*, donuts) and spend that currency throughout the game. Some mobile games would supply you with a steady dribble of gems for free, giving you a taste to convince you to open your wallet—another technique ripped straight from casinos (or drug dealers). Some of the studios behind these "freemium" mobile games even hired psychologists to try to figure out the best way to keep players addicted.

Throughout 2013, as *Dungeon Keeper* grew and absorbed developers from the other prototype teams, including Dave Crooks and Dave Rubel, two things became clear: (1) that *Dungeon Keeper* would be Mythic's next game after *Ultima Forever*; and (2) that *Dungeon Keeper* would rely on timer microtransactions, allowing players to pay to speed things up. The mandate from EA was that all of their mobile games had to be free-to-play, and that *Dungeon Keeper* needed to emulate the success of other games that let you pay to play more quickly.

EA gave Mythic specific targets for KPIs—key performance indicators—like revenue and player numbers. "A lot of our discussions were not just about money, but about retention," said Alec Fisher-Lasky, a designer on *Dungeon Keeper*. "How do we keep players engaged? How do we give them rewards that feel fair?" Most often, the point of comparison was *Clash of Clans*, a popular tower-defense game in which you'd build a village, train troops, and raid other players. *Clash of Clans* had earned billions of dollars from impatient players eager to bypass its many timers.

Developers at Mythic were skeptical of this business model. To many people who had grown up playing traditional PC or console games, it seemed predatory and unethical.[3] Even as Mythic's staff knew they had to transition to mobile gaming—"pivot to mobile" was the phrase tossed around most frequently—many were wary of the transition. "The culture of Mythic was great, and all the people were awesome, but everyone who had been there a long time, they were old-head gamers," said Dave Crooks. "The idea of chasing *Clash of Clans'* business model was for some, including myself, a bitter pill to swallow." Of course, they all knew that Mythic had been struggling financially, and that this was the type of game their corporate owners wanted. They'd grumble about it, but they would still make it happen.

The people tasked with conveying EA's wishes were called

---

3 Of course, video games were predatory and unethical before most people even knew what a video game was—back in the arcade days, many designers would make their games as difficult as possible so that you'd keep popping in quarters. Mobile microtransactions seemed like a newfangled invention, but they were actually a natural evolution from that old-school model.

product managers, or PMs, and they would fly to Mythic frequently from their base in Redwood Shores, armed with market research and charts full of numbers from *Clash of Clans*. Throughout *Dungeon Keeper's* development, there were all sorts of conflicts between Mythic's developers and EA's PMs. Each faction had a very different idea of what a successful video game looked like. From the PMs' point of view, the Mythic people had very little experience making mobile games and didn't seem invested in the project, while from the Mythic developers' point of view, the PMs were clueless about game design and solely concerned with money. "You've got this situation where the game team says, 'We want to do this thing,' and this PM—who is there maybe two days out of the month and has no idea what designing a game loop is—comes in and says, 'Here are the things we're doing,'" said Dave Crooks. [4]

During one meeting, an EA product manager asked Crooks what he was working on. Crooks said he was designing traps for *Dungeon Keeper* and walked the PM through his list of ideas, which included an ice trap that would freeze enemies, knocking down their hit points and slowing their movement. "[The PM] said, 'Man, it slows *and* does damage? That sounds overpowered,'" recalled Crooks. "I was like, 'What the fuck are you talking about?'" For Crooks, this was a microcosm of a bigger problem—the tension between creatives and executives that so many game developers have faced over the years, from veterans like Warren Spector to newcomers like himself. How could this PM offer an educated perspective on a

---

4   For the rest of us who might also not know what a "game loop" is: think of it as the core "loop" of activities a player might do in a video game. In the popular shooter *Destiny*, for example, the loop is to take a mission, shoot a bunch of aliens, collect the rewards that pop out, and repeat. Generally, the goal of a game loop is to be fun and satisfying in both short- and long-term doses.

game's design when they couldn't even understand why an ice trap might both slow enemies and do damage?

In August 2013, Mythic's long-in-development *Ultima Forever* finally launched on iOS. It landed with a thud, receiving middling reviews and very little attention, and the bulk of Mythic moved on to *Dungeon Keeper*, hoping this next game would drive more buzz. There were reasons for Mythic to be cautious moving forward, though. Those critics who had actually paid attention to *Ultima Forever* had slammed the game's free-to-play mechanics and micro-transactions. "*Ultima Forever*'s design goes to some evil places," wrote the game critic Rich Stanton, noting that the game constantly used "sleight-of-hand" to bleed real money from players. *Dungeon Keeper* was shaping up to feel just as exploitative, if not worse, but there wasn't much the developers could do about it. "Free-to-play games are not, I think, what most people there would have wanted to work on," said Dave Rubel.

On a raw level, Mythic's developers were happy with the way *Dungeon Keeper* felt to play. It was a lot like *Clash of Clans*, but it had a quirky sense of humor inspired by the original Bullfrog games. The developers enjoyed their testing sessions, in which they'd carve out dungeons and build traps to zap enemies. Problem was, the main reason they were having so much fun was that during tests, they could disable all of the timers.

As *Dungeon Keeper* coalesced, it became clear that having to wait around or pay real money just to get things done was not a par-ticularly enjoyable experience. People who played games like *Clash of Clans* might have grown accustomed to the timers, but Mythic's developers hated them. There were heated battles between Mythic and the EA PMs over the timers' length and frequency—battles that the EA product managers would almost always win. "There was one day that they said, 'I think we're going to double all the timers,'" Crooks recalled. "I remember them explaining it to me: 'We think timers can get pushed harder.' I said, 'I don't know, man. I wouldn't play this, but maybe some other people will.'"

From EA's perspective, this was just how the mobile business model worked. The product managers valued statistics and numbers above all else, and they had loads of data showing that iPhone and Android players were perfectly fine with timers that lasted hours or even days. *Clash of Clans* was the ultimate example of this. In fact, to say that *Dungeon Keeper* took inspiration from *Clash of Clans* would be like saying Instagram Stories borrowed a couple of ideas from Snapchat.

The tutorial screen for *Clash of Clans* introduced the player to the game's premium currency (gems) by granting some for free and encouraging the player to spend them with the following message: "Now's not the time to be stingy. Spend some green gems to speed things up!"

There's a popular meme in which two images are posted side by side with the caption "Hey can I borrow your homework?" followed by "Yeah, just change it up a bit so it doesn't look obvious you copied." The tutorial screen for *Dungeon Keeper* introduced the player to the game's premium currency (gems) by granting some for free and encouraging the player to spend them with the following message: "This is no time to be stingy! Spend a few more Gems to instantly rush the building of this trap."

■ ■ ■

As 2013 rolled along, the atmosphere at Mythic grew stranger. The developers came in every day and did their jobs, but they were growing concerned that *Dungeon Keeper*'s upcoming release would be controversial. "Individually, within the studio, people would look at each other in the eye and go, 'People are going to hate this,'"

Crooks said. "You're like, 'Yeah, I know. But we have to make it.'"
It was like they were on a cruise ship headed straight for an iceberg.
Even though everybody knew they were about to crash, there was
no way to turn the ship around. "When you have this mandate that
there have to be a bunch of timers in the game, and the timers have
to be skippable to make money, it's hard to say, 'Well, the timers
suck,'" said Brent Sodman. "What are you going to do about it?"

Dave Crooks, unsatisfied with what he was doing at work, began
talking to Sodman and Dave Rubel about going independent. Crooks
and Rubel had already tooled around with some indie projects together on the side. That was how they'd met, before Rubel helped
Crooks out with the *Desert Strike* prototype and got a programming
job at Mythic. Sodman, who had grown close to Crooks since their
first encounter at the airport a year ago, wanted to be involved as well.
These days, Sodman and Crooks lived together in an apartment down
the street from Mythic's offices, and every once in a while they'd get
together and brainstorm ideas for games alongside close friend Joe
Harty, an unemployed artist, and Crooks's girlfriend, Erica Hampson,
a sound designer who would also later come to work at Mythic.

With *Dungeon Keeper* failing to inspire them, the group started
to talk more about developing a game on their own, and soon
enough what had started as a hobby became a serious aspiration.
They started making plans to save money, and eventually set a finite
date for themselves based on each of their financial goals. At the
beginning of 2014, Crooks and crew took the unusual step of telling
the studio about their plans. They had a lot of respect for Paul
Barnett and Carrie Gouskos (who had been promoted to director
of studio operations) and didn't want to screw the company over.
The group explained that they planned to leave in August, and that
they were sharing the news months in advance so that Barnett and
Gouskos had ample time to replace them. "In a different situation,

we never would have told anyone," said Crooks. "We felt it was the honorable thing to do."

Before then, however, they had a game to launch. On January 30, 2014, *Dungeon Keeper* came out for iPhones, and it turned out the developers had been right to worry. The reviews were *scathing*. Critics and video pundits detested the game, and throngs of gamers joined the chorus of anger, trashing *Dungeon Keeper* on Reddit and Twitter. EA marketed the game as the revitalization of a beloved franchise—"a twisted new mobile take on the 1990s cult strategy game," the press release said—but in reality it felt like someone had added a bunch of demons to *Clash of Clans*. Whereas the old *Dungeon Keeper* games required players to strategize and manage their resources, the new one just kept asking you to spend money on gems. Fans were already inclined to dislike EA—this was the company voted "Worst Company in America" two years in a row in a tournament held by the website Consumerist, beating out the likes of Comcast and Bank of America—and this game seemed to prove all of their worst assumptions right.

Wrote Dan Whitehead, a critic for Eurogamer:

What we have here is the shell of Bullfrog's pioneering strategy game, hollowed out and filled up with what is essentially a beat-for-beat clone of *Clash of Clans*. Every function, every mechanism, every online feature has been tried and tested already by Supercell's money machine and EA is following behind, drooling like a Pavlovian dog. That's what stings the most: not that *Dungeon Keeper* has gone free-to-play, but that it's done so in such soulless fashion.

Maybe the game would have been less of a disaster if it wasn't called *Dungeon Keeper*. What set people off most wasn't that EA and

Mythic had made a microtransaction-packed phone game, but that the two companies seemed to be exploiting a beloved old franchise. A game like this would have been most appealing to gamers who played primarily on phones—people who wouldn't mind timers because they played only in ten-minute bursts—yet it had the skin of a game adored by hard-core PC gamers. *Dungeon Keeper* quietly accumulated a small audience of fans who didn't care about the timers, but the internet outrage was deafening.

Dungeon Keeper's launch day was not pleasant for the staff of Mythic Entertainment. People sat at their desks in silence, unable to stop themselves from reading through the nasty comments and awful reviews. As was custom in video game culture, gamers sent messages saying they hoped the developers of *Dungeon Keeper* would go kill themselves. ("Working in the games industry, you kind of get used to that one," said Sodman.) The staff got together to drink, some lamenting that they should've known this was going to happen. Of course *Dungeon Keeper* was going to elicit reactions like this. Combining microtransactions and nostalgia was not a formula for success. "There were a lot of sad people at the studio," said Crooks. "A lot of people were like me, though. They just said, 'Well, duh. Obviously.'"

Paul Barnett's plan to steer Mythic to the shores of mobile gaming hadn't gone as planned. Now, even the studio's most optimistic employees realized that they might be out of lifeboats.

■ ■ ■

On the evening of May 28, 2014, Brent Sodman got a call from Dave Crooks that felt a lot like what had happened at the airport two years earlier. Sodman had gone home for the night, but Crooks was working late and had some news. "He said, 'Dude, you might want to come to the studio and grab your personal belongings,'" said Sodman. "'Because I'm pretty sure the studio's getting shut down tomorrow.'"

This time, Crooks had much stronger proof that Mythic was closing. Carrie Gouskos had left the main office to use the bathroom. When she came back, her key card wasn't working. Crooks went outside to check his own key card—same problem. It couldn't have been a technical error, because the janitor's key card still worked. When Crooks got back into the office, he looked at the dozen or so employees who were still there and told them that they'd better start packing up their things. Then he called Sodman. "I said, 'That's convincing evidence, but I don't have anything to grab,'" Sodman said. "I woke up the next morning and went in early, because I figured it was going to be a bad day."

Gouskos was told to head to the nearby Marriott hotel for an 8:00 a.m. meeting. When she arrived, EA executives and HR people were already there, preparing for what was about to happen. Frank Gibeau, the head of EA's mobile department, gave her the news: Mythic was closing. "It wasn't heartless," Gouskos said. "It was warm and kind." Gibeau had been the man responsible for EA's purchase of Mythic, and he had always been fond of *Dark Age of Camelot*—even, it was said, holding executive meetings within the game—so he appeared to feel guilty that they had to shut down the company. Yet it was hard to justify keeping Mythic alive. The once-lucrative studio had been losing money for years, and the transition to mobile had clearly not worked out, as evidenced by *Ultima Forever*'s tepid response and *Dungeon Keeper*'s critical backlash. "The vibe was: 'We know the studio's not making enough money; we can't keep doing this; we've tried a couple things,'" Gouskos said. "And, 'We are going to try to find a home for everybody.'"

An hour later, the management team drove to Mythic's office to give the studio the news. Word of the malfunctioning key cards had gotten around, so when Gibeau got up to tell them that the studio was closing, few in the room were completely shocked. Still, it was crushing. Many of the developers were close friends, and they knew that not a lot of them would remain in Virginia. "Everybody cried," said Gouskos. "Even people you wouldn't think would be crying." Perhaps because Mythic was the only big video game studio in Virginia, or because so many of them spent time together on weekends and after work, the staff there saw it as a special place. Later, one former Mythic employee said they hadn't "worked anywhere else that had that kind of spark."

Video game studio shutdowns often feel unfair and inhumane to the people involved. Sometimes they come out of nowhere, as with 38 Studios and Big Huge Games, and sometimes hundreds of employees might lose their jobs because of shortsighted strategies concocted by millionaires in a corporate boardroom. With Mythic, however, many staff members felt like there wasn't much else EA could have done. There was frustration at EA's heavy hand in the making of *Dungeon Keeper*, but if anything, it felt like Mythic had gotten to stay alive two or three years more than they should have. "We weren't making money," said Gouskos. "What was EA supposed to do?" All of Mythic's staff got severance packages, and EA tried to move some of them to its other mobile studios.

It was a storm of complicated emotions for Dave Crooks, Dave Rubel, and Brent Sodman. They didn't want to see the studio shut down, and many of their friends would now wind up leaving Virginia for jobs elsewhere in the industry. Yet the Mythic severance would give them life jackets as they plunged into the risky waters of independent game development. As they all went to a nearby bar to drink and reminisce, the three developers began to realize that they'd be able to start their dream project three months earlier than they'd planned. "I remember somebody came up to us and said, 'Honestly, this isn't so bad for you guys,'" said Sodman. "I said, 'Yeah, I hate to say it, but it's not that bad.'"

Closing a studio like *Mythic* wasn't an easy or straightforward process, Gouskos would soon discover, because they had so many online games that either needed to be shut down or transferred elsewhere. Earlier in the year, one of Mythic's original founders had started a new studio and bought the license to maintain *Dark Age of Camelot*, and Mythic had shuttered *Warhammer Online* in 2013, but the mobile games were still online. EA offered a handful of developers time and a half for the next three months if they kept working out of the Mythic offices to help shut things down, and Gouskos was put in charge of this group. She helped close *Ultima Forever* and relocated the operations of *Dungeon Keeper*—which had been patched over time to make its timers less harsh and actually still had some players—to a different studio within EA. Toward the end, she packed up computers and consoles. "There were a lot of practical things," Gouskos said. "Anything that was worth something needed to be locked up."

It turned out that Mythic had a whole lot of objects that were indeed worth something—in addition to expensive computer equipment, the studio had accumulated years' worth of promotional material and cultural artifacts. Gouskos found closets stuffed full of posters for *Warhammer*, statues for *Dungeon Keeper*, and truckloads of shirts, pins, lanyards, and other swag.[5] When Mythic had

---

5   One of the more bizarre decisions EA had made while promoting *Dungeon Keeper* was to print foam devil horns in the shape of the shocker—the sexual hand gesture—which Carrie Gouskos, recognizing how bad an idea it would be to disperse, had stuck in the back of a closet as soon as they'd arrived. Now, with the studio shutting down, she had to dispose of two thousand foam shockers. "Of course every employee wanted one," she said. "I said, 'No one gets to have this.'"

inherited the *Ultima* license, someone had sent them all the gear from the old Origin offices, and Gouskos found all sorts of relics, including awards made out to Warren Spector and Richard Garriott, which she mailed back to them. On one of the walls was a massive *Ultima* painting by the artists Brothers Hildebrandt that was said to be worth hundreds of thousands of dollars, but EA quickly took care of that one. "An army of people came in," said Gouskos. "One of the things they did was took it off a wall, put it in a room, and locked the door."

Gouskos spent those final days walking around Mythic's office like a zombie, tears on her face during the day and inane reality shows on her television at night. She packed boxes and closed contracts with external vendors, marveling at how many companies they had to work with, from the people who delivered the bagels to the folks in charge of the fire extinguishers. At the end of it all, she had the honor of being the final employee that Mythic Entertainment ever had—something that nobody else could say. "I was the last person," said Gouskos. "There's a picture of me leaving the office. I turned the lights off, and walked off, and nobody walked into Mythic again."

■ ■ ■

The day after the Mythic shutdown, as the rest of the studio's former employees tried to figure out what to do next, Dave Crooks kicked his master plan into gear. He, Brent Sodman, and Erica Hampson turned their apartment's living room into a makeshift office space, where Dave Rubel and Joe Harty would join them every day. "It was definitely an adjustment," said Hampson. "So many of us crammed in there, day in and day out." Less than a week after Mythic closed, the five of them started an independent company called Dodge Roll

Games.[6] The plan was to live off their savings for as long as it took to make and release their first video game, then see if they could generate enough revenue to keep going.

That first game would be called *Enter the Gungeon*—a name that popped into Dave Crooks's head one night and never left. It would take inspiration from popular indie games of the past few years, like the dungeon-crawling action game *The Binding of Isaac*, which had launched in 2011. Just like *The Binding of Isaac*, *Enter the Gungeon* would be played from a top-down perspective and, pivotally, it would be a "roguelike" game. A roguelike, named after the classic game *Rogue*, was a game characterized by two main systems: (1) dying would kill your character permanently, forcing you to start again from the very beginning; and (2) the levels were generated randomly, so that every new playthrough felt different. Some roguelikes let you keep certain weapons or perks even after you died, so it always felt like you were making some sort of progress, but the goal was to create replayability— every time you lost, it was tempting to start again and see how much further you could get. From a game developer's perspective, rogue- likes were the Holy Grail, generating hours and hours of playtime at a fraction of the development cost of a purely handcrafted game.

In *Enter the Gungeon*, you'd play as a "gungeoneer" battling off the "gundead" on a planet called "Gunymede," seeing how much progress you could make and how many weapon puns you could stomach along the way. The characters would be cute and squishy— protagonists with big heads and dots for eyes, monsters shaped like

---

6 Erica Hampson, who wanted to freelance for other games as well, technically worked as a contractor rather than a cofounder of the company. "I think I was more of a question mark at the beginning than the other guys," she said. "I think they were pretty devoted with the idea of going indie. They really stuck their necks out there and took the risks, while I was more wishy-washy."

bullets, and beautiful two-dimensional dungeon levels drawn by Joe Harty. You'd pick a hero and descend into the gungeon, collecting dozens of weapons ranging from traditional (pistols, machine guns) to absurd (a T-shirt cannon, a banana). Then you'd try to survive swarms of bullet-spraying monsters and bosses, knocking over tables for cover and hunting for chests that featured useful new items and guns. If you were lucky, you'd find good enough gear and play well enough to make it to the bottom of the gungeon, but most of the time you'd get killed along the way. Once you died, you'd start again from the beginning, armed with new knowledge and slightly better dodging skills.

Crooks, Sodman, Hampson, Harty, and Rubel had been casually working on a demo of *Enter the Gungeon* before this ("Kind of for fun, kind of for learning," said Sodman), but now that Mythic was closed and their jobs were gone, it was time to double down. Part one of their plan was to find a publisher. For a while now, as the Dodge Roll crew concocted schemes for life after EA, they'd been drawn to the idea of working with a partner to help them handle marketing, PR, legal deals, and all of the other fiddly stuff a video game needs outside of what's actually in the code. They didn't want to take outside funding right away, but it would also help to have a publishing partner as backup in case the game took too long and they ran out of money.[7] One name kept coming up: Devolver, the small publisher behind a number of popular indie games, including a similar top-down shooter called *Hotline Miami*. "Devolver had a pretty sterling reputation for treating people right, which I think continues to this day," said Sodman.

---

7   They didn't want to bother with crowdfunding on Kickstarter, which seemed like it'd be a full-time job on its own. "I didn't want to deal with customers before the game was out," said Dave Crooks.

It was late May 2014, and E3 was just a couple of weeks away. That would be a good opportunity to track down Devolver, or one of the other publishers that descended on Los Angeles every year for the massive video game trade show, and pitch the demo for *Enter the Gungeon*. Through their old boss, Paul Barnett, the Dodge Roll crew got in touch with one of Devolver's partners, Nigel Lowrie. They asked if they could show him their game. *Sure*, Lowrie wrote back. *But it's going to be pretty loose.*

The team booked Crooks a flight to Los Angeles and started scrambling to finish their prototype for *Enter the Gungeon*, which consisted of a floor, a boss, some enemies, and a dozen different guns. Crooks asked an old Mythic friend if he could crash in their L.A. hotel room, then headed off to E3 with no plans or appointments other than a vague commitment from Devolver. "Dave bought an E3 pass with his savings and I bought him a plane ticket with my savings," said Sodman. "We put the prototype on his laptop, put the laptop in his backpack, put the backpack on his back, and put him on an airplane." Crooks had no contacts and no experience pitching games to publishers, but if anyone was going to pull this off, it was going to be the guy who had talked his way into the video game industry by charming his college professor. "Everyone else on the team had the feeling that if anybody could squeeze water from the stone, it was going to be Dave," said Sodman.

When Crooks got to Los Angeles, he went up to strangers and started introducing himself. He recognized Rami Ismail, an indie game celebrity and one of the minds behind *Nuclear Throne*, and immediately went over to say hi. Ismail put him in touch with some other colleagues and soon Crooks was schmoozing with all sorts of key video game industry figures. He networked with indie publishers like Midnight City (an ill-fated branch of Majesco) and executives from PlayStation, impressing them with his charisma and the demo for *Enter the Gungeon*, which was slick and fun to play.

At one point, Crooks went to the Xbox booth in the Los Angeles Convention Center, fighting his way through crowds in search of someone who looked like they might work there. One guy in an Xbox T-shirt caught his eye, so Crooks went up and introduced himself. Did this guy work for Xbox? *Yes.* Did he want to hear about Crooks's game? *Sure.* As Crooks started telling his story, the Xbox guy's eyes looked glazed, like he had spent most of his day listening to random video game pitches from strangers. But when Crooks mentioned that Dodge Roll was made up of ex-Mythic employees, the guy perked up. "He said, 'Wait a minute, Mythic?' I said, 'Yeah.' He said, 'Oh man, my brother was the art director there five years ago.' Immediately then it clicked over into—okay, now I'm actually listening."

The next day, Crooks headed over to the parking lot across the street from the convention center where Devolver set up shop every year.[8] He flagged down Nigel Lowrie, who said he had a bunch of other appointments and would meet with Crooks as soon as he could. Devolver didn't typically take developer pitches at E3—they were mostly there to show their games to press and other exhibiting partners. Lowrie had a host of other meetings with journalists who were in attendance to play Devolver's demos, so his schedule was packed.

Crooks grabbed some of the free food and beer, then sat down in the parking lot. Then he waited. And waited. "I was there for six hours," Crooks said. "By the time I'd actually pitched *Gungeon* to

---

8 For years, rather than buy booth space on the E3 show floor, Devolver has used the parking lot across the street—both to distinguish itself and to poke a little fun at the big trade show next door.

Nigel, I had drank at least ten smallish cups of beer just to settle my nerves."

Finally, Lowrie grabbed Crooks and brought him into one of the silver Airstream trailers they used for meetings. As they sat on the couch and made small talk, Crooks pulled up his laptop and loaded *Enter the Gungeon*, then tried to gauge Lowrie's reaction as he played the demo. "Nigel is the nicest, warmest dude in the world," said Crooks, "but man, I could not read him at all." Lowrie sat there stone-faced, nodding and asking procedural questions. How long did they need to make it? What platforms did they want the game to release on? "I got out of it, called my team, and said, 'I don't know,'" said Crooks. "I had no idea what he was thinking."

Crooks flew home to Virginia, feeling good about the trip even if he wasn't sure where they stood with Nigel Lowrie. Other people had said they liked *Enter the Gungeon*, and it seemed like Dodge Roll would have multiple options even if Devolver turned them down. The market for digital indie games was just getting wider in the summer of 2014, and the console makers were on the hunt for games that could boost their lineups on the newly launched Xbox One and PlayStation 4. After his networking successes at E3, Crooks now felt like they could get meetings with anyone, and he planned to keep hustling with other publishers over the next few weeks and months if Devolver didn't work out.

But they really wanted Devolver to work out.

A week later, Crooks got a call. It was Nigel Lowrie. He said Devolver wanted to publish *Enter the Gungeon*, and asked if Crooks and crew were still interested in making that happen. "I was like, 'Holy shit,'" said Crooks. "That was a very good day."

It turned out that despite his poker face at E3, Lowrie had instantly fallen in love with *Enter the Gungeon*'s demo. Usually, the video game pitches he saw were rough, requiring heavy explanation and a lot of imagining what a game might look like with more time and money. Often, Lowrie needed to fill in the blanks in his head. *Enter the Gungeon*, on the other hand, was so polished that it felt like he could jump in and play it right away. "I remember thinking, 'This is great,'" said Lowrie. "I was genuinely excited." It helped that the Dodge Roll crew wasn't asking for money, and it *really* helped that they had all come from an established video game studio, so they knew how games were made. Lowrie pitched *Enter the Gungeon* to the rest of his partners at Devolver and got everyone on board. "I said, 'This is the real deal,'" said Lowrie. "I think everyone was pretty geeked about it."

Now, after getting their first choice of publisher, the Dodge Roll team had to get back to development. "It was a weird moment because we were so caught up on this laser goal, and it immediately worked," said Dave Rubel. "Then we were like, 'Oh, okay, now we have to make the whole game.'" Back in Virginia, the newly independent group of developers took their demo and began expanding it, adding new levels, enemies, and guns. For the next few months, they kept working out of their living room, tooling away at whatever inspired them most on a given day. "We got a little more organized as time went on," said Joe Harty. "It was pick-up-sticks at the beginning."

Originally, Dodge Roll had pitched the game to Devolver for an April 2015 release, but as 2015 actually started, it became clear that wasn't going to happen. There were too many levels left to design, too many monsters to create, too many pieces of the game to polish. "That's when we really got serious," said Dave Rubel. "Wow, this is taking a long time, and we have a lot of stuff we want to put in this game." What that meant was crunching—working many long nights and weekends—to finish *Enter the Gungeon* in the next year. Eventually, they ran out of money and asked Devolver for an advance on what they hoped would be the game's future proceeds, which was just fine with Nigel Lowrie. "I don't think there's ever been a game that's been on time that we've worked on," Lowrie said. "[*Enter the Gungeon*] was always showing progress."

For Crooks and Sodman, it became a struggle to both live and work together. The two men, close friends since they'd first met at the airport, were now on top of each other 24-7, intensifying what may have otherwise been standard, workable creative conflicts. "The way we worked together was just poisonous," said Crooks. "Things that I asked for and reactions I got to them, I perceived as bad. I don't have a whole lot of white-glove treatment: 'Hey this looks good, but could you maybe do this?' I'm more like: 'This is wrong; this is wrong; this is wrong.'"

Crooks was a perfectionist, the type of designer who would polish each aspect of the game to a fine sheen before moving on to something else, while Sodman liked to bang out rough versions of tasks and then refine them later, which led to some big fights. "I didn't take criticism super well," said Sodman. "You combine a person who generally has been told he's doing a good job and doesn't take criticism very well, and then you take a guy who basically only gives feedback negatively, you've got a formula for danger there."

What further exacerbated the tension were Crooks's trips. Once every month or so, Crooks would fly to a gaming convention to show the game to fans—E3, PAX, the PlayStation Experience, Gamescom, and so on. As people played, he'd watch and scribble notes, meticulously writing down everything that they disliked, and then he'd bring home the feedback, arriving back in Virginia with a giant list of problems that they all needed to solve. "It got to the point where me coming back from a show was a stressful moment for the team," said Crooks. But the rest of his team hadn't been there watching players and getting their feedback, so they didn't feel the same sense of urgency that Crooks brought home with him. They just knew that every time Crooks came back from a show, they had to overhaul a whole bunch of work. "I definitely think that made the game much better, but it also came with a lot of stress," said Crooks. "I didn't know what I was doing in terms of people management."

There was no denying that fixing every problem Crooks discovered made the game better, but constant changes to the game could be excruciating for the people behind it. "There were hundreds of tasks. I'd wake up and work my ass off to finish twenty of them," said Sodman. "Then I'd wake up the next day and I'd have thirty new tasks." Every night, Sodman would go to sleep a few hours before Crooks, and as he lay in bed, all he could hear was typing. "I knew he was making new tasks for me," Sodman said. "I'd go to sleep every night hearing that for a couple hours—being really angry and sad and tired."

The work days just kept getting longer toward the end of 2015 and into 2016, much to the Dodge Roll team's dismay. "The last part of development on *Gungeon* broke all our brains," said Sodman. "We were all tired, all stressed." Sodman, an outspoken leftist who had moral compunctions against crunch, was particularly shaken by the workload, although at least it felt like they were doing it for themselves. "We did crunch very hard, and it sucked, don't get me wrong, but it's a huge difference crunching for a game that you know you have revenue share in," Sodman said. "If the game is better, I make more money." The hours and planned release date weren't mandated by Devolver—they'd already delayed the game a year and could certainly ask for more time—which perhaps made it worse. It was self-imposed crunch. "We all had a strong desire to not let each other down," Sodman said. "If we all work really hard, the machine works well. We had a feeling that it was what we needed to do."

Everything was miserable for the Dodge Roll crew—except for *Enter the Gungeon*, which was shaping up to be fantastic. It was challenging, satisfying, and consistently fun. In early 2016, as the Dodge Roll team prepared for an April launch, they got in touch with some *Binding of Isaac* Twitch streamers who were looking for something new to play. In exchange for some marathon stream sessions, Dodge Roll offered them early access to *Enter the Gungeon*. Tens of thousands of people watched the streams, building up buzz and driving solid preorder sales. In the weeks before launch, Nigel Lowrie called to tell them it looked like they were going to be in good financial shape. "We so made the right game at the right time," said Dave Rubel. "I don't know that we'll ever hit that timing combination ever again. But it worked phenomenally well for us."

When *Enter the Gungeon* finally came out on April 5, 2016, it was a huge success. The game was excellent—spelunking through the dungeon was snappy and addictive, and as soon as you died (a frequent occurrence), you'd immediately get the urge to start a new run. *Enter the Gungeon* didn't sell the millions of copies that a big-budget EA game might have been expected to sell—and it might have been seen as a failure if they were still at Mythic—but it was lucrative for the founders of Dodge Roll Games. "It was enough for me to purchase a place to live eventually," said Sodman. "It was enough for me to pay off my mom's credit cards for her."

Money was nice, but the developers at Dodge Roll Games were burned out, and as soon as the game came out, they all needed a break. They knew that continuing to live and work out of the same apartment for sixteen hours a day was an unsustainable way to live. Dave Crooks did what he'd thought about doing a few years earlier and moved to Japan, while Brent Sodman relocated to Kansas so his wife could go to graduate school. "By the end of *Gungeon*, we were not friends," Crooks said. "We were very unhappy with each other for reasons that now seem trivial."

As the Dodge Roll crew recuperated, they decided not to start their next project right away. During those last months of *Enter the Gungeon*'s development, they'd cut a lot of content to ship the game, and their computers were full of half-completed weapons, enemies, and rooms. Rather than drag all that work into the recycling bin, the team decided to finish it and put it in an update for *Enter the Gungeon*. They wouldn't sell this update as downloadable content—rather, they'd give it away for free to anyone who owned the game, a very different approach than the mobile-game models that Mythic had embraced. "The purpose of this update explicitly was to put in stuff we wanted to finish," said Sodman. "We felt bad charging for that, and so we said, 'Okay, we'll put it out for free.'" It wasn't an entirely selfless move. They knew that putting out a free update would help drive buzz and lead to a few sales, even if it might not be quite as lucrative as paid DLC.

In January 2017, Dodge Roll put out what they called the *Supply Drop* update to *Enter the Gungeon*, and they were shocked to see just how much of a sales spike they saw. The *Supply Drop* update brought in a whole new wave of press and attention, which they kept in mind as they worked on yet another update, *Advanced Gungeons & Draguns*, for release in the summer of 2018. Each update led to more sales, as did console ports to the Xbox and especially the Nintendo Switch (the game had originally launched on PC and PlayStation). It was a strange and exciting trend: *Enter the Gungeon* became more successful the longer they worked on it. Just like The Molasses Flood had learned with *The Flame in the Flood*, the developers of *Enter the Gungeon* were realizing that in the modern video game industry, day-one sales were just a small part of a game's success. What really mattered was what happened afterward. "Gungeon's best month of sales was its twenty-fourth month of being sold," said Sodman. "I'd always heard about the long tail, but I'd never expected we'd basically be able to reset the sales of our game two years after it came out."

Crooks and Sodman eventually repaired their relationship—it helped that they were no longer living, working, and breathing on each other at all hours of the day—and they both wound up moving to Austin, Texas, although not as roommates. By the end of 2018, all of Dodge Roll had grown sick of working on *Enter the Gungeon*. The game had been more successful than any of them could have imagined, but there was only so much time they could spend on the same game without driving themselves nuts. They decided that they'd release a third and final update that spring. Then they would move on to something else.

"*Gungeon* was going to be six months, small, just get our name out there, get some kind of income in, some kind of cohesive experience of making a game start to finish, prove we can do it, then figure out what's next," said Dave Rubel. "I worked on that game for five years."

■ ■ ■

On April 5, 2019, three years after *Enter the Gungeon* launched and nearly five years after Mythic closed, Dodge Roll released the game's final update, *A Farewell to Arms*. Just like the previous two updates, it was full of new bosses, guns, and modes, and it led to yet another sales spike. The team then decided to move on to something else—a spin-off that would release later that year called *Exit the Gungeon*, followed by other projects they'd been thinking about developing.

In the end, Mythic's closure had almost been a boon for Dave

Crooks, Brent Sodman, Dave Rubel, and Erica Hampson, all of whom had found the type of financial and creative success they'd never found while working at the studio. What was particularly remarkable about *Enter the Gungeon* was that it cultivated a community of positive, supportive fans—something that had seemed unimaginable in the wake of *Dungeon Keeper*'s internet rage. "I was really scared of what it would mean to have a Reddit and stuff, because I'd seen lots of horror stories, and experienced a lot of that at Mythic," said Sodman. "But at least to this date, Dodge Roll's relationship with our fan base is really positive."

The creators of *Enter the Gungeon* never forgot about their time at Mythic, a studio that had been formative and essential to their livelihoods. In fact, they ensured that Mythic's memory would live on forever in their game. Alongside the release of *Enter the Gungeon*, the Dodge Roll crew put out a piece of DLC that would give players access to a special weapon: the Microtransaction Gun. Using this gun would allow you to convert your in-game gold to various objects—like green gems—and fire them at enemies. It cost extra money to purchase.

"Everyone involved in the production of this gun thought it was a bad idea, but the higher-ups made them build it anyway," read the official in-game description. "Later, management shut down that gun factory for making a gun no one liked."

CHAPTER 9

HUMAN COSTS;
HUMAN SOLUTIONS

Ask any veteran video game developer their least favorite thing about the industry and you'll probably get a different version of the same answer: It treats people poorly. It chews them up and then spits them back out, leaving nothing but gristle and bones behind.

Joe Faulstick was one of those people. He started his career in 2003 as a tester for the iconic video game company Atari in Massachusetts, where he worked for half a year before he was caught up in a mass layoff. "That was basically my start in the industry," Faulstick said. Soon he got a call from an old friend, Bill Gardner, who asked if he wanted to come manage the QA team at a studio called Irrational Games. *Absolutely*, Faulstick said, joining Irrational as a tester and then becoming a producer on the first *BioShock*, which nearly destroyed his relationship with his girlfriend thanks to perpetual crunch. "We'd only see each other on weekends because I worked so late," Faulstick said. "And a lot of times I'd have to work that Saturday. Or I'd be so tired that I would cancel our plans for that weekend."

Faulstick managed to turn things around and salvage the

relationship (and that girlfriend would later become his wife) by vowing to improve his work-life balance. After *BioShock*'s release in 2007, nobody else at Irrational wanted to crunch again either, so things were pleasant for the next few years—until the summer of 2010, when the studio revealed *BioShock Infinite* to the world. "We crunched leading up to that and didn't really stop afterwards," Faulstick said. The hours were hard enough on their own, but Faulstick also had a tough time dealing with the brutal criticism that was ingrained in Irrational's culture. There were only so many times he could get yelled at by Ken Levine for screwing up. "In other places that'd be a hostile work environment," said Faulstick. "Part of the challenge in the games industry is, if you feel that's the only place you can be or the only place you want to be, you don't want to be a rotten egg."

In 2011, Faulstick quit Irrational to be a freelance consultant, agreeing to continue working on *BioShock Infinite* but no longer interested in staying there full-time. In 2012, he decided to move to Redmond, Washington, for a job at Microsoft. He stayed there for two years until he was laid off in July 2014. A few months later, he and his wife moved to San Francisco, California, so he could be a producer at Crystal Dynamics on *Rise of the Tomb Raider*. That lasted eight months. "I was willing to pay back the relocation fee to go get another job," Faulstick said. "That was where I had the worst work-life balance of my life. They make the mistake of scheduling for crunch—they plan it."

Faulstick took a new job as a producer at 2K's offices in Novato, which didn't require a move, but as he spent the next few years working on games from a publisher's perspective, he started to feel like he was part of a broken system. Over the past year he'd seen 2K Marin and Irrational shut down, and watched a continuous cycle of layoffs both at 2K's other studios and at neighboring companies in the Bay Area, like Telltale Games. "Your average game company, even big publishers like 2K, they can't necessarily focus on the long-term—focus on the game after next—because a lot of what they're able to do depends on the success of the current game they're working on," Faulstick said. "That's the reality they're in."

Faulstick started getting antsy and paranoid, worrying about what might happen if he was laid off again. Did he really want to have to keep moving across the country every time some bean counters decided that they couldn't keep him employed? "If this opportunity doesn't fully work out, or if god forbid we ship a project and then we're not fully planned or ready to move onto what's next, we have to lay off a good amount of staff," Faulstick said. "If I was affected, I wasn't that concerned about being able to find a job, but there would be a 95 percent chance we would have to move again. . . . It felt untenable."

So in 2018, Joe Faulstick decided to leave the video game industry. He and his wife packed up and moved to Raleigh, North Carolina, where he took a job in software development making programs and websites. It wasn't quite as glamorous as gaming, but the pay was better, the work-life balance was a massive improvement, and he felt like he was part of an industry that placed more value on its workers. "I'm not worried about what's happening tomorrow anymore," Faulstick said. "That's not to say the company won't have layoffs, but I don't have to worry about moving my family."

Like Zach Mumbach and countless others, Joe Faulstick left a field that didn't care to keep him. How, then, do you solve this problem? How do you create a system where games get made without churning through workers like a factory assembly line?

Put another way: How do you fix the video game industry?

■ ■ ■

Video game programmer Steve Ellmore wasn't too surprised when Irrational Games shut down. He said as much to his friend Gwen Frey over drinks at a dive bar near the office on the afternoon of February 18, 2014, when they found out their studio was closing. Ellmore was experienced enough to see how big a problem it was that they didn't have a new project after *BioShock Infinite*, and he knew that the studio couldn't support a staff that large for too much longer. He had a feeling that, at the very least, there would be layoffs. "I had read the writing on the wall," Ellmore said. "It was almost a relief when we got the announcement that the studio was closing. Because now everything made a lot more sense. This situation obviously couldn't continue, and the people in charge knew that this situation couldn't continue, so they were at least doing something about it."

Plus, he had a plan. "Everything just clicked into place at that point," Ellmore said. "'Now I know what I'm going to do.'"

Many years earlier, Ellmore had studied computer science at the University of Sheffield in the United Kingdom, where he grew up. He'd always wanted to be a programmer, working not just on video games but on the tools that made it possible to create video games. He loved working with engines—a catchy term for code that game developers reuse from project to project—and as he got older, he dreamed about making a living by solving people's technical problems. In 1996, Ellmore got his first video game job, as a localization engineer for a kids' software company, helping adjust text boxes and deal with the other fiddly problems that emerged when you tried to translate a game from English to other European languages.

A few years and one failed start-up later, Ellmore moved to the United States for a job and eventually wound up at Midway, a game studio in Chicago, Illinois, that had started off as an arcade company, taking the likes of *Space Invaders* and *Pac-Man* from Japan and distributing them in North America. By the time Ellmore joined in 2001, Midway was a video game console developer and publisher, best known for a series of gory fighting games called *Mortal Kombat*. The series was a cultural touchstone, but Midway had become dysfunctional, with a revolving door of top executives and yearly operating losses in the eight and nine figures.

While leading Midway's technology team, Ellmore met another programmer named Steve—Steve Anichini, who became a friend and confidant. The two of them grew close working together on games like *Stranglehold*, developed in collaboration with the film director John Woo (whose project with Warren Spector never came together). *Stranglehold*'s main gameplay hook was allowing the player to slow down time to take out enemies, which made for a fascinating technical challenge that the two Steves enjoyed solving. Even as Midway crumbled around them, Anichini and other members of the *Stranglehold* tech team found that they got along well, and they loved working for Ellmore, who was a gregarious leader. "A lot of people, if they like their direct manager, they'll put up with a lot from the rest of the organization," said Anichini.

At the beginning of 2009, the two Steves started talking about what they'd do when Midway finally shut down. They briefly talked about starting their own company, but their plans never quite coalesced. Instead, Ellmore got on the phone with a friend at Irrational Games, which was just starting up *BioShock Infinite* and needed programmers. Ellmore convinced the studio not just to hire him, but his whole team—an unusual move, but one that worked out nicely for a studio that was looking to expand. "I think this industry undervalues teams and team dynamics," said Ellmore. "They're all too ready to dissolve great teams with synergy."

It was a package deal. In April 2009, the two Steves and two of their other Midway colleagues, Mike Kraack and Kris Munson, shipped off from Chicago to Boston, where they'd handle engine and technology work for Irrational Games.[1] Together, they did all sorts of tasks for the *BioShock Infinite* team, ranging from elaborate lighting enhancements to tool optimization that would allow the designers to work as efficiently as possible. Over the course of *Infinite*'s long and crunchy development, the engine team grew close, bonding over long hours and technical challenges.

When *BioShock Infinite* came out in March 2013, it quickly became clear that something was wrong at Irrational. Discussions about the studio's next project tapered off, and Ellmore's tech team stopped getting new requests and assignments. They decided on their own to start porting *BioShock Infinite* to the new consoles, the Xbox One and PlayStation 4, but it wasn't an officially sanctioned project—they just needed something to do. "When the engineers are just left to their own devices, that's a bad sign," said Steve Anichini, who started again bringing up the idea they'd had years earlier to start a company of their own. After *BioShock Infinite*'s rocky development, the idea of sticking around for another lengthy project was too exhausting to imagine. "Personally, I didn't know if I had it in me to do another five-year game," Anichini said.

One day in February 2014, Anichini arrived late to the office and learned he'd missed a surprise morning meeting. "It was halfway done," said Anichini. "I thought I'd just find out what it was later,

---

1   Midway went bankrupt just a few months later, although a number of its staff stayed in Chicago to form a new studio called NetherRealm that would helm the *Mortal Kombat* games moving forward.

and I'd just get started on some work." He was at his computer for just a few minutes when, suddenly, one by one, his programs began logging him out. Notifications flooded Anichini's computer screen, informing him that his log-ins and passwords were no longer working. At the same time, Ken Levine was in the kitchen, telling the staff of Irrational that he was shutting down the studio. A few minutes later, Steve Ellmore walked into the room. "He said, 'Well, I guess we're doing our own company,'" recalled Anichini.

Over the next few weeks, as the rest of Irrational's former employees flew out to interviews and attended job fairs, Ellmore and Anichini put together a PowerPoint presentation detailing their plans for this new company. Then they invited a few other members of the tech team to Ellmore's house for a pitch meeting. "We had to move quickly because we knew that a lot of people on our team were going to get offers from all these companies," said Ellmore. "We wanted to be there with an alternative. 'This is going to be a real thing. We're really going to make it happen. This is going to be viable. You should consider this along with the other offers you get.'"

The pitch was simple: using their savings and the severance money they'd received from Irrational's closure, Ellmore and Anichini would start a new company, and they'd try to bring along a few other members of their team. This wouldn't be a traditional game studio. They didn't want to enter the boom-or-bust world of game development by making their own original video games. Instead, they would form a tech outsourcing house, selling their services to companies all across the world. They'd fix bugs, write complicated code, and help companies port their games to new platforms such as the PlayStation 4 and Xbox One and, later, virtual reality devices like the Oculus Rift. Their tagline was simple: "Shipping games is hard. Let us help."

It was an enticing pitch for a few reasons. Nobody in Ellmore's crew would have to leave Boston for new jobs, and they'd all get to keep working together. "They were the smartest group of people I'd worked with," said Mike Kraack. "And the fact they wanted me with them, that stokes your ego a bit.... The compensation was on par with every other place I was getting offers from, and I wouldn't have to move. So it was a win-win-win." To Kraack, it felt like a viable business model. Launching a start-up was always a risk, but if there was any discipline in the video game industry with more demand than supply, it was programming.

They called the company CodeBeast, later changing it, after some trademark issues, to Disbelief. At first they thought there would be a lull as they started negotiating contracts, but to the Steves' delight, they already had deals in place by the end of May, just three months after Irrational closed. One of their old friends from the Midway days, Dave Lang, had founded his own outsourcing-focused studio called Iron Galaxy, and he offered Ellmore some contract work. "I remember saying, 'Are you crazy? You're helping me set up a company that's going to compete with your company,'" recalled Ellmore. "He said, 'Don't worry about it—shipping games is hard, and everybody needs people who can ship games.'"

In the coming years, Disbelief would take on technical contracts for all sorts of games, both big and small. They worked on major franchises like *Gears of War* and *Borderlands*, and they even collaborated with some old friends. When Gwen Frey needed some technical assistance on her solo puzzle game, *Kine*, Disbelief was her first call. When Ken Levine's new studio, Ghost Story Games, had engineering problems, they went to Disbelief. By 2021, the Steves had expanded their company to twenty-five people across two offices, in Boston and in Chicago (where Anichini had returned to be closer to his family). Irrational's closure had, in the end, led them to unexpected comfort, success, and, most important, stability. "There's going to be consolidation, and there's going to be winners and losers," said Steve Ellmore of the video game industry. "And I guess I'm not that worried about it, because we sell the shovels."

■ ■ ■

A look at Disbelief might be a glimpse at the future of the big-budget video game industry. It's a model that aims to solve or at least mitigate the volatility problem that has driven people like Joe Faulstick out of games. The staff of Disbelief don't have to worry about their next game flopping and their company shutting down. A contract ending or a project getting canceled isn't going to destroy Disbelief, because their eggs are in several baskets. There will always be new technical challenges, new platforms, and new problems to solve as the graphical fidelity of video games races forward. "I think the future is going to be: there's a small team in charge of the creative vision, and then all of the other work is outsourced," said Ellmore. "There has to be a network, an ecosystem of companies that do good work in order to make this happen. But I think that's the future of game development."

The ideal Disbelief customer, Ellmore likes to say, looks something like Ghost Story Games: a small operation with creative ambitions and good funding. In fact, when Levine's new studio reached out to Disbelief in the years after Irrational's closure, something interesting happened. The people at Ghost Story wanted a specific graphical rendering feature, and Disbelief came back to them with an estimate—it would take about six months to finish. "Now if we were full-time employees still working for Irrational, we would've just started working on it, because what else are we going to do?" said Ellmore. "But we told them it was going to take this long, with this much engineering investment, and what it would take to maintain it. They said, 'Well, it doesn't sound like we want to do that.'"

That was the key difference between the Disbelief crew working as an internal team at Irrational and existing as an outsourcing house. When a game studio has to pay for every single hour of an engineering team's time, its leaders have to think twice about outsize technical requests—they can't just go to the engineers on a whim and ask them to get something done. "That, to me, even though we lost out on the gig, is the system working," said Ellmore. "Teams are supposed to make decisions about how they're going to spend money, not just blindly do it."

Of course, outsourcing is nothing new to the video game industry. For many years, big publishers and studios have relied upon contractors from all across the world to do all sorts of work. Two Los Angeles–based companies are ubiquitous in the production of big games: Blur for cinematic trailers and Formosa Interactive for sound design. A look at the credits for 2019's *Call of Duty: Modern Warfare* reveals outsourcing companies in India (Dhruva); Spain (elite3d); Vietnam (Glass Egg); China (Red Hot); and many others. For years now it's been cheaper to hire artists in Shanghai than in San Francisco, which big companies have used to their advantage.

But Disbelief is unique in some ways that are worth examining. A few years into the company's life, the Steves decided to create a flat, transparent salary policy, ensuring that every single title at the company had the same pay. They built a spreadsheet with titles—Junior Programmer, Programmer 1, Programmer 2, Senior Programmer, and so on—and listed an accompanying salary for each one, along with specific criteria for how to get promoted. It was a radical move, and, to libertarian-minded video game programmers who preached meritocracy above all, might have been a massive turnoff. To the owners' surprise, though, the policy turned out to be a selling point for the company. When Steve Anichini put up a blog post explaining their open salary policy in May 2018, he started getting applicants who had seen the post and wanted to be part of that kind of culture. Disbelief's employees were also thrilled about the change. "You knew what you had to do to get promoted," said Elizabeth Baumel, who spent three years at Disbelief's Boston office. "It was awesome. I wish every company ever would do that."

Disbelief also maintains a staunch anticrunch policy, although the two Steves have disagreed upon how to enact it. (Anichini wants to ban overtime entirely; Ellmore says he wants to keep things more flexible—just in case.) When employees do put in extra hours, Disbelief gives them vacations right away. "Usually at a big company like Irrational, you'll crunch for a year and then they'll give you a month off," said Disbelief programmer Kris Munson. "When I've had to crunch here, we've been doing it one-to-one. You work forty hours extra in a week, you get a week off." Disbelief charges clients for every single hour it works, which helps make up the difference (and encourages those clients to pick practical deadlines).

The downside to all of these perks is that Disbelief will always be subservient to the people who are signing their checks. Unless they decide to develop a game on their own, a scenario that the Steves call unlikely, Disbelief's engineers will never lead the creative direction of a project. Their technical decisions will always be limited to what their clients want. They'll never work on a game from beginning to end, getting the satisfaction of watching a project morph from concept illustrations and PowerPoint presentations into a work of art that millions of people play, like *BioShock Infinite*. "This is not my ideal job," said Munson. "My ideal job would be to be embedded in an AAA team, and not be a contractor. But having gone through all the BS that goes along with that, I think I'm happier now."

Besides, how many people really get all that much input into a game's direction? In big-budget AAA development, it's the directors—the Warren Spectors and Ken Levines of the world— who get most of the creative control. Artists and designers can take ownership of their own little domains or specialty projects, but of the two hundred people who worked at Irrational, there were many whose jobs were simply to follow orders, and many more who had to throw away weeks' or months' worth of work when Levine rewrote a scene. Engineers like the Disbelief crew wouldn't even be in those meetings. "It's not like we had a ton of creative input on *BioShock Infinite*," said Steve Ellmore. "We didn't write the story. We didn't design the characters....From my perspective, I just facilitated. I made it happen. And so to a large extent, my job is the same these days as it always was."

This is one vision of a sustainable model for video game development: dedicated outsourcing houses that a group of core creative leads can hire as needed. During the first year of production on a brand-new franchise, when a game is designed mostly through paper and prototypes, the artists and designers might not need too many engineers. But at the end, when it's time to fix the bugs and crank up those frame rates, a team like Disbelief can come in and help get the game out the door. "There are large periods of time where you don't need a tech team because you're working on the concept for your game," said Mike Kraack. "That's part of why studios shut down—they say, 'Well, we don't need this whole gigantic team of people behind games, so we're just going to [lay off] and then we'll rehire later.'"

Today, an average AAA video game company might have two hundred or three hundred employees while outsourcing art and levels to hundreds more. Imagine, then, a world where the video game company is just fifteen or twenty key creative leads. Rather than hiring people for each new project—only to have to then lay those people off when they're not needed, or if the game fails—what if those creative leads rely on a network of specialized companies across the world? "Disbelief provides an amazing service to anyone who hires them," said Joe Faulstick. "Why can't there be an equivalent of Disbelief for people who are really great at making first-person shooter levels? A small, eight- to ten-person studio with a track record of making great levels in the Unreal Engine?"

Say you've made a video game about a mustachioed plumber trying to defeat a malevolent turtle and now you're trying to develop a sequel. Let's call it...*Super Plumber Adventure 2*. You're the creative director, working on the dime of a well-respected publisher, and you've hired a few key people to work out of your office: an art director to set the visual tone for the game; a design director to decide what the jumping and fireball mechanics will look like; and an engineering director to determine how the game's code will function. If you were an indie house like The Molasses Flood or Dodge Roll, you might be able to stop there, making a small-scale game with just a handful of people, but this is AAA, baby. To reach the graphical fidelity and technological innovations your publisher is expecting, you'll need a staff of hundreds of people. If your game doesn't look pretty enough, Reddit will make fun of it.

In today's video game industry, you'd probably take a scattershot approach, hiring a bunch of proper full-time employees and another group of full-time employees who are actually contractors, working out of your offices but technically employed by an outside company, allowing you to pay less for their services and avoid pesky perks like "health care" and "vacation time." Three years later, when the game comes out, you'll need to lay off all the people you don't need anymore. And you'll have to pray to the god(s) of your choice that the game sells well and your publisher doesn't decide to shut you down.

What, then, would another model look like? What if, rather than trying to recruit a staff of artists and designers to make *Super Plumber Adventure 2*, you found a team in Utah that comprised experts at designing platformer levels, a studio in New York devoted to modeling gorgeous three-dimensional monsters, and an engineering house in Brazil with a suite of technology that's perfect for your game's needs? In the same way that a car might be assembled from parts made all across the globe, your big-budget game could be created by groups of specialists who worked remotely. There would be some challenges, no doubt—talking through creative disputes is hard enough face-to-face, let alone across multiple time zones, as 2K Marin and 2K Australia once learned—but wouldn't those problems be preferable to layoffs or a closure?

If each of those specialty companies treated its staff as well as Disbelief has—embracing anticrunch policies and transparent salaries—perhaps video games could be made without chewing people up. Maybe they'd no longer have to pick between moving every three years and leaving the video game industry entirely. "I feel like the small contract studio is a model that is going to last," said Disbelief's Mike Kraack. Like every other game developer, Kraack had his own layoff story—his first video game job was at a game studio in Indianapolis that shut down just as he was starting his fifth year.[2] "I've been avoiding buying property since my first house in Indianapolis," Kraack said. "Now I'm thinking maybe it's

---

2 That studio, Sunstorm, was responsible for popular deer hunting games and shuttered in 2003. "Even though my brother had worked at a video game company before me, and his company closed, I thought mine would be fine," said Kraack.

time to buy a condo. I don't feel like I'm going to be leaving Boston anytime soon."

The idea of a video game industry made up largely of specialized contract studios has been bandied about by a lot of people. In fact, it's something that was seriously discussed by a group of developers we've met before—a group of designers and animators in Maryland who were also the victims of a studio shutdown. A group whose members still, years later, call it the best time of their lives.

■ ■ ■

Back before Big Huge Games was hit by a Curt Schilling–shaped asteroid, the members of Joe Quadara's combat pit liked to joke that they should start a company together. The crew of designers and animators, who would play silly games and compete over trophies, loved working together and were thrilled with the praise they'd received for *Kingdoms of Amalur: Reckoning*'s combat system. Quadara, the competitive-minded designer who led the team, even had a name in mind for this hypothetical company: Just Add Combat. "That was something we sort of jokingly said at the time, but it was probably a good idea," said Justin Perez, the designer. "What if we got together and were a traveling band of people that made combat?"

It was never too serious a consideration, though. When Big Huge Games suddenly stopped paying employees and shut down nine days later, there was no time for any of them to think about starting a company. They were too busy scrambling to pay rent and find new jobs. Some moved over to the short-lived Impossible Studios, while others flew off to new cities, and the idea of a specialty combat team fizzled before it could get off the ground.

After Impossible Studios closed in 2013, Quadara moved back

to San Francisco and spent a year at Crystal Dynamics, where he'd started his career, then took a job on the publishing side of game development at 2K's offices in Novato. "I'd gone through two studio closures in a year, and in both cases did not expect or anticipate them," Quadara said. "And I felt there was something I was missing, so being on the publishing side, I thought, could teach me what was going on." 2K provided plenty of educational material. He started in 2014, a year after 2K Marin was killed. And in 2015, a year later, Quadara had to watch the publisher shut down 2K Australia as well, which was rough. He'd worked with a lot of the people there.

Quadara mostly enjoyed being part of a big publisher. It was challenging and rewarding in new ways to work on several games at a time rather than dedicate years of his life to a single project as he had in the past. He also learned some of the dark financial wizardry behind publicly traded companies, where all that really matters is fiscal quarters. "When you have a game that is projected to not sell so well, like *The Bureau: XCOM Declassified*, you might hang on to it for longer than you want to," Quadara said, "just so you can release it in the same fiscal year as a *Grand Theft Auto* or a *Red Dead Redemption*."[3] For three and a half years, Quadara worked out of 2K's Novato hangar, coordinating with developers all across the world to help them finish games. "I got really good at the work," he said. "But it was getting kind of boring. I was getting my job done two days out of the week—the other three I was playing *Street Fighter* or trying not to make a nuisance of myself."

Quadara reached out to one of his mentors, a veteran game designer named Eric Williams who worked as a consultant

---

3   *The Bureau: XCOM Declassified* came out on August 20, 2013. The megasensation *Grand Theft Auto V* came out on September 17, 2013. Take-Two's fiscal quarter ended on September 30, 2013. Needless to say, it was a profitable quarter.

specializing in combat. The two had crossed paths when Quadara started at Big Huge Games back in 2008. Williams, who had worked on many of the *God of War* games, was consulting on what would become *Kingdoms of Amalur: Reckoning*, and often encouraged Quadara to become a freelance consultant as well. "When we met, he said, 'You could be doing this right now,' and I just didn't believe him," said Quadara. "When that became an option for me, he was instrumental in giving me confidence." Encouraged by his wife to take the plunge, Quadara decided to quit 2K in the fall of 2017 and start his own consulting business. When he told his bosses at 2K what he planned to do, they offered to be his first client, which was a relief. In the months and years to come, he found success in the consulting world, attracting clients both big and small who were mainly looking for help with combat.

It might have seemed like the natural move would be for Quadara to start reaching out to his old combat pit and see if he could get the gang back together. Some of the designers and animators who had worked with Quadara at Big Huge Games called it the best work experience of their lives—surely if he called, they'd answer? Maybe Just Add Combat could finally become a real thing.

But all these years later, Quadara didn't actually believe that the idea could work. "It's not something I feel is a viable business model," he said. "You'd have to line up enough work for everybody on board. You'd have to keep rates competitive enough that people feel like they can't just do it themselves." The largest challenge, Quadara said, would be getting past the hubris of other video game developers, many of whom tend to overestimate their skills and underestimate the challenges they have to face. (The scientific term for this phenomenon is called "being human.") As an example, Quadara said, a company recently reached out to him saying they were shipping a game in ten months and needed to build twelve boss battles—could he help? Absolutely not, he told them—a single proper boss battle might take three months to build, and that was with an experienced team. "The personnel required and expertise required is just off the charts," Quadara said. "And no one wants to actually pay for it when they're not on fire."

When I proposed the model of a video game industry in which a core creative team works with specialty contract houses across the globe, Quadara was skeptical. "What I've found is that there are roles that are easy to outsource and roles that are harder to outsource," he said. It was easy for developers to off-load the behind-the-scenes engineering work to a company like Disbelief without causing too many disruptions. But for moment-to-moment action like combat, Quadara said, it'd be tougher to work from a distance. "The line of outsourceability is inversely related to how close to the player experience you get," Quadara said. After all, the Big Huge Games combat pit had been successful because they were able to iterate quickly, and they could do that because they all worked in the same room.

Quadara had grown less interested in combat since his days at Big Huge Games, even if many of his clients knew him as the go-to guy for satisfying, challenging video game battles. In recent years, as game developers faced culture wars and harassment campaigns from whiny gamers who didn't want to see the industry grow more diverse, Quadara moved sharply in the opposite direction. "I'm way more interested in having creative voices that aren't male power fantasies," Quadara said. "I find that the teams that are more approaching healthy diversity, they tend to not have as much combat."

In other words, Just Add Combat probably isn't going to happen. Quadara, like most veteran developers, thinks the industry needs to change in some big ways. He just doesn't know if the specialty outsourcing model is the way to go. "We can't ramp up a team full-time anymore and then just lay them off—it's unsustainable," Quadara said. "We have to solve it somehow. I don't see the industry surviving the way it continues."

There's another option—one that could provide the benefits of a company like Disbelief to more workers at other video game studios. It's an option that's been discussed quite a bit. And in recent years, it has seemed more feasible than ever before.

■ ■ ■

On March 21, 2018, at the Game Developers Conference in San Francisco, California, two hundred people packed into a warm conference room for a roundtable discussion on unionization in the video game industry. Drilling noises from nearby construction drowned out many of the speakers, but you could still feel the buzz of energy in the room. There was only one microphone, chauffeured by a GDC staffer between people who wanted to share stories about how the video game industry had failed them. One said they'd burned out of game development due to overwork; another said that they'd worked nine months straight of crunch only to receive, at the end of it all, a single week of paid time off.[4] They talked about how unionizing the video game industry might solve some of these issues, giving workers a seat at the table and allowing them to draw up contracts that enshrined fair pay and proper benefits.

Game developers had discussed unionization many times in the

---

4   This sort of compensation is far more common across the video game industry than the five-figure bonuses that Zach Mumbach described receiving at EA.

past, but it was at this GDC that the conversations gained serious momentum, led by a grass-roots group called Game Workers Unite that had been founded earlier that month. During the conference, members of Game Workers Unite handed out pamphlets and offered to have one-on-one conversations with anyone who was curious to hear more. "We love the games these people make, but you can't kill people in the process," one of the organizers, who went by the name Emma Kinema, told me then. "It's just not okay."

The roundtable was called "Union Now? Pros, Cons, and Consequences of Unionization," but over the course of an hour, only one person mentioned cons and consequences: the panel's moderator, who clearly opposed unions. The moderator was the head of the International Game Developers Association, a loose nonprofit that organized events and seminars for people who made games. And, as it turned out, she had plenty of her own horror stories from the video game industry—it was Jennifer MacLean, the former CEO of 38 Studios.

MacLean responded to most of the people who spoke at the roundtable with skeptical questions, offering anecdotes about the downsides of unionization and arguing that organizing wouldn't fix every single problem that the video game industry faced. In a separate interview with me the day before at a Marriott nearby, she'd made similar comments, arguing that unionization wasn't a panacea for the industry's ills. "Generally when a studio closes, it's because they run out of capital, they run out of access to cash, and unions won't help with access to cash," MacLean said then.[5] "We cannot expect unions to solve everything that's wrong with the games industry."

---

5 MacLean declined to chat further for this book.

Of course, she's technically correct. Unions aren't a cure-all for everything that ails the video game industry. Moving the goalposts like that is a common rhetorical argument from people who oppose unionization, but the reality is that a union might have helped prevent the company MacLean helped run from upending the lives of hundreds of people. If the staff of 38 Studios had secured some sort of collective bargaining agreement, they might have demanded more transparency or even a guaranteed severance policy. Unions couldn't have prevented 38 Studios from running out of money, but they might have forced Curt Schilling and the rest of the company's management to wind down the studio before it could get to the point where it could no longer afford to pay staff.

Put another way: the bulk of 38 Studios employees would have likely preferred to be laid off in March with two months of severance over coming to work one day in May and finding out that they weren't getting paid anymore.

As I write this book in 2020, discussions over unionizing are ongoing. It remains to be seen whether a big US video game studio will take the plunge (some game studios in countries like Sweden are unionized), although the majority of game developers are in favor of organizing—a GDC survey conducted in January 2020 found that 54 percent of polled developers wanted unions to happen in the games industry. Of the remainder, 21 percent said maybe, 16 percent said no, and 9 percent said they weren't sure. It seems inevitable that the video game industry will organize at some point—the questions are when and how.

The staff members of Disbelief aren't unionized—when I asked Steve Ellmore, he said there was a concern it would lead to their losing customers—but in practice, the company essentially acts as an engineering union, negotiating with clients and protecting its workers thanks to policies on crunch and salary transparency.

Rather than be subject directly to the whims of a creative director like Ken Levine, the staff of Disbelief will always be protected by a contract they sign with their clients, similar to a union's collective bargaining agreement. One problem with this model, however, is that it's dependent on the generosity of management. If the Steves decided one day to change their policies, or if Disbelief were swallowed up by a larger company, those perks might simply disappear. Unions could help solve that problem.[6]

The downsides of unions, as presented by their opponents, include bureaucracy, inefficiency, and significant fees. During our chat, MacLean suggested that if video game companies started organizing, it would encourage bosses across the games industry to rely on cheap outsourced labor elsewhere, or to favor the companies that weren't union shops. What MacLean couldn't do was offer a better solution—other than a nebulous wish that the video game industry had more "access to capital"—which essentially meant maintaining the status quo. That's a tough reality for many video game veterans to accept.

Every new layoff or studio closure is evidence that the video game industry needs more protection for its workers, and unions are an essential, inevitable part of that equation. Jen MacLean is right about one thing, though—a union can't stop a company from running out of money. Maybe nothing can. Maybe there's no way

---

6   I can speak from personal experience here—at Gawker Media, we organized in 2015, which helped protect us from potential problems when our company went bankrupt in 2016 thanks to a vengeful billionaire and we were purchased by a corporation. Our new owner, Univision, had to maintain all of the benefits we'd enjoyed in the past. In 2019, when we were sold to a private equity firm called Great Hill Partners, our union contract again ensured that we were able to keep solid health insurance and competitive salary minimums. Of course, the union couldn't protect us from Great Hill's other catastrophic decisions...but that's a story for another book.

to prevent risky business decisions in an industry so fickle and driven by hits.

Maybe we should be looking at this problem from another angle.

■ ■ ■

On Thursday, February 27, 2020, Carrie Gouskos was brought into a meeting with her leadership team to talk about the spread of a highly contagious virus. After the closure of Mythic Entertainment in 2014, Gouskos had stayed at EA for a few years, moving to Austin, Texas, to supervise teams on mobile games like *The Simpsons: Tapped Out* and *Star Wars: Galaxy of Heroes*. Then, in the fall of 2019, she took a job as a top producer at Bungie, the developer of *Destiny*, in Seattle, Washington, where people had just begun reporting positive cases of a novel coronavirus that led to a debilitating disease called COVID-19.

At this point, the words "social distancing" had become part of America's national lexicon, and it was becoming clear that the only way to thwart COVID-19 was for people to avoid physical interactions. Gouskos and other leaders at Bungie were providing hand sanitizer and giving employees extra paid time off for the virus, but they were starting to suspect that they'd need to take more drastic measures soon. As they entered the weekend, they began plotting out what it might look like for Bungie to work remotely. How would they set up a virtual network? What would meetings look like? What kind of equipment would they need? "We did a worst-case example of what if every tester, engineer, and artist needed a new computer," Gouskos said. "Our IT went out looking for prices. On Monday I think they wound up buying four hundred laptops."

On March 2, they asked a few dozen people to stay home as a pilot to test out their workflows, and by the following Tuesday,

March 10, all of Bungie was told to go home and stay home. By the end of the month, the bulk of the video game industry (and much of the world) had switched to remote work as part of this bizarre new reality, and nobody knew how long it might last. Suddenly, an industry accustomed to working in physical offices and studios across the globe was almost exclusively virtual. An industry that had driven so many workers to drop everything and relocate their families for new jobs now found itself forced to build virtual offices for them all.

There were hiccups, of course. With schools and day cares closed, working parents found themselves pushed to the brink trying to get anything done. Gouskos found herself putting out fire after fire as servers went down, controllers stopped working, and staff struggled with the emotional toil of the pandemic's devastation. But while productivity took a hit at Bungie and other companies—a few developers across the world estimated that they were operating at 70–80 percent capacity during the crisis—the work was able to continue. (Bungie would later delay the next *Destiny* expansion from September to November of 2020, citing the pandemic's unique challenges as the main reason. But the expansion did come out.)

As the pandemic dragged on, a new question began to come up in video game industry circles: If game developers can work remotely now, why can't they always? Gouskos found that there were drawbacks to a virtual workplace. Isolation, she said, can drain creativity. "Our best collaboration happens when we're face-to-face," she said. "You miss the human craving element of seeing a person in the hallway. You can't manufacture that. The connection you get is not something I think you can replicate artificially. I do think really good creativity comes out of that."

Yet Gouskos could also sympathize with video game industry veterans sick of moving across the country every time they lost their jobs or got new ones—after all, she was one of them. "This is giving us an opportunity to think about how we can be more tolerant of that," said Gouskos. "In my brain I'm always trying to plan for the worst outcome. If one person in the group gets to be remote, what does that mean? I think those are challenges Bungie is willing to take on and consider."

When the artist Thomas Mahler left Blizzard Entertainment in 2010 to move back to his hometown of Vienna, Austria, he knew he wanted to found an independent game studio. But the engineer with whom he wanted to start the company lived in Israel. So when Mahler started Moon Studios, he decided they would have no office or home country—they would be a virtual company. "We realized that, actually, this is a really good thing for us," Mahler said. Their first hire was a programmer in Australia, and over the years they found artists in Russia, designers in Poland, and a writer in Japan. By 2020, Moon Studios had released two hugely successful games— a gorgeous platformer called *Ori and the Blind Forest* and its sequel, *Ori and the Will of the Wisps*—and consisted of eighty employees who all worked remotely. Before COVID-19, it was one of the largest video game companies to operate entirely virtually. "We literally have people from all around the world," Mahler said. "It's one of the things that has really helped us. We can pick up talent that's superstrong, but would never get the opportunity to move or relocate."

It's not a perfect model—Mahler told me a few people have quit because they grew too lonely—but for Moon Studios, operating as a virtual office solved a lot of problems. Nobody had to worry about getting visas or moving to expensive cities. When the developers put in extra hours—a trap that's easy to fall into when your day isn't broken up by commutes—at least they were at home, where they could cook their own meals and tuck their kids into bed. Every year, Moon Studios would hold a company retreat, renting a European castle and flying everyone out to be together for a few days ("There's a lot of castles and villas that are just empty for most of the year," Mahler said). The rest of the time, they'd use organizational software to communicate about the progress of their games and hold regular video meetings every week. "The only thing you don't have is the watercooler moments," Mahler said.

Some indie companies have taken remote work to a more extreme level, like Sonderlust Studios, which was founded by three people in Vancouver, Toronto, and Maryland, all of whom had roots in those cities and didn't want to leave. They knew that communicating via text-based messages on email and Slack wasn't ideal—in text, tone can get lost, and responses can take way too long. So they set up a virtual office via video conference. Whenever someone at Sonderlust started their workday, they'd turn on their webcam and log onto a Zoom call, where all of their coworkers would be waiting, sipping coffee and plugging away at their game. During office hours, they'd all hang out in boxes on the screen like the Brady Bunch as they worked and talked. (They could keep the window minimized if they didn't want to get too distracted.)

For Lyndsey Gallant, one of Sonderlust's three cofounders, this sort of virtual office was the ideal way to work. It allowed for the social atmosphere of an office without forcing them all to change home cities, and, just like Moon Studios, they could hire talented new staff no matter where they lived. They didn't have to lose time commuting or waste money renting an office, yet they could all still talk face-to-face whenever they chose. "The instability of the games industry is galling," Gallant said. "Anything we can do to change that and make it better, we should."

It's hard to imagine that sort of virtual office working quite the same way at a big-budget studio. Four hundred people hanging out on the same conference call would be a recipe for bedlam. But it's easier to imagine a world where, say, the art team is all on one video call while the programmers are all on another, and where everyone is always jotting down notes and communicating to ensure they don't lose anything along the way. "I think it's going to take a modicum of bravery to try to reexamine: Why do we work the way we work? Why do we make games the way we do?" said Gallant. "How do we adapt that to this new way of working?"

Getting hit by a layoff or a studio closure will always be a terrifying experience, but as so many game developers have come to learn, the scariest part is knowing you might have to move across the world for your next job. It can be challenging—and sometimes even impossible—for anyone with a family or close ties to their city to relocate, which has led countless people to bail on the industry, like Joe Faulstick did. If game developers could work from anywhere, that problem might not be as severe. Layoffs and studio closures might not hurt as badly. "I can't even imagine what it would be like to have a world of opportunities open to me without having to uproot my entire life over and over," said Liz Edwards, an artist who has worked at big game studios in England and Canada.

Sometimes, even game developers who aren't laid off have to live like nomads if they want to stay in the industry. Jordan Mychal Lemos, a writer for video games, has had to move across the world for gigs at developers like Ubisoft and Sucker Punch, to the point where he's considered leaving for other fields. "It's one of the worst parts about this industry without a doubt," he said. "I did two [states] in three years and may have another soon, and I'm not sure how many more I can do before I'm completely done with it."

If there's no way to make the video game industry less volatile, perhaps there's a way to make it more viable. Many of the solutions explored in this chapter would require big systemic changes—

changes that might be necessary, but will take big investments of both time and money before they can happen. But if there's one action video game companies can take today to help solve the problems that so many of their workers have experienced over and over again, it's to allow more developers to work remotely. It wouldn't cost much. In fact, it'd save them money. And it might change the video game industry forever.

EPILOGUE

As I wrote this book between 2018 and 2021, more than a dozen video game studios shut down. There was Capcom Vancouver, the developer behind the long-running *Dead Rising* series; and Carbine Studios, maker of the online game *WildStar*. A small studio in Austin, Texas, called QC Games closed its doors in 2019, having failed to build a substantial audience for its four-versus-one multiplayer game, *Breach*. Boss Key Productions, a studio founded by former Epic Games designer Cliff Bleszinski, shuttered in 2018 after its games *LawBreakers* and *Radical Heights* flopped.

Perhaps the highest-profile of these closures was a company called Telltale Games, located in San Rafael, California. Telltale had a long and turbulent history, marked by several reorganizations and executive shifts, but it was also a landmark in the games industry. Founded in 2004 by a group of ex-LucasArts employees who had worked on point-and-click adventure games like *Monkey Island*, Telltale quickly found a niche for itself in the gaming world. Telltale's games were often episodic, like TV shows, released in five or six installments over the course of a year or two. Unlike many of its peers, Telltale focused first and foremost on telling stories. Familiar mechanics like branching dialogue and puzzle solving became conveyor belts to transport the player from one story beat to the next. The company was treasured, particularly by video game writers. Whereas writers were close to the bottom of the food chain at many other studios, Telltale gave their ideas top priority.

In 2012, a Telltale team co-led by Sean Vanaman—the same Sean Vanaman who was part of the Disney intern group that came up with *Epic Mickey*—released an episodic set of adventure games based on the popular zombie series *The Walking Dead*. Starring a criminal named Lee Everett and his proxy daughter, Clementine, the games had pathos and narrative decisions that felt consequential. This character "will remember that," the game would state whenever you made a choice that mattered. (That wasn't entirely true, but the illusion of characters keeping track of your actions was powerful enough.) Whether you were selecting which NPC to save from certain death or trying to decide whether or not to give a gun to a zombie-bitten girl so she could use it to commit suicide, the options were tragic and memorable. *The Walking Dead* became the surprise hit of 2012, winning Game of the Year awards and convincing companies across the world that they needed to work with Telltale.

Over the next five years, Telltale expanded rapidly, snatching up license after license and applying the same formula to them all. There were Telltale games based on *Batman*, *Game of Thrones*, *Borderlands*, *Guardians of the Galaxy*, and even *Minecraft*. Some of these games were popular, but the business model wasn't ideal—working with other companies' licenses meant giving those other companies a cut of the profits. The episodic schedule made for near-impossible deadlines, which led to lots of nights and weekends for Telltale staff. Over time, fans grew tired of the Telltale formula. Telltale games in 2017 looked a lot like *The Walking Dead* had in 2012, and new ones seemed to be coming out every month, oversaturating the market.

In November 2017, following a string of expensive flops, Telltale restructured, laying off 25 percent of its staff (ninety people) and installing a new CEO, Pete Hawley, in hopes of establishing a new direction. On September 21, 2018, Telltale abruptly shut down, laying off hundreds of staff with no warning and no severance. Investors had reportedly pulled out at the last minute, which left Telltale out of cash—the 38 Studios story all over again. It was a shocking move that sent ripples across the video game industry and tore hundreds of lives apart.

There was Nick Mastroianni, a sound designer and one of Telltale's earliest employees, who had previously been laid off during the 2017 restructuring. Unable to find another job, he'd applied to Telltale again during the summer of 2018, this time accepting a new role as a cinematic artist. Just one month after starting, he was called into an all-hands meeting along with the rest of his coworkers, where they were all informed that they had thirty minutes to pack up their things. "You know when shit just snowballs and gets so bad that you can only laugh?" Mastroianni said. "It was like that for me—'Is this really happening?'" When Hawley told employees that the company couldn't afford to pay severance, there were mutters and curses. "One of the people I worked with was talking about how they wouldn't be able to pay rent for the next month and they weren't sure what they were gonna do," said Mastroianni. "I said, 'I got a big couch—come over.'"

JD Straw, a veteran writer who had spent two stints at Telltale, was sitting on a plane with his wife on September 21 when his phone started blowing up with Slack notifications—people talking about how it was great to work together, how much they'd miss one another, and how to stay in touch. Panicking, Straw started texting his manager and then his manager's manager, working up the chain in an attempt to figure out what was happening. Then he was logged out of his work accounts. Just as the plane was about to take off, he finally got a text back from a colleague saying that Telltale had shut down. "My wife of course says, 'What's going on—were you fired?'" said Straw. "I said, 'No, the company's gone.' It was a great weekend." In the months that followed he took contract work, wrote his own projects, and drove for Uber and Lyft to help pay the bills.

Derek Wilks, a cinematic artist who was just twenty-three years old when Telltale shut down, had moved from Webbville, Kentucky (population 1,095), to the San Francisco Bay Area just three months earlier for what he thought was his dream job. He'd gotten an offer after making some impressive *Half-Life* videos on his YouTube channel. It was his first time in California and his first time more than a state away from Kentucky, and he and his wife spent a few weeks living out of a hotel before they found an apartment near the Telltale office. When the company closed, Wilks and his wife couldn't even afford to fly home, until a Twitter drive from charitable observers raised them around $500. "I had enough money to split two plane tickets with that," Wilks said. "It was pretty crazy." When he got back to Webbville, he moved back in with his family, applying for other video game jobs and hoping that something might come up. "At first I felt like it was a bad omen or something, that maybe I shouldn't be in the games industry," Wilks said. "Now I feel like it just happens."

■ ■ ■

What Cassandra Lease misses most are the people. You hear that often from developers who have burned out of the video game industry. As we sat at a coffee shop in Somerville, Massachusetts, one cold Friday in January 2019, she sounded a lot like many of the other video game castaways I encountered while writing this book.

Lease started her video game career as a quality assurance tester at Turbine, the developer of online games based on *Lord of the Rings* and *Dungeons & Dragons*. In April 2012, she took a job at Irrational Games, where she began testing levels for *BioShock Infinite*. By the end of the fall, she was working twelve-hour days and being asked to come in on weekends to help catch the game's bugs. Irrational had a lot of perks, she said—there were catered meals, free movie vouchers, and managers that seemed to care about their people— but the hours were brutal. "That entire period is just a blur to me," Lease said. "We got overtime pay—that part was very nice. But there's a point at which the pay can't really make up for the fact that you have no time whatsoever."

In February 2013, a month before *BioShock Infinite* came out, Lease and a group of her colleagues were called into a room and told that their contracts were ending. The company needed only a few testers to stay on for the DLC, so this was good-bye. As a way of saying thank you, the company gave them all keychains. "The contract didn't really specify an end date, but we knew that most of us were going when the game shipped," Lease said. "It wasn't unexpected, but it was still a little abrupt."

Lease applied for another video game testing job, but it was on the West Coast, and she soon decided that she didn't want to move across the country for another position that might turn out to be ephemeral. Testers didn't get much respect at video game companies, where they were often perceived as unskilled workers and made close to minimum wage. To advance your career and make a decent salary, you'd either have to move into another field (like design or production) or become a manager, which required a completely different set of skills. Instead, Lease decided to leave games to be a tester at a mobile software company. A couple of years after that, she moved to an education company as a QA engineer, a job that came with a pay bump and benefits. "I was making $12 an hour during my time [at Irrational]," Lease said. "Now I'm working in educational software making $31 an hour."

Between sips of hot chocolate, Lease told me that she loved games and missed getting to work on them, although she didn't miss the way the video game industry treated its workers. She said she wished game developers would unionize. She said she wanted to share her experiences in hopes that one day, things might change. "I was tired of the instability, the low pay, the long hours," Lease said. "If the pay were higher and the hours were better and the benefits were better, I might go back."

▪ ▪ ▪

At the very beginning of this book, I wrote that when a video game presents you with an unexpected, unfair catastrophe, you pretty much have two options: you can push forward, fighting through setbacks and trying to keep making progress, or you can hit the reset button and try again.

That's not entirely true, though. There's a third option: Change the game dramatically. Band together with your colleagues to crack it open, fix the glitches, and tear out all the unfair parts.

Build an organized system in which your successes and failures are determined by your own choices rather than circumstances beyond your control. What would such a game look like? How long would it take to patch the frustrating bugs, overpowered enemies, and broken mechanics out of existence? I think it's worth finding out.

ACKNOWLEDGMENTS

Thanks first of all to everyone who took the time to speak with me for this book. It's no small thing to tell stories about your life to a journalist, especially when those stories get tragic and painful. But I'm honored to be able to share them, and I'm grateful to all the people who talked to me both on and off the record.

Nothing but love and gratitude for my agent, Charlie Olsen, for all the texts he sends me about *Destiny*. Also, for working with rapid speed to save this book after a shake-up at another publisher left its fate in doubt. Without Charlie, this book would not be in your hands (or on your screen or in your ears) right now. The *Destiny* texts are pretty great, too.

A big thanks to my editor, Wes Miller, for his thoughtful edits, patient responses, and careful shepherding of this book along the road to publication. Thanks to Alli Rosenthal, Morgan Swift, Carmel Shaka, and the rest of the Grand Central team for all their help on this project. And thanks to Lyndsey Blessing, Claire Friedman, and everyone else at Inkwell Management.

For reading early copies and providing some critical feedback, thank you to Matthew Burns, Nathaniel Chapman, Brett Douville, Kirk Hamilton, Seth Rosen, Kim Swift, and others who asked not to be named.

Never-ending love and thanks to my family: Mom, Dad, Safta, Rita, and Owen. And to my newer family: Pam, David, Jonah, and Maya.

I don't think Berry is old enough to read this book just yet. Right now she still prefers *Goodnight Moon*. But I hope that by the time she does read this book, it feels less like relevant reporting and more of a chronicle of how the video game industry used to be. And I hope she knows that I love her more than anything else in the world.

Finally, thanks to my partner, best friend, wife, first reader, and constant companion, Amanda. If I was going to be forced to quarantine for a year, at least I got to do it with you.

ABOUT THE AUTHOR

Jason Schreier is the author of *Blood, Sweat, and Pixels* and a reporter at Bloomberg News, where he covers the video game industry. Previously, he spent eight years at Kotaku, one of the biggest video game websites in the world. He has also covered games for *Wired* and has contributed to a wide range of outlets including the *New York Times*, *Edge*, *Paste*, *Kill Screen*, and the *Onion News Network*. He lives in New York with his wife and daughter.